The Battered Wife

Books from Christians for Biblical Equality
122 W. Franklin Ave. Suite 218
Minneapolis, MN 55404
Phone (612) 872-6898
Fax (612) 872-6891
E-Mail cbe@minn.net
www.ChrBibEq.org

Books from Christians for Biblical Equality
.V. Franklin Ave., Suite 218
neapolis, MN 55404
Phone (612) 872-6898
Fax (612) 872-6891
E-Mail cbe@mim.net
www.ChrBiblEq.org

The Battered Wife

How Christians Confront Family Violence

NANCY NASON-CLARK

Westminster John Knox Press
Louisville, Kentucky

Scripture quotations from the New Revised Standard Version
of the Bible are copyright © 1989 by the Division of Christian Education
of the National Council of the Churches of Christ in the U.S.A.
and are used by permission.

Book design by Jennifer K. Cox
Cover design by Pam Poll
Cover photograph courtesy of SuperStock

First Edition
Published by Westminster John Knox Press
Louisville, Kentucky

This book is printed on acid-free paper that meets the
American National Standards Institute Z39.48 standard. ∞

PRINTED IN THE UNITED STATES OF AMERICA
97 98 99 00 01 02 03 04 05 06 — 10 9 8 7 6 5 4 3 2 1

Library of Congress Cataloging-in-Publication Data
Nason-Clark, Nancy, 1956–
  The battered wife : how Christians confront family violence / Nancy Nason-Clark. — 1st ed.
    p.   cm.
  Includes bibliographical references and index.
  ISBN 0-664-25692-9 (alk. paper)
  1. Church work with abused women.   2. Wife abuse—Religious aspects—Christianity.
I. Title.
BV4445.5.N37   1997
261.8'327—dc21   97-23724

CONTENTS

Preface   vii
Introduction   xv

1 The Social and Cultural Context of Abuse in the Family   1

2 The Bases of Christian Family Life   21

3 The Abused Christian Woman   37

4 Evangelical Clergy and Wife Abuse:
   Knowledge and Response   57

5 The Pastor as Counselor   83

6 Women-Helping-Women: Transforming
   Victims into Survivors   109

7 From the Steeple to the Shelter: Challenges to Sacred
   and Secular Cooperation   139

Notes   161
Subject Index   181

PREFACE

My journey in writing this book has been made pleasant because of the multitude of people I have met along the way. But it has been both intellectually and emotionally challenging. Talking about violence is like that: it touches each of us at the core of our being.

I have been privileged to work with several wonderful graduate students over the last few years, many of whom caught and shared (and refined) my vision of the need to examine religion and violence against women: Lori Beaman; Christy Terris; Lisa Hanson; Michelle Spencer; Susan Chalmers-Gauvin; Dawne Clark van Every; Amanda Henry; and Anne Stapleton.

The Religion and Violence Research Team began when I called my colleague and friend Dr. Lois Mitchell, of the Social Action Commission of the United Baptist Convention of the Atlantic Provinces in Canada, to see if she wanted to work together with me on an initiative exploring the role of faith communities in responding to the needs of abuse victims. Three other people were invited to join us: Sheila McCrea, then Wesleyan Women International Director of the Atlantic District of the Wesleyan Church; Terry Atkinson, a Baptist pastor; and Lori Beaman, a feminist lawyer who was affiliated with the New Brunswick Coalition of Transition Houses. While the original vision was mine, the Team has worked in a collaborative fashion for more than four years. Over this time, our mission and goals have expanded as has our program of research. All the Team members have provided input into this book, though the writing has been my sole responsibility (with the exception of chapter 3, which has been coauthored with Lori Beaman).

There have been friends and colleagues who have been particularly supportive: Nancy Tatom Ammerman, Helen Rose Ebaugh, Adair Lummis, Baukje Miedema, Helen Ralston, Angela and Jeremy Furzer, Mary Jo Neitz, Jim Spickard, Meredith McGuire, Peter Beyer, William Stahl, Kathleen Kufeldt, Gail Murphy-Geiss, Loretta Morris, and Dale Sollows. The lieutenant governor of the Province of New Brunswick, Margaret Norrie McCain, serves as an exemplary model for any Canadian woman interested in researching violence against women, and I wish to acknowledge what a source of inspiration she has been.

I am grateful for financial support for my research program and that of the Religion and Violence Research Team from the following sources: the Louisville Institute for the Study of Protestantism and American Culture, the Social Sciences and Humanities Research Council of Canada, the Victim Services Fund of the

New Brunswick Department of the Solicitor General, the Lawson Foundation, the Women's Program of the Canadian Secretary of State, the Constant Jacquet Research Award of the Religious Research Association, the Muriel McQueen Fergusson Centre for Family Violence Research, the Fichter Fund of the Association for the Sociology of Religion, and the University of New Brunswick Research Fund. Participating denominations have also provided some financial support as well as in-kind donations of time or other material resources. I am particularly indebted to James Lewis of the Louisville Institute for his enthusiastic endorsement of my work and to Jon Berquist of Westminster John Knox Press for his splendid support along the way.

I am writing these words of appreciation as I approach my fortieth birthday, and for me it is a time to look back, not only on the process of researching wife abuse and writing this book, but also on my growth and development as a scholar and a committed member of a faith community. I want to acknowledge my parents' generosity for my educational background, not without some personal costs for my mother, who felt that I should never have gone that far from home, and my father, who had friends tell him that daughters should be prepared for marriage, not careers. Thank you for silencing those voices in your mind.

For half of my life, David has been my partner, and we have shared the joy of setting and meeting personal goals, not least of which includes raising our daughters. When we were undergraduates we used to share a worktable in the library, when we were doctoral candidates we pored over our empirical data at the computing center at the University of London, and though we have separate offices in our home now we have not lost the companionship that we shared in those early days. And for that I am truly grateful—it is support that I take for granted but could not do without.

There were times I wondered (and doubted) whether I would ever be able to meet the time deadline for the book's completion. As my panic became vocalized within my family, my two little girls, Christina and Natascha, of their own volition added Mommy's book to their list of nightly prayer requests. Thank you for trusting God on my behalf.

Throughout the pages of this book there are many voices to be heard: battered religious women, churchwomen active in ministering to one another, clergy, transition house workers, pastoral counselors, and members of congregations. It has been a tremendous privilege to share so intimately in the lives and experiences of others. I thank all of them for their time, their honesty, and their commitment to soul-searching concerning the issue of religious faith and violence against women. I trust that the account that follows addresses the pain and the healing process accurately and sensitively.

In the late spring of 1995, I was asked to deliver a plenary address at a workshop celebrating the completion of an eighteen-month interfaith family violence initiative in Eastern Canada titled Gethsemane's Comfort. As I prepared for and offered my address, I became intrigued and challenged by what messages the Garden of Gethsemane offers to those who wish to respond pastorally to victims of violence.

As a prelude to this book on Christianity and violence, it seemed fitting to ponder for just a moment some of the images that Christians might glean from the familiar scene set in the Garden of Gethsemane: Jesus' prayer to God for strength, the sleeping disciples unaware of the support they may offer, the "kiss" of betrayal, the soldiers, the exchange of coins, the arrest.

These images have been impressed on most Christian believers since the time they were children. Yet, as familiar as they are, these images provide a context for introducing the complexities and contradictions inherent in the study of religion and violence.

As a sociologist, I have come to learn the important role that stories play in helping families, churches, and communities make sense of their unique and collective experiences. The stories of scripture too play an important role in the life of the individual believer and of the faith community.

By reflecting for a moment on the pain and hope of Gethsemane, this prelude seeks to sensitize the reader to the power and reality of the hurt, betrayal, and long-term consequences of violence directed against those we purport to love. It offers a moving account of the partnership between God and human suffering.

While the word means olive press, the name "Gethsemane" refers to a garden across the Kidron Valley from Jerusalem, close to the Mount of Olives. Jesus and his small band of disciples went there often—it was a safe place, a place of refuge; a place to rest and receive spiritual strength and renewal. But it is best known as a place of betrayal. The disciple Judas knew where to take the soldiers, guards whose mandate was to arrest Jesus of Nazareth. Judas knew the spot where Jesus sought respite, for they had gone there together on many occasions. The garden that had offered shade in the heat, refuge from the crowds, sustenance for the human spirit, and privacy to communicate with God was the place where the beloved teacher was betrayed, wounded by someone who was loved and trusted.

This story reminds us that even where we feel the greatest refuge from the strains and pressures of contemporary life, we can also be the most vulnerable. The Garden of Gethsemane serves as a warning for us all—but especially for women and children—that we can be wounded and betrayed by those to whom we are closest and whom we trust.

But Gethsemane represents more than just pain and human anguish. It also signals hope, renewal, and strength to combat even the greatest challenges that betrayal can bring. This narrative reminds us that there are resources both within and beyond the human person that can transform a woman or man, girl or boy, from vulnerability to strength, from fear to calm, and from desperation to hope. So what hope does Gethsemane offer?

To respond pastorally to a victim of violence is to support that individual in finding the inner strength to leave the garden—and to work through the pain and betrayal to human wholeness. It offers hope while never diminishing the reality of the pain; it provides the basis for growth and independence without denying the fear of the unknown. Ultimately, it reveals the complexity of human relationships and provides a model of the partnership between God and human suffering.

The potential for partnership between the secular and the sacred in the struggle to end violence is immense. Yet, as this book will reveal, the road to achieving it is rather long. There are both opportunities and obstacles, cooperation and conflict. In the pages to follow we will consider how churches and their leaders have responded (or failed to respond) to the needs of abuse victims. We will also examine the reluctance of both secular and sacred caregivers to work together toward empowering women victims to gain control over their choices and ultimately their lives. And we will consider how churchwomen themselves have attempted to reduce the suffering of other women, sisters in the faith as well as women in the wider community.

Motifs of pain and hope also characterize the analysis of how contemporary Christianity is responding to abuse within its midst and within the larger society of which it is a part. Some churches have identified violence against women and children as a priority for ministry; others seem unaware of the suffering. Some religious leaders are knowledgeable and trained to support victims through the long healing journey; others offer pat answers and unhelpful (even harmful) advice. And some religious victims have found strength and support within their faith communities to work through the pain to wholeness, while others report anger and disappointment in the leaders of their faith traditions.

There is no simple solution to the problem of violence that invades relationships and homes. And there is no simple way to analyze how religious institutions have ministered successfully or ineffectively, or have failed to minister at all to victims—as well as perpetrators—of abuse. But the difficulty of the task should not sidetrack its importance.

The research described in this book attempts to address the relationship between Christianity and violence from divergent perspectives—that of clergy, woman victims, congregations, women's groups, youth, and the individual experiences of people of faith. It is one of the first attempts to tell the different parts of the story of what happens when religious people seek or receive counsel within their faith tradition. As we might expect, not everyone has the same story to tell. Yet, betrayal and hope—themes of the Garden of Gethsemane—help us to understand in part the journey from victim to survivor.

Listening to the Voices

When my daughter was four-and-a-half months pregnant with twins . . . her husband left her. We had him . . . three nights in a row out in front [of] our house, threatening to murder her, to burn our house down. We had friends sittin' up all night with us, takin' turns. My husband ended up having a nervous breakdown . . . The police were there probably up to three hours every night. We had him on tape threatening to kill her. The RCMP [Royal Canadian Mounted Police] picked her up. They hid us behind a building all day on a hot Saturday with a baby . . . while they escorted her to another area . . . He was never once arrested. He pulled his pants down in the middle of the street and urinated at the police officer.

(Woman #7, Focus Group #7)

But when a man picks up his wife and throws her . . . on the street three times in front of a whole audience . . . I mean is a man really supposed to be allowed to do that in front of the children? . . . This is what happened in my family, [to] my daughter, last year, downtown.

(Woman #21, Focus Group #28)

He had her up against the wall, pounding against the wall . . . and I was saying, "Cool it, cool it, man, cool it, cool it, cool it." And then she would yell at him, and he'd pound her again . . . So anyway then he turned on me and grabbed me and he lifted me like this, had me right on my toes . . . Eventually he left her . . . and killed himself. . . . She had a real commitment to that marriage and to that family not to leave him and she put up with abuse and abuse and abuse.

(Clergy Interview #500)

Satan is tearing apart the family and if men . . . [were] living the way God has designed them to live there wouldn't be an abused woman on the planet.

(Woman #1, Focus Group #12)

I'm a friend . . . [to some abused women] but also I'm safe, just a safe place to go.

(Clergy Interview #543)

I thank the Lord that I'm a great big two-hundred-pound guy because . . . I've had a husband who was violent against his wife haul and hit me and all I could think about was "these glasses cost me two hundred dollars and I don't want to get them broken." So I put my fists up and I said, "Go for it!" . . . If a man is screaming at me, as in this case, I don't coward down . . . If another man can try to intimidate me, great big two-hundred-pound guy, what makes me so friggin' mad is another man would do that to [his wife] . . . I see the violence against women and it makes me mad, and there's a lot of it going on.

(Clergy Interview #373)

I think this idea that we've been talking about, this coming alongside of, is a Christian responsibility for us as women. I think battered women have a tendency to feel, you know, very low in spirit, like they're not worth anything, you know, or have any purpose . . . We need to be encouraging one another . . . The scripture speaks to that . . . Men perhaps ministering to men, couples ministering to the couple . . . It doesn't take a professional necessarily to come alongside of a needy family . . . just a loving, caring concerned people reaching out to hurting people.

(Woman #4, Focus Group #6)

You know, when his first marriage broke up, I mean he, he not only beat his wife, but was endangering his children's lives. The second marriage broke up because he was beating up on his wife and was making comments that caused her to be really scared for the safety . . . of particularly the oldest daughter . . . His third marriage broke up when his third wife finally got tired to death of putting up with the pressure and the frustration . . . and was getting beat. And then she complained to her family and to her pastors. She wished somebody had told her. Well, I told the pastor and he agreed to do the wedding [anyway].

(Clergy Interview #277)

And I think that . . . a woman, you know, that's been abused will come to probably a woman in the church first even before the pastor.

(Woman #4, Focus Group #17)

I get a phone call, guy says, "I'm in jail, I've been accused of sexually assaulting my daughters and I need help". . . He used to throw kids' tricycles against the wall, he used to frighten, his anger and his volatile activity . . . He was the only male in the house, pushed the wife . . . They stayed away from him, even though they lived under the same roof . . . Both Christians, heavily involved . . . highly public leader in the church.

(Clergy Interview #514)

There's a mutual submission involved in marriage because Christian wives are said to submit to their husbands, but husbands are said to love their wives in sacrificial love, with Christ being the example . . . Love is . . . patient and kind and gentle and never fails, keeps no records of wrongs, so yeah, I think the idea of Christian love is the foundation of any marriage. It's the living it out that's the challenge.

(Clergy Interview #336)

I don't propose divorce or separation to any of the couples that I see at all . . . My focus in counseling [is] healing of relationships. Healing our relationship with God and healing our relationship with our self . . . healing our relationship with one another, that's my focus.

(Clergy Interview #552)

I would never say to a couple, [or] to a woman, or to a man, "You've got to stay in this relationship because God says you've got to stay in this relationship," I think that's hogwash.

(Clergy Interview #350)

There has to be a balance . . . of the spiritual counseling and the practical.
(Woman #4, Focus Group #17)

A few years ago while going through the ordination process in the United Methodist Church, I was asked to serve on the board of directors of a local shelter for battered women and their children. When the shelter women (board and staff) found out I was a clergyperson, they were obviously nervous. They all knew of clergy who had sent women back to batterers to pray harder or be more submissive. . . . During the same period I went to my Board of Ordained Ministry to continue my process toward full ordination . . . My paperwork that year included descriptions of my work at the shelter . . . In my interview, I was asked if I hated men, and if I was an angry feminist. . . . Ironically, I saw my work at the shelter as part of my call to ministry. . . . The shelter's hesitance about religion and the church's fear of feminism meant that both were curious about me.

(Letter from an ordinand sent to me in 1995)

I've grown up in the church and you're not supposed to get [a] divorce, you know. You married this guy and you're supposed to stick it out for better or worse and it's really a hard decision to finally leave. It's one of the hardest decisions I've ever made.

(Woman #2, Focus Group #1)

INTRODUCTION

The Research

Violence is so prevalent in our society that we assume it to be normative behavior. Whether we listen to the world news on the radio or watch it on television, we are exposed daily to numerous stories about violence: countries at war, terrorist attacks, or ethnic uprisings within nation-states vying for greater political or economic power for those of common ancestry. At the local level too, newsworthy events focus heavily on acts of violence: armed robberies, sexual predators, gang warfare, or isolated acts of aggression. As spectators of these repeated scenes of violence, it is easy to believe that the greatest threats to our personal or community safety lie outside the institutions we claim as sacred: the family and the church.

For long periods of time our society has *assumed* that men, women, and children equally enjoy both physical care and emotional well-being within the confines of their family home. Yet over the last twenty-five years evidence to the contrary has been accumulating. For millions of women and children, home life is replete with danger and marked by fear and tension. The reality and pervasiveness of violence in American and Canadian families cannot be denied. What is still denied in many circles, however, is that religious institutions have a role to play in both responding to the needs of abuse victims and reducing the violence that characterizes so many families.

This book grows out of a conviction that religious and secular institutions need to work together in common purpose to reduce and ultimately eliminate violence against women and other forms of family violence. The research data described and analyzed in the pages to follow are built on a continuing program of research conducted by the Religion and Violence Research Team of the Muriel McQueen Fergusson Centre for Family Violence Research at the University of New Brunswick, a team that I coordinate.[1]

The multidisciplinary Team is composed of both academic researchers and community partners, working in collaboration to understand more fully the role of churches and clergy in responding to the pain and suffering caused by violence in the family context. It was created with the specific purpose of addressing a gap in the current scholarly literature about violence against women and other types of family violence—the role of religion. While the Team's mandate is research-specific, its guiding policies are action oriented. Thus, the driving force of our program of research is to assist clergy, congregations, and individual men, women, and young people in faith communities to work toward reducing violence and responding with compassion to empower those who suffer the hurt and humiliation of abuse.

The following questions capture some of the Team's initial interest in the issue of family violence and religion: Do faith communities ease or intensify the suffering of victims of family violence? What difference does involvement with a specific faith community make in a battered woman's life? How do various faith traditions respond to the needs of victims—or perpetrators—of family violence? What is the role of a spiritual counselor in meeting the needs of hurting women and children? To what extent do churches and other faith traditions utilize secular community resources and refer parishioners outside of the religious community for help? Do secular counselors involve religious caregivers in cases where they know clients to be committed to a particular faith tradition? Is cooperation and collaboration possible, or even desirable? At the very early stages of our thinking about these issues, it became clear that very little empirical work had been done in this area.

As we approach the year 2000, the pressures and demands placed on both pastors and parishioners continue to escalate. So too do the complexities of the problems and stresses experienced by not only the people within the household of faith, but those living in the communities where churches serve. At times all these demands can seem overwhelming. Whether clergy, churches, and congregations respond fully and effectively to victims of male violence against women and other forms of family violence is one such challenge. As with most pressing social problems facing the church and the world, there is no simple solution, for there are many pieces to the violence puzzle. First and foremost, there are the practical needs of woman abuse victims and their families. Second, there is the victim's journey toward healing and wholeness, a long and painful process where continued support and services are critical. Third, there is need to break the cycle of abuse, which means services and support for both victims and offenders and their families. Fourth, churches need to ensure that their people and their leaders are knowledgeable about the dynamics of violence and compassionate in both offering services and making referral suggestions to those needing assistance. Fifth, there is a need to be proactive in faith communities in advocating and supporting violence-free family living.

Portions of this book will consider these various intersection points between churches and the issue of family violence. We will examine how clergy, religious women's groups, transition house workers, and abused women connected with faith communities talk about their experience of offering or receiving help. Moreover, this book will demonstrate that there are both pockets of support and resistance within evangelical denominations and within local congregations when it comes to responding to the issue of violence against women.

Like the subject of abuse itself, the story of the involvement of faith communities is complex: this book will document areas of strength and weakness; examples of innovative programs and of regressive advice; narratives of the contribution of religious faith toward the healing process, and others where religious experience worked against healing; clergy who were trained and experienced in helping abuse victims and their families and those who were not; secular workers who were open to the involvement of clergy in supporting abused women, and others who were not; and the myriad stories of the involvement of people of faith in the struggle to promote violence-free family life and to respond to those whose reality contrasts with that ideal.

One of the unique features of this book is that it is built on the reported experiences of over a thousand clergy and lay people from a wide range of evangelical churches, representing small and large congregations as well as urban and rural contexts, supplemented by the experiences of a small number of transition house workers. The research design includes survey data, focus group discussions, participant observation, and in-depth interviews.

Outline of the Research Initiative

Study 1 was a pilot project that examined tensions, contradictions, and collaboration between clergy and transition house workers in selected regions of Eastern Canada, with a goal of identifying areas of cooperation and coordination. Twelve different sites were chosen, and both clergy and shelter workers were interviewed in those locations. In many ways, the results of Study 1 influenced the design of subsequent projects, not least by emphasizing the important role played by churchwomen's groups in support of the transition house movement.

Study 2 was a quantitative study involving all pastors of United Baptist and Wesleyan churches serving in Atlantic Canada. The data collection covered clergy experience with woman and child abuse, knowledge of family violence issues, and referral practices related to violence and abuse. A total of 343 clergy (70 percent response rate) participated in this phase of the research program.

Study 3 was built on the results of the clergy survey and involved personal interviews with a sample of 100 evangelical ministers in various locations across the Atlantic Provinces. In addition to a more in-depth examination of clergy experience and knowledge of woman and child abuse, this research focused specifically on pastoral counseling approaches with abused women and the advice and support they offered to families in crises.

Study 4 explored the unique and specific needs of evangelical churchwomen who suffer abuse and the responses of women within the evangelical church to the needs of abused women. It involved focus group interviews in 30 churches, representing rural, urban, and small-town contexts. A total of 247 women participated in these focus group interviews. Follow-up personal interviews with 94 individual women were conducted as part of a further project.[2]

Study 5 is a smaller project which explored the role of youth groups and youth pastors in responding to the needs of young people associated with evangelical churches. It draws on data collected from 10 church youth groups and interviews with selected youth pastors.[3]

Study 6 examines family functioning within evangelical churches from the perspective of individual men and women connected to evangelical churches. Designed as a congregational study, it employs a sample of 24 churches representing rural, urban, and suburban settings.[4]

Taken together, these projects portray a comprehensive picture of how churches, their leaders, and the individual men and women who support them think about—and have experienced—the relationship between religious faith and family violence. While this book focuses primarily on the evangelical sector of contemporary Christianity, our research program has now been extended to include collaborative projects with the Anglican Church of Canada, the Maritime Conference of the United Church, and the Maritime Division of the Salvation Army.

The book is organized into four sections: the social, cultural, and religious context of abuse; evidence of the pervasiveness and seriousness of abuse in families of faith; current attempts to respond to victims of abuse and their families by clergy and their congregations; and working toward new solutions and new partnerships.

Two chapters will be devoted to exploring the cultural and religious environment in which any discussion of violence against women and other forms of family violence must be contextualized. Here we will address such questions as: What is the role of male-female power inequities in understanding the frequency and severity of wife abuse? What happens when children witness their mother as victim and their father as aggressor? Why has the role of religion been virtually ignored by the social science community when it comes to understanding violence in the family setting? Why is there so little religious discourse on abuse and so much on family hierarchy? Does conservative religious ideology put women followers at greater risk of abuse? Does an evangelical Christian worldview negate or augment the possibility of breaking the cycle of violence?

The second section of the book—evidence of abuse in faith communities—is divided into two chapters, one that explores what conservative religious women do when they are abused, while the other chapter considers the demand for pastoral counseling on behalf of women, men, and children who are victims—or perpetrators—of violence in the family context. Questions we will address in these chapters include: Where do Christian women turn when they have been victimized by their husbands? What factors impede a religious woman from disclosing her abuse? What services do religious abuse victims use and are they helpful? How knowledgeable are clergy about wife abuse? What training and experience can they offer families in crisis? Are they willing to make referrals outside the faith community, and how often do they do so?

The third section of the book will explore current attempts by churches, women's groups, and clergy to respond to the needs of abuse victims and their families. In chapter 5, we will consider in some detail the advice clergy offer to abused women and their families. We will also examine both the spiritual and the secular (or practical) components of their counseling or response to abuse victims. Within this chapter we will ask: How does a clerical counselor differ in perspective from one trained in the discipline of psychology or social work? What do clergy, as an occupational group, believe they have to offer victims—or perpetrators—of family violence? What does counseling mean to a religious leader, and how does it differ from counseling offered in a secular context? What advice do they give a battered woman or an abusive man?

Chapter 6 will consider how women-helping-women has become the model of women's ministries within evangelical circles. We will look at the level of involvement of religious women in offering practical and emotional support to women victimized by their husbands. This chapter will examine to what degree evangelical women are hampered or encouraged in their efforts to deal with violence as a result of their traditional understandings of women's role in the family, church, and general society.

The fourth section—and final chapter—of the book will offer a look down the road and into the next century. Here we will ask about emerging partnerships between secular and sacred service providers. As fiscal restraint becomes the prerogative of modern governments and social services are trimmed to meet constricting budgets, churches and secular organizations will be forced to think about new ways of working together. From the point of view of secular agencies, churches have several enviable characteristics, not least of which includes space, an army of volunteers, and a mission to help those in need. From the point of view of religious institutions, secular agencies often have a critical mass of professional knowledge and experience, as well as links to other services and to those in need of such services. In this chapter, we will consider examples of bridge building between sacred and secular personnel committed to ending violence against women and other forms of family violence. Can we be optimistic about partnership as we move to the year 2000?

When I am asked to offer an address on violence against women—to clergy or religious audiences—I often include the phrase "beyond belief" in my title. For these words capture some of the complexities, contradictions, and ambiguities that arise out of our multifaceted examination of contemporary Christianity and battery. The nature and pervasiveness of male violence against women is *beyond belief* for those men and women sheltered personally from the devastation of violence in their childhood or adult homes. The silence about wife abuse amid the burgeoning Christian family literature is also *beyond belief*. And then there are the data we examine from clergy, women abuse victims, transition house workers, and women connected to local congregations. Here too the words *beyond belief* ring true: sometimes in terms of the extraordinary compassion and support that is offered; sometimes a reflection of the regressive advice and insensitivity that characterizes churches' response to victims and their families.

Finally, the phrase *beyond belief* offers a challenge to those of us who want to reduce and eliminate violence in our communities and in our churches. For it is indeed *beyond our beliefs* that action will come. The struggle for survivors, the healing journey and collaborative ventures between the sacred and the secular, all necessitate direct human intervention. To comfort and empower women victims and to fight the structures that give rise to their suffering is a monumental undertaking. But, then, the mission of the Christian church has never been for the fainthearted.

1

The Social and Cultural Context of Abuse in the Family

The Family Is Sacred . . . *but It's Not Always Safe*

The Christian church holds firmly to the belief that the family is an institution ordained by God. With the Bible on their side, churches argue that God planned for men and women to choose partners for life and to share life's journey, in good times and amid trials. Through toil and celebration, fathers and mothers have been instructed to love and nurture their children and to pass on the story of faith and obedience. From pulpits and within the hearts of like-minded believers, the message is cherished: *The family is sacred.*

But there is a startling reality the Christian church needs to face. Many, many mothers and children in our neighborhoods—and in our churches—do not experience the family as God intended it to be. Rather than being provided a safe haven from the pressures and strains of contemporary life, for millions of women and children "going home" is something to fear.

At least one woman in six in the United States and Canada has experienced a violent episode at the hands of her husband within the last year.[1] Furthermore, more than one woman in every four has at some time in her adult life experienced a violent outburst from her partner.[2] Every day scores of children witness their father strike their mother or are the victims of parental rage themselves.[3] This violence affects church families, too. Each year, pastors report an increasing number of victims of family violence who seek their counsel.[4] Wife abuse is not isolated in the inner city, nor is it a direct result of poverty, alcoholism, or unemployment.[5]

No community or church is immune to the problem of violence in the home. In fact, women are more likely to be harmed by their husbands than they are by strangers. Statistically speaking, it is far more dangerous to go home than to walk city streets alone at night. In the words of Marilyn French, violence represents individual men's physical war against women, creating a climate so pervasive that it produces fear in all women, whether or not they have ever actually been a victim of violence.[6]

While the purpose of this book is to understand the response of contemporary Christianity to violence in the family, it is important to contextualize that discussion against the backdrop of the emerging information about the prevalence of violence against women (and children) in our society, and of theoretical formulations concerning the nature and cycle of abusive family patterns. While this chapter cannot possibly be exhaustive in its scope or presentation, the goal is to *highlight several issues related to abuse that will guide our later discussion about the Christian church and its response to this major social problem.*

Is Family Violence a New Problem?

Violence against women, as well as other forms of family violence, is not new. What has changed during the last ten to fifteen years is women's willingness to report it and a growing openness on the part of the helping professions (such as medicine or social work) to listen to women's stories of abuse and to respond to their needs.[7] Shame, embarrassment, guilt, and fear have kept and continue to keep many women from telling anyone else what takes place within the four walls of their homes. Abused women have often blamed themselves for being poor wives or mothers. They have excused their husbands' behavior. They have hoped or prayed for change.

When a woman musters the courage to tell a friend, a family member, or a pastor her life experiences, she may be ridiculed, dismissed, or accused of lying. Could a man who seems so nice in other contexts actually be violent at home? The answer—though few are willing to admit it—is "Yes."

From a historical perspective, the "right" of husbands to beat (or even kill) their wives is embedded in Roman law.[8] Implicit within this right of husbands to subjugate their wives by force was the belief that wives needed to meet some standard of conduct, and that those who failed would be chastised. The historical context within which battering emerged and flourished is rooted in male domination of women both within and outside the family.[9] Eighteenth- and nineteenth-century legal definitions of the criminality of assaults on wives viewed woman battery as noncriminal as long as no visible marks remained[10] or if inflicted by a stick no thicker than the thumb—hence the phrase "rule of thumb." Clearly the Judeo-Christian religious framework played a supportive role in the development of patriarchal attitudes toward women, though it has been the subject of much debate as to whether such values are *inherent* in this belief system.[11]

Within the secular society, there was a growing literature on child abuse by the mid-1960s, though violence toward wives received little public attention until the 1970s. In fact, prior to 1970 there was not a single article to appear in the popular *Journal of Marriage and the Family* (begun in 1939) with the word "violence" in the title[12]. According to Murray Straus, one of the most prolific researchers in the area of family violence, three factors were influential in the emergence of violence in the family context within the 1970s: (1) an increasing sensitization toward violence in all corners of society; (2) the emerging second wave of feminism, which brought women together in "consciousness-raising" groups to share their life experiences; and (3) theoretical challenges within the discipline of sociology that advocated abandoning a consensus model of society in favor of a more conflict orientation.[13]

But part of the silence was the notion, too, that what happens in the home is a private matter. Because family violence occurs behind closed doors, it is hidden and removed from public scrutiny. By the 1970s, however, new legislation required the reporting of child abuse, and shelters for battered wives—though few in number—were established in various locations across the continent. Many of the first studies of battered women collected their data from the lives and experiences of women who sought refuge in a transition house.[14]

What Is Abuse?

Family violence includes all forms of violent or abusive behavior that occur within intimate relationships. While deliberate acts of physical violence or abuse tend to be most closely identified with family violence, other abusive behavior can include willful neglect and sexual, emotional, or financial abuse as well as threats of intended aggressive acts. The most common victims of family violence are women, children, and the elderly, though men too can be abuse victims. Violence in the family always involves the abuse of power and control to hurt, shame, or humiliate another person through intimacy and shared experience.[15] The consequences of family violence are far-reaching and enduring for its victims: in addition to physical and emotional pain, there is the violation of the trusting relationship which may never be resolved. For religious victims, their spiritual journey may be adversely affected as well.

Defining and naming violence that takes place between family members has been, and continues to be, a difficult and sensitive task. Some early understandings of violence included behaviors ranging from shoving and pushing to throwing objects, choking, or breaking bones.[16] Yet such definitions tended to limit abuse to what could be identified by physical injuries or by a medical examination. As a result, other forms of abuse—like emotional abuse—remained hidden.[17] Current literature on violence tends to be far less restrictive in its scope or definition than was true in the past.[18]

While definitions of violence have broadened over time,[19] naming the behavior still sparks debate.[20] Grass-roots feminists have worked diligently to reveal the extent of male violence against women[21] and to establish services for the victims of that violence.[22] As a result, they label the behavior as male violence against women and strongly resist any notion that abuse is a family issue.[23]

Feminists claim that resistance to the term wife abuse reflects their gradual loss of control of the issue to both the state and powerful professions. In this way, they believe, the grass-roots women's organizations are being marginalized and effectively silenced in their work to end violence against women, and to politicize male anger and control.[24] Lost in this "mainstreaming" of the wife battery movement, then, is the feminist analysis of male violence as a form of social control.[25] And as a result, the challenge to the core values and institutions that perpetuate male privilege is ignored.[26] In its place, professionalism and careerism within the battered woman's movement has created discrepancies and inequities between the voices of the survivors and the voices of the caregivers.[27] As we will discuss at length in a later chapter, *naming the problem* of violence within a family context has important and far-reaching implications for one's response to it as well as the potential steps to eliminate it.

Understanding the Context of Wife Abuse

Though family violence most often occurs "behind closed doors,"[28] it does not take place in a vacuum, but rather in a carefully crafted context of shame and secrecy, upheld by pervasive societal beliefs in the privacy and sanctity of the family.[29] Ultimately, it is reinforced by a society that teaches that people with power have the right to control those who are "worth less" than they are.[30] Moreover, it happens within a cultural milieu that glorifies violence as a "problem solver and as entertainment."[31]

To be sure, there are paradoxes and contradictions in most human relationships. Within violent families these paradoxes are profound, "the love and sometimes hate, the affection and sometimes violence, the pleasure and the wounding, the attachment that, in many cases, continues in spite of the abuse."[32] Feminists continue to highlight the connections between wife battery and women's subordinate position in the family.[33] In a sense, wife abuse exposes the danger of the patriarchal family structure for women and sets the stage for male control. Moreover, it contributes to the isolation that individual women feel.[34]

In their ground-breaking study *Violence against Wives: A Case against the Patriarchy,* Dobash and Dobash argue that the seeds of wife-beating lie in the subordination of females and in their subjection to male authority and control.[35] They write:

> This relationship between women and men has been institutionalized in the structure of the patriarchal family and is supported by the economic and political institutions and by a belief system, including a religious one, that makes such relationships seem natural, morally just and sacred.[36]

Joy Bussert claims that as long as theological traditions cling to submission as the theory for male-female marital relations, then battering will inevitably continue to be the practice.[37] Patriarchy provides a social structure of ownership of women by men that makes it possible for men to do "whatever they want with their woman."[38] Denial and silence in religious communities about wife abuse, then, may not only immobilize religious victims but inadvertently encourage the behavior of perpetrators.[39] As a result, the churches' silence about sexual violence has been regarded by some as an act of complicity.[40]

Since the rights, roles, and responsibilities of men and women have been institutionalized and continue to exert their power through the promotion of gender inequality, the cultural and religious milieu is conducive to abuse within the family. Several religious feminists believe that both the misappropriation and misinterpretation of the Bible augment the problem of woman battery.[41] To be sure, violence against women under patriarchy has been fostered by religious thought and practice, if only inadvertently.[42] In essence, it is the combination of a belief in male authority, the objectification of women, a sociocultural system that forces women to be economically dependent on men, and the ability of batterers to use physical force with relatively few legal or social consequences that accounts for why family violence is so pervasive and why a disproportionate number of victims are women.[43]

While it is inaccurate and insensitive to speak for all women as if mere female embodiment erased a woman's individual characteristics—such as social class, culture, ethnicity, religion, race, age, or disability—violence in many ways disregards women's individuality.[44] Yet women of color,[45] or immigrants,[46] or poor women,[47] or disabled women[48] differ in terms of their response to that abuse and the social structural support available to them.[49] These differences notwithstanding, all women live with the fear or reality of violence.[50]

The Prevalence of Violence against Women

There are three major sources from which social scientists obtain data concerning wife abuse: clinical samples, official statistics, and random sample surveys. It is important to highlight the different sources, for indeed each offers part of the picture needed to understand the frequency and context of wife battering. Clinical samples are by far the most frequent source of data on family violence; these studies are conducted at shelters where abused women have sought safety, or data is collected by clinical researchers within their practice of psychology, social work, or medicine.

Research data obtained at a transition house, or shelter, offers rich, in-depth material of the experience of violence from the point of view of the woman victim. Because her escape from a violent home is relatively recent, the battered woman in a shelter environment is able to offer the researcher valuable insights about the context and dynamics of the abusive home, including her decision to leave. Yet, as important and moving as these accounts are, they tell only part of the story of wife abuse. Many women never leave the men who abuse them or seek professional help or advice. Moreover, women with independent resources do not typically seek refuge in a shelter. Consequently, the data obtained from clinical samples cannot be generalized to the entire population of abused women. While studies conducted in a clinical setting offer the researcher perhaps the most detailed look at violence directed toward wives and partners, it is important to understand that they are limited in some respects, most notably in terms of the generalizability of the research findings. Because most abused women do not seek shelter at a transition house or therapy from a professional, clinical studies tell us only one part of the struggle of victims.

A second source of data is official statistics, including those compiled for police records or, in the case of child abuse, the statistics collected by social service departments as citizens respond to mandatory reporting legislation. Yet, unfortunately, many cases are never reported. And for wife abuse, there is currently no legal mandate to report suspicion. As a result, official statistics, though important, tell only a very small part of the story of wife abuse. As well, these data are often limited to prevalence rates and therefore tell us little about the factors and circumstances that accompany violence against women.

A third source of data concerning violence in the home is collected through random sample surveys. The expense of undertaking this form of research initiative generally necessitates that the amount of information gathered from each participant is rather limited. Yet one of the main advantages of the random sample technique is that the results can be generalized back to the population from which the survey was drawn (e.g., all women 18–75 living in the state of California; all women in Eastern Canada over the age of 21). Typically, though, random surveys do not contain the wealth or detail of data generated from clinical samples, and often the response rate is very low. Thus, if we are intent on understanding as much of the picture of abuse as possible, more than one research strategy is imperative. With this overview of the research strategies open to those interested in family violence issues, we turn to consider the incidence rates of wife abuse.

In 1993, Statistics Canada conducted a national survey of 12,300 women (aged 18 years and older) concerning their experiences of physical and sexual violence and their perceptions of personal safety. This was the first national survey of its kind anywhere in the world to ask a large random national sample of women about violence perpetrated against them. According to the Statistics Canada survey,[51] three in ten Canadian women currently or previously married or coupled have experienced at least one incident of physical or sexual violence by their partner, violence that is consistent with legal definitions of these offenses and hence against the law. One in six currently married women reported abuse by her spouse and one in two women with previous marriages reported abuse by that previous spouse. The data confirm that women face the greatest risk from the men they know.[52]

The Violence against Women Survey reveals that many women experienced ongoing violence from husbands or live-in partners: 63% of women who had been assaulted by a current or past partner had been victimized on more than one occasion, 32% more than ten times. One in every three of the women who had been assaulted by their partners feared for her own life at some point during the abuse. Women who reported having a violent father-in-law were at three times the risk of abuse (36%) of women with nonviolent fathers-in-law (12%). And the study reports that children witness the violence against their mothers in approximately 40% of violent households. In sum, then, these data indicated that for most abused women abusive episodes are chronic, extending over a long period of time. Repeated incidents of violence far outnumber isolated acts of aggression in the life of a woman victim.

Alcohol was also found to be a prominent factor in women's reports of violence, for abusers had been consuming alcoholic beverages in more than 40% of violent incidents. Women who lived with men who drank regularly were at far greater risk of assault than women who lived with partners who didn't drink at all. Almost one in two (45%) wife assault incidents resulted in injury, though in only 28% of the cases did women report seeking medical attention; 90% of incidents were reported to have an emotional effect on the victim. Weapons were used by 44% of violent spouses—16% of the women reported having a gun or knife used against them.

Despite the pervasiveness and repetitive nature of the violence directed toward women by men, few wife assault victims reported incidents to the police

(26%), and in only 24% of the incidents did victims seek the help of a social agency. Only 8% of women victims of wife abuse contacted a transition house and 6% stayed there at some point. Women reported that they relied mostly on friends and neighbors (51%) and family (42%) as a source of support. A small proportion of women disclosed the violence to a physician (9%) or a religious leader (2%). According to these data, victims in 22% of violent incidents told no one about their experience prior to disclosing it to a Statistics Canada telephone interviewer.

The Statistics Canada study updated what had been a widely proclaimed rate of about one in ten women per year who suffered abuse at the hands of male partners.[53] The one-in-ten Canadian figure had been extrapolated from information on the number of physically battered women in transition houses and the number of divorces filed on the ground of physical cruelty, though it was often acknowledged to be an underestimate.[54]

One of the major researchers in the United States for the study of family violence is Dr. Murray Straus, of the Family Research Laboratory at the University of New Hampshire. This team has developed what is known as the Conflict Tactics Scale, for identifying the form and frequency of violent acts between family members.[55] Though the scale has come under intense criticism from some other researchers,[56] to which the originators have attempted to respond,[57] it nonetheless does clearly allow us to dispel any notion that violence in the family is rare. The 1975 National Family Violence Survey conducted by this team of researchers was the first large-scale study of violence in a representative sample of American families.[58] That initial survey was replicated a decade later.[59] For over twenty years, they have argued that about one in six couples report at least one violent incident per year, and that when the referent period covers their entire relationship, the figure rises to over one in four.[60]

Other estimates place the proportion of women who are abused by their husbands in the United States from 30 percent to 60 percent.[61] Depending on the questions asked and the research sample utilized, estimates vary. Despite these differences, however, we can conclude that violence is common among partners who purport to love each other. And spouse abuse is most often men victimizing women. No matter how you define abuse, and irrespective of the manner in which you collect the data, a significant proportion of women in North America suffer physical cruelty at the hands of their husbands or partners each year.

Clearly the battery of women takes place in homes across the nation, with epidemiological research demonstrating that violence cuts across every demographic level measured. It happens in all social classes, though it may be even more difficult to detect among the more affluent members of society. It knows no ethnic or religious boundaries, though particular groups of women, like immigrant women or those involved in very closed religious communities, may be especially vulnerable when abused.[62] Throughout later chapters of this book, we will consider in detail some of the particular needs and presenting issues of religious women who are abused, particularly those who seek help from within their faith community from other women or from religious leaders.

Marital Rape:
A Specific Form of Wife Abuse

Diana Russell in 1982 obtained some of the first direct evidence about the rates of marital rape in the population at large.[63] In her study of 930 women residents of San Francisco aged eighteen and over, 14 percent of the 622 married women reported that they had been forced to have intercourse with their marital partner against their will; another 2 percent had experienced other types of forced sex. In 1985, Finkelhor and Yllo conducted a study in Boston among a representative sample of 326 women about whether a spouse, or person with whom they were living as a couple, had ever used physical force or threat of force for sex.[64] Exactly one in ten married women answered in the affirmative.

Within our society, the concept of marital rape has been regarded as "a contradiction in terms," with the vows "I do" offered at the marriage ceremony interpreted as a "statement of permanent consent to sex."[65] Women raped by their husbands lose their confidence to form and sustain enduring intimate relationships, since the sexual violation shatters their ability to trust others. As Kersti Yllo and Donna LeClerc have pointed out, "a woman raped by her husband has to live with her rapist, not just a frightening memory of a stranger's attack."[66]

Sexual violence is, without doubt, an act of violence, hatred, and aggression. As Marie Fortune has argued, no matter how sexual violence is understood—from a clinical or legal perspective—violence is the common denominator.[67] For the religious victim of marital rape, attitudes and values associated with her faith community may make it especially hard to disentangle what rights she has to her own body and whether it is her wifely duty to submit to forced or even violent sexual acts whenever and wherever her husband chooses.[68]

The Abusive Cycle

Lenore Walker describes three stages that occur in most abusive relationships: tension building; the crisis; and the aftermath.[69] In the first, or tension-building phase, the abuse victim tries to please the batterer and keep his world calm, acting as a "tension manager."[70] But according to Walker's research all the victim can do at this point is to influence the timing of the crisis: if she is able to behave in a way that pleases the abuser, phase two (the abusive acts) is delayed; if she "misbehaves," she speeds up the crisis. The second phase, or crisis period, is when the most serious injuries occur. But Walker cautions against focusing too exclusively on the discrete events of phase two, for to do so minimizes the repetitive and escalating danger of the abusive cycle. The final phase of the cycle—the aftermath—involves contrition and loving behavior and was observed in about two thirds of the 1,600 cases Walker studied in 1984.[71] During this period, there are pleas for forgiveness and the offer of gifts, but the acceptance of these may simply perpetuate or reinforce the abusive behavior. While there is no one profile of spouse abuse, there are some patterns that can be detected by the trained observer.[72]

The Intergenerational
Transmission of Abuse

Violence is learned behavior. More than half of all abusive men experienced *or* witnessed violence in their childhood homes.[73] Sons who watch their fathers' aggressive acts toward their mothers are far more likely to abuse their wives in the future.[74] In fact, the previously mentioned Statistics Canada study revealed that women with violent fathers-in-law are three times as likely to suffer assault by their partners as are women with nonviolent fathers-in-law.

Estimates suggest that between 50 and 75 percent of wife abusers experienced or witnessed severe violence in childhood.[75] More specifically, the Family Research Laboratory at the University of New Hampshire found that sons who have witnessed their fathers' violence have a 1,000 percent greater rate of wife abuse than sons spared this childhood experience.[76] These researchers conclude that each generation learns to be violent by participating in a violent family. Canadian psychologist Peter Jaffe and colleagues found among a sample of school-age boys that exposure to family violence may be as harmful to the child as physical abuse.[77] The recent Statistics Canada Violence against Women Survey found compelling evidence for the cycle of violences being passed on from one generation to the next.

Further evidence for the intergenerational transmission of violence comes from the case studies of Rosenbaum and O'Leary, and of O'Leary and Curley.[78] In these studies, abusive husbands were more likely to have experienced or witnessed abuse as children than a control group of men who were in dysfunctional but nonviolent relationships. In fact, the witness or experience of abuse was the critical distinguishing factor between these two groups of men.

Witnessing violence has a long-term impact. Given that at least one in three battered wives report that their children have observed the violence against them,[79] it should concern the church greatly that the next generation of abusive men are now small boys watching their mothers suffer.

Not only is violence transmitted intergenerationally, there is also an intragenerational cycle as well. Kalmuss and Seltzer found higher rates of spouse abuse in remarried families.[80] Using data obtained from the 1976 National Survey of Family Violence, they found that remarried adults who had been divorced were substantially more likely to have observed physical aggression between their parents than were adults who had never been divorced. Furthermore, they found that spouse abuse was more likely in families in which one or both partners had been divorced.

Those who have studied the intragenerational cycle of abuse contend that research results support the belief that divorced couples carry behavioral patterns from previous marriages into remarriage, bringing certain negative components of their marital repertoire into remarriage. Although we ought to be concerned to break the cycle of violence that is transmitted from one generation to another, we ought also to be concerned to break the chain of abuse that travels from marriage to remarriage within the same generation.

What Do We Know about Abusive Men?

The data available on abusive men come from three main sources: in-depth interviews with abused women who are reporting on the characteristics and behavior of their abusive partner(s); random sample survey data gleaned from national or regional studies, where a proportion of the respondents self-identify their abusive behavior; and participants in programs for men who abuse their wives or partners.

In their book *Behind Closed Doors,* Straus and colleagues contend that the lower a husband's economic and prestige resources relative to that of his wife, the greater the tendency to use physical violence to maintain a male-dominant power position within the family. As such, then, abuse may follow husbands' unemployment or difficulties with the labor force. Other researchers have also found that negative work experiences for men are associated with violent acts perpetrated against their wives.[81] As the number of stressful work events increases, this may impact on a man's perceived ability to cope at the place of employment and at home.

Low self-esteem is a factor that is often associated with aggressive behavior, and not surprisingly has been implicated in wife abuse.[82] Abusive husbands are more likely to perceive their wives' behavior as threatening to their sense of self. Data on abusive men and low self-esteem support the idea that the probability of violence is increased when a man with low self-esteem perceives that his sense of self is being threatened.[83] Others contend that the higher level of general aggression in wife batterers interacts with characteristics in their family of origin, poor communication skills, and a lack of self-confidence in a fashion that makes spouse abuse more likely.[84]

In a small-scale interview study of abusive men who had participated in a Boston-area counseling service for batterers, it was revealed that both *excuses* and *justifications* were common responses by the men to account for their personal acts of aggression.[85] In a chapter titled "How Men Who Batter Rationalize Their Behavior," James Ptacek documents ways that abusive men use *excuses,* thereby denying full responsibility for their actions. Here are the words of two participants:

"It's taken the edge off my self-control. That's what I call it, being intoxicated. It's taken my limits off me and let me do things and become disruptive in a way I would not become."

"It was all booze. I didn't think. I didn't think at all. I was just like a madman. It was temporary insanity. I really, all's I really wanted to do was crush her. There was nothing there but I wanted to cause pain and mess her looks up."[86]

While some abusive men *excused* their behavior by blaming alcohol, others engaged in *justification:* "I never beat my wife. I responded physically to her"; or "[She was] not injured. She bruises easily"; or "I'd yell at her, and scream, and stuff like that, and maybe I'd whack her once or twice, you know, but I wasn't going to kill her."[87]

The issue of male entitlement—of services and of emotional support from the women they love—seems to be a central feature in understanding the behavior of batterers.[88] Frequently the literature on abusive men has argued that the root of "male entitlement" is patriarchal religion,[89] despite the fact that many authors have demonstrated that the Bible has given at least as many messages to treat women well.[90] Yet, regardless of the impact or role of religion, it has been generally assumed that women's lot in life is to meet male expectations of her and to expect punishment if she is unable to meet or prevented from meeting that ideal.[91]

According to James Ptacek, the interview transcripts of the abusive men in his study revealed that the men were "motivated by a desire to silence their partners, to punish them for their failure as 'good wives,' and to achieve and maintain dominance."[92] And the abusive behavior they subjected their partners to met its objectives. Their wives were silenced—taught a lesson, as it were—and the batterer reinforced his control over both the relationship and his partner. The maintenance of power and control by an abusive man is central to any feminist analysis of wife battery,[93] though the standards these men set for the specific women they abused were often arbitrary and unspoken.[94]

Despite the fact that some couples equally initiate abusive acts,[95] it is most often the man who controls whether or not there will be violence in the home.[96] Data on abusive men suggest that when certain family background factors exist (like observing their father hit their mother), when there are multiple stressors (like marital discord or employment stress), and when certain personality characteristics exist (such as low self-esteem) male violence against wives is more likely to occur.[97] Social work professor Larry Bennett claims that most of the violent men he has counseled insist that their female partners were abusive with them as well, but interestingly none of these men "were afraid to go home at night."[98]

While abusive men may blame their violent behavior on alcohol,[99] it is not a primary cause of violence against wives, for more than half of abuse cases occur in the absence of drinking alcoholic beverages.[100] Still, we should not underestimate the relationship between alcohol and violence—since there is a strong correlation between alcohol use and physical violence in the home.[101] It is important to remember that men who abuse their wives when drinking heavily also abuse them when sober.[102] As a result, some researchers have hypothesized that wife abusers may become intoxicated in order to carry out a violent act.[103] Thus, contrary to conventional wisdom, excessive alcohol consumption cannot explain abuse in isolation from other factors, though families where substance abuse occurs share a variety of characteristics with abusive families, including the intergenerational transmission of the problem, frequent crisis states, victim blaming, and isolationism.[104]

Why Do Women Remain with Abusive Partners?

For women who have never been in abusive relationships and who have not witnessed abuse in their childhood home, the question that seems so puzzling is "Why do women remain with men who are abusive toward them?" While the answer for any individual woman is complex, there are several common features.

Fear is the number-one reason why women stay with men who abuse them. They fear further violence and they fear for their children.[105] For many women, the impact of repeated abuse is paralyzing terror, a fear that grips them so fully that it rules their actions, their decisions, and their daily routine. This fear means that many battered wives spend their lives keeping the secret of their abuse from family, friends, and neighbors.

In her book *Battered Wives,* Del Martin contends that although women who are abused give many reasons or rationalizations for staying, fear is the common denominator.[106] Because of the pervasiveness and power of fear (including the fear of reprisal), abused women stay in violent homes rather than fleeing to a neighbor's or a shelter. As a result, Martin believes, many battered wives spend more energy in keeping the secret of abuse and in trying to salvage self-respect than in any attempts to extricate themselves from their dangerous environment. From clinical samples of abused women, it is clear that fear leads to a sense of hopelessness, which itself is a form of loss of control.[107] And it is important to remember that the violence does not stop when the battered wife leaves her abusive husband;[108] sometimes it intensifies as women seek help,[109] or after they have left.[110]

Finances are a critical factor in understanding why women remain with their abusive partners.[111] Economic dependency and a woman's lack of resources are directly linked to her choice to stay in an abusive relationship. A sense of hopelessness pervades her life. She may not have advanced training or education, she may not have worked for pay since her children were born, or she may have a very low paying job with few benefits and no security. Besides, some violent men are good providers financially. For scores of women, this means they see no way out of a life of abuse.[112]

Within our contemporary society, a paycheck offers women both a sense of self-esteem and a measure of self-worth: it is tangible evidence that someone deems your labor worthy of pay.[113] For women who have worked as housewives and mothers full-time, considering it "a labor of love,"[114] and within an economy that is constricting rather than expanding, entrance into the labor market appears formidable. As a result, Gelles has concluded that the fewer resources a battered woman has at her disposal and the lower her power, the more probable it is she will remain in an abusive home.[115] Sullivan and Rumptz argue that a woman's economic dependence on her husband is a major factor in whether or not she returns to an abusive home from a shelter or other safe place.[116]

Fantasy of change, or a glimmer of hope that the violence will someday cease, also keeps battered women with their abusive partners. There is a pattern to abuse, whereby after an abusive episode there may be remorse on the part of the husband or partner and a promise to turn from his violent ways. Although few violent men do change, many abused women cling to that hope year after year.[117]

For service providers, abused women's hope for change can be particularly frustrating.[118] In fact, clinical studies reveal that it often takes dozens of abusive incidents for an abused wife to leave her abusive husband the first time, and then several separations before a woman who has been beaten will relinquish her faith and trust for change.[119] In this way, leaving becomes not a single act but a process.[120] Regarding that process of leaving, Marden and Rice conclude that there are four dimensions to how abused women use hope as a coping mechanism: hope for change in the violent behavior; hope for personal survival; hope as something to cling on to in the midst of uncertainty; and hope for control of the situation.[121] For some pastoral counselors, trust and hope do not simply augment the healing process, they *are* healing[122]; certainly clergy are well immersed in the language of faith and hope.[123]

There are many other reasons why women feel reluctant to leave abusive homes. Some feel the marriage must be saved no matter how much suffering occurs; others feel guilt and responsibility for men's abusive actions, believing in part that as wives they have failed to be "tension managers"[124] in the home, and still other women believe they deserve the abuse.[125] Some contend that since their husband is a batterer, he must be a sick man, and therefore he really needs their help.[126] Yet as Deborah Prieur has observed, women living with battery are not passive. They try to stop the abuse, but concurrently "they try to meet their social-assigned responsibility for keeping their relationships and families together."[127]

In their study of rural Canadian women, Merritt-Gray and Wuest contend that rather than conceptualizing abused women as passive victims, survivors in their study counteracted abuse from its inception, by relinquishing parts of "the self," minimizing the pain and consequences of the violence, and fortifying their personal defenses against it.[128] Consequently, women need social and structural support to help them justify their termination of an abusive relationship and conclude that for them "enough is enough."[129] For Christian women who are abused, other dynamics as well may be important in understanding why women stay in abusive relationships.

Religion and Violence

Organized religion provides a context for learning and transmitting religious — and often secular—beliefs, values, and practices.[130] As such, religious organizations and their leaders may be uniquely situated to alter, or at least challenge, attitudes that reinforce violence within the family. It has long been established that ordained ministers, priests, and rabbis play a central role in responding to the mental health needs of the North American public.[131] As such, they are viewed as "gatekeepers" active in both counseling and (less often) referral of individuals who seek their help.[132] Some researchers have noted that clergy occupy only a peripheral status as front-line mental health workers.[133] Still others regard clergy as part of a "funnel effect" for mental health problems, whereby people first seek help from family or friends, then from a minister or physician, and only then from a professional counselor.[134]

Over the last two decades, there has been a growing call among religious writers to condemn power abuses within the family.[135] Moreover, there have been several impressive initiatives launched with the specific goal of addressing the role of denominations, churches, or clergy in responding to abuse victims and their families.[136] Psychologist Andrew Weaver argues that "domestic violence is probably the number one pastoral mental health emergency."[137]

On the other hand, religious organizations, at least historically, have been in a position to reinforce gender attitudes and practices that may give rise to violence against women.[138] Whether conservative Protestant theology deters or exacerbates violence within the familial setting is an empirical question. In one of the few studies to assess religious variations in spousal violence, Bartkowski and Anderson, using American data from the National Survey of Families and Households, argue that they found no clear evidence that men or women affiliated with conservative Protestant denominations are *especially* prone toward violence directed at their partners.[139] Using a Canadian sample, Brinkerhoff, Grandin, and Lupri report that conservative Christian men do not abuse their partners significantly more often than men of other religious persuasions.[140] Yet, to be sure, some tenets of the worldview (e.g., the condemnation of divorce) restrict a woman's options once abused.[141] Even recognizing abuse can be especially painful for deeply religious people.[142]

In their book titled *Abuse and Religion: When Praying Isn't Enough,* Horton and Williamson[143] argue that each year more abuse victims, perpetrators, and family members seek help from clergy and religious leaders than from all other helping professionals combined.[144] Still, many (if not most) leave clergy offices dissatisfied, uninformed of their options and unprotected from further abuse.[145] For the religious victim, abuse strikes at the heart of one's selfhood, self-concept, and sense of sacred self.[146] Because religious values may be in conflict with certain treatment options, it is important that secular counselors understand the needs of religious victims[147] and that clergy maintain ongoing pastoral care and spiritual support even for abuse victims already in secular psychotherapy.[148] Yet, as Horton and Williamson[149] have pointed out, the dilemma facing religious victims is that the dual nature of their presenting issues—religion and abuse—mitigate against treatment sensitive to both of these concerns: treatment options offer help in one area while typically excluding the other.[150]

The relationship between theology and psychology has at times been stormy, perhaps in part because of the competing frameworks for the cure to damaged emotions.[151] Corroborating evidence of this competition between secular and sacred caregivers is the finding that while orthodoxy of religious beliefs has not been found to be related to whether or not an individual seeks help for personal or family problems, it is related to the source from which help is sought.[152] Thus, individuals who are linked to conservative churches tend to begin their search for answers to personal problems by looking within their own faith community first.[153]

Violence and Religious Service Providers

Whether or not they feel "called" to counsel abuse victims and hurting families, or whether they have adequate or any training that would specifically enable them to do this, clergy across North America are being asked to offer advice and support to women, children, and men who have experienced violation or abuse.[154]

Horton and Williamson[155] argue that although clergy and other religious leaders are sought out more frequently than all the other helping professionals combined, their ability to understand abuse within their theology of family life is woefully limited.[156] Only by listening to "the voices of the violated" can the "reconstruction of our theologies" occur, writes Lois Gehr Livezey, a professor of Christian social ethics.[157]

In the few isolated U.S. empirical studies that have considered the involvement of clergy in the lives of abused women, it has been reported that between 16 percent[158] and 40 percent of women who have been battered sought advice from clergy.[159] Frequently they were disappointed.[160] In one sample of 350 battered women, 28 percent sought help from local clergy. The primary responses these women reported having received from clergy were (1) a reminder of their marital responsibilities and the advice to "forgive and forget"; (2) a suggestion that they avoid church involvement; and (3) "useless advice," based on religious doctrine rather than the woman's own needs.[161]

In 1988 Bowker[162] reported the results of two studies of religious abuse victims and the services they reported having received from clergy. In a combined non-random sample totaling 1,000 women, recruited mainly from an advertisement in *Woman's Day* magazine, he found that one third of the abused wives received clerical support and 10 percent claimed that their husbands had also received support. In terms of perceived effectiveness, clergy rated lower than most other formal sources of help that abused women received. As a result, Bowker concludes that while clergy have far more contact with battered wives than previously thought, they are relatively ineffective in their efforts to help abuse victims.[163]

Findings from a smaller sample of 187 women who qualified as being abuse-free for one year prior to the study, revealed that 54 percent of religious victims and 38 percent of nonreligious victims turned to clergy for assistance in dealing with their abuse.[164] While many in this Horton, Wilkins, and Wright sample were critical of clerical support and advice, they were also critical of the help they received from secular resources; in fact, 25 percent of their sample reported that no outside intervention at all was effective in responding to their abuse. Thus clergy were not necessarily singled out as the most ineffective counselors; few victims felt that any service was especially helpful to them, and one in four said no intervention demonstrated effectiveness in their experience. These authors also revealed that religion proved extremely helpful to many victims and was believed to be life-preserving to others; eleven women in their sample reported that their personal religious beliefs prevented them from either taking their own life or the life of someone else.

In this same study,[165] those victims who enjoyed positive experiences with their religious leaders reported that they had received "validation" and "approval." Women who were most positive about the help clergy offered noted that their religious advisors had "agreed that safety, even divorce or separation, was imperative or at least acceptable for the battered victim."[166] On the other hand, the criticisms of religious leaders focused mainly on (1) not understanding the woman's feeling of being trapped in a dangerous relationship; (2) a lack of understanding about abuse or a minimization of it; (3) no practical advice offered; (4) being blamed or made to feel personally responsible for the abuse; and (5) expressing a sense of helplessness to escape or change the situation.[167]

A small segment of the Horton sample of abused women had remained in the marital relationship that had once been abusive, the violence had stopped (with the relationship abuse-free for a minimum of twelve months), and the women reported general satisfaction with the marital relationship. Looking more closely at these data, the researchers found that higher levels of religiosity "increased chances for an abuse-free, happy future,"[168] particularly so if both partners claimed to be religious. Horton and colleagues concluded that the religious victim appears to stay married longer and goes to greater lengths to save the relationship.

Clergy themselves are aware of how ill-prepared they are in the area of pastoral counseling,[169] particularly in the area of wife battery.[170] While some clinical researchers have suggested that clergy show little promise as counselor-trainees,[171] most argue that clergy are highly skilled as empathic listeners and are thus well suited to the role of counselor.[172] As more women enter the ranks of ordained clergy,[173] their performance of counseling roles may well enable them to offer a unique service to the needs of abused religious women.[174]

In sum, then, pastors are sought out by some abused women, but those women generally report that they have been dissatisfied with the help they have received from their clerical leaders. Part of the problem lies in pastoral counselors' lack of understanding of the prevalence and nature of abusive relationships and the longer-term impact of abuse on the woman victim. Given the nature of the clerical profession, and the opportunities for ongoing training and workshops, it appears that pastors' lack of educational exposure to issues of abuse could be addressed.

Responding to the Abused Religious Woman

Throughout this chapter, it has been revealed that many women suffer physical violence and other forms of abuse at the hands of their husband or partner. Even though violence knows no religious, class, ethnic, or geographical boundaries, services for abused women and their children tend to be scattered, lacking the cohesiveness and interagency cooperation necessary to bring a swift response to the pain of abuse victims. There is a growing recognition that legal and social services need to be involved in interagency cooperative ventures to guarantee safety for victims and due process for offenders.[175]

For religious victims of wife abuse, the lack of coordination and trust between personnel representing various community services poses several dilemmas. First, when religious victims seek secular services, the importance of their faith perspective and religious belief system are often underestimated. Many agency counselors feel handicapped in working with religious victims whose values may be in conflict with certain treatment options.[176] They may neither respect their religious values nor understand how to work within the victim's religious framework.[177] In fact, Holden, Watts, and Brookshire[178] argue that secular counselors report that they are very poor at challenging erroneous religious ideation.

Some secular therapists hold the position that if victims value their marital relationship they do not value their personal well-being.[179] Many community counselors have told religious victims that it was their religion that, in fact, caused the abuse[180] rather than regarding a woman's religious faith as a vital component of an authentic coping process. Because religion and the family are often considered to be parts of a symbiotic relationship, anything that is perceived to threaten one institution can be construed as potentially harmful to the other.[181] King found that a majority of evangelical Christians in his midwest U.S. study reported that they would be reluctant to seek help from a professional counselor for fear that their faith would be misunderstood, unappreciated, or ridiculed, though women were more likely to seek such help than men.[182]

As a result, then, clergy have an instrumental role in breaking the silence surrounding abuse in families of faith.[183] Furthermore, clergy have unparalleled opportunities to both educate the faithful and offer support to victims, their families, and abusers.[184] Just as ministers need to recognize that battering, not divorce, destroys abusive marriages,[185] so too secular therapists must recognize that abuse, not religion, degrades women.[186]

As a result of the apparent disinclination of secular and sacred counselors to work together, religious victims of abuse have little help within their faith perspective to make sense of the violence they are enduring. One consequence of the lack of coordinated assistance to religious abuse victims is that they tend to assume that the violence is either God's will or their own fault. On those occasions when clergy condemn abuse publicly from the pulpit or in private counseling sessions, they begin to dispel such misguided (but common) beliefs of religious victims.[187]

Several writers have pointed to the important role that clergy might play in assisting victims and their families—as well as perpetrators—once a case of abuse is before the legal system.[188] Others have suggested that clergy embark on a process of preparing their congregations to combat abuse through joint lay/clergy initiatives.[189]

Some writers have highlighted particular issues that clergy need to be aware of in terms of counseling abuse victims and perpetrators, including the danger of the save-the-family ethic,[190] the reluctance to engage in mandatory reporting of child abuse,[191] the preponderance of clergy who stress wifely submission in a vacuum devoid of husbandly love,[192] the potential to overstep emotional boundaries in the clergy counseling relationship,[193] and premature forgiveness of the abuser.[194]

We will explore more fully this last point about forgiveness. Marie Fortune argues that premature forgiving of the abuser (on the part of the clergy counselor or the victim), coupled with the admonition to forget the pain, actually thwarts rather than augments the healing process for the victim. As a result, the intervention of clergy—while well intentioned—may actually prevent healing from taking place in the life of the victim. From the perspective of the violent man, the forgive-and-forget mentality of some religious counselors enables abusers to continue to circumvent accountability for their actions. Fortune labels forgiveness before justice as "cheap grace," and contends that the most charitable and compassionate act that the church can offer is to take seriously the timing and the power of forgiveness to bring healing.[195]

Pastoral Responses to Victims of Abuse

Clinical psychologist James M. Alsdurf conducted a study in the 1980s among clergy in Protestant denominations in the United States and Canada designed to evaluate the pastors' experience with wife abuse and their theological presuppositions in the areas of marriage, divorce, and marital roles that might impact on the assistance they offer abuse victims.[196] Since fewer than 10 percent of the 5,700 questionnaires were returned, Aldsurf cautions that the results are both tentative and limited. He credits the low response rate to pastors' lack of interest in the problem and even denial of wife abuse.

The weaknesses of the study (most notably the very low participation rate among clergy) do, in large measure, limit what we can learn from it. Yet, tentative though they are, a number of interesting findings emerge. The vast majority of clergy in that study had counseled a woman who had been physically abused by her husband. One in three pastors reported that they questioned an abused woman's report of violence, with 35 percent claiming that wives overestimate the husband's responsibility for the violence. One in four pastors held that wives should submit to their male partner and that God would honor that submission by either stopping the violence or giving the woman victim the strength to endure it.[197] Pastors calling for wifely submission and spiritual endurance were opposed to advising a victim to protect herself through either legal or medical assistance. Moreover, their data suggests that pastors are more committed to the concept of marriage than they are to a woman's physical safety in it.

Other researchers offer corroborating evidence that many abused women seek out pastoral help.[198] With few exceptions[199] response rates from clergy to mailed surveys have been very low, hampering researchers' ability to draw decisive conclusions. Martin argues that clergy do not take a proactive role in addressing wife abuse; rather they wait for victims to seek out their help.[200] McHugh and Wood reported that clergy were hampered in their efforts to help abuse victims by their lack of education in counseling or battery, though they found that ministers with specialized training were more likely to recommend that victims contact transition houses and secular counseling agencies for safety and help.[201]

Religion and Violence:
Concluding Thoughts

This chapter has highlighted the frequency and nature of male violence against women that occurs in the family setting. Since wife battery is not linked to any specific religious, cultural, ethnic, or social class characteristics, it is pervasive and all women are potential victims. It is a significant problem within the general society and within faith communities as well. For the abused religious woman, locating services that understand and empathize with both her faith journey and her experience of violence is a major challenge. Battered Christian women have some unique problems and special needs that set them apart from nonreligious women victims. As a result, many religious women seek out help from their spiritual leaders in such times of crises. But, the response of pastors has been ineffective at best, while sometimes clergy are guilty of sending a woman back home to a continued cycle of violence.

Certainly, religious and nonreligious service providers can benefit from enhancing their referral network to include each other and thereby augment the healing process.[202] Many religious women who have suffered battery at the hands of their husbands desire support and care from *both* their faith community and secular agencies.[203] Ultimately the struggle to stop violence in our homes and within our communities requires religious and secular wisdom.[204]

It's hard now, 'cause I'm only 20, but if I meet a guy at [the] bar, it's very hard because all they want to do is sleep with you. But I find that guys at church, they just want to marry you. Like I'll go out there and like within like half an hour into your conversation they'll ask you about kids and . . . when you want to get married. And you're like "Whoa, wait a minute, I've got the rest of my life here."

(Woman #2, Focus Group #7)

Like I heard you mention mental cruelty. Like I don't know how much, but I don't think that there's a married woman in this room that hasn't broke out in tears from her husband at one point or another. But sometimes I get afraid when what, what you might think is abuse to me really is not. And sometimes when we have people that are trying. . . . But what I don't know [is] where that fine line is.

(Woman #6, Focus Group #6)

We as Christians believe in the sacredness of marriage [and] because of that I think you need to treat the whole family. . . . Reconciliation . . . counseling . . . if the situation is so violent, then yes . . . divorce may be the only option.

(Woman #13, Focus Group #26)

I'm a public health nurse. . . . I find . . . women within a church circle, particularly evangelical, often feel that they shouldn't be complaining, that this was part of their vows, and that they really [are] very different from the other side of society. . . . This is part of the submission.

(Woman #6, Focus Group #10)

God "hates divorce" (Mal. 2:16).

(Dr. James Dobson, *Love Must Be Tough*, p. 231)

2

The Bases of
Christian Family Life

The celebration of *family life* and *family values* has been embraced so fully by contemporary evangelical churches that one might be tempted to conclude that it is indeed a cornerstone in their theological foundation. With these buzz words on their lips, and the associated warm feelings they produce in their hearts, conservative preachers and counselors across Canada and the United States have sought to define marriage and family patterns, *Christian style*.

Blueprints and specific patterns of family living have been rushing off the Christian press for the last thirty years, selling literally millions of copies. These writers have enormous influence and popular support, among not only laity but clergy and pastoral counselors as well. If we are to understand how contemporary Christianity conceptualizes the rights and responsibilities and the roles of men, women, and children in family life, we have to pay serious attention to what these books teach ordinary churchgoers, not just the religious elite, about God, the church, and the family. This chapter seeks to introduce some of the key players in the rapidly expanding *Christian family literature*.

While much of their message would be familiar enough to women in the post–World War II era, it has been repackaged in some unique ways for a more contemporary audience. Mothers have a particular, but not exclusive, role as caregivers, though men are encouraged to be more affiliative and nurturing, especially with their children. Keeping the family "true to the faith" is tied to the heartstrings and energies of women, though men are heralded as the spiritual leaders. Through the "keeping of promises" Christian men are to set themselves apart from the attack on the family by secular forces. As "reapers of those promises" and "memory makers," women watch the home fires, for secularism, individualism, and materialism spread quickly, like a virus, from one family member to the next. In this way, women become the emotional thermostats of the inside of the home (or its heart), as men wage war with the forces of evil outside.

While the language of war and hearth may be a bit melodramatic for mainstream Christianity or the secular culture, the underlying message is familiar there too: women's sphere revolves primarily around the private, domestic domain, while men's sphere revolves primarily around the public domain of paid work.

Historian Randall Balmer, in an essay exploring the relationship between fundamentalism and femininity, argues that fundamentalist religion idealizes woman as a self-sacrificing wife and mother whose energies and devotions are occupied with the tasks of running the home rather than with the external world in which it is located.[1] Anthropologist Karen McCarthy Brown contends that fundamentalism's response to the stress and anxiety created by modernity has been to reinforce and extend the boundaries of women's and children's lives.[2] Such a process, which we might label *gender inerrancy,* is predicated on the notion that the worlds of men and women are very distinct, and as such gender roles, expectations, and performance standards need to be clear, differentiated, and nonnegotiable.[3] It is the rigidity of the gender scripts, together with their supernatural blessing, that renders them inerrant. Men and women, of course, err in their performance of these gender messages, rebel against them, or fail to understand the importance of them. The task of the burgeoning Christian family literature, then, is to set the boundaries, the lines of demarcation between men and women in the family and within the church, in a clear and encompassing manner.[4]

While the voices telling religious men and women how to live their lives within the family context may be clear and audible, social scientists have argued that there is far more latitude in how conservative Protestant family members interpret and render operational these gender messages than one might expect.[5] Yet distinctiveness is a central feature in how evangelical and fundamentalist families understand their own religious and social lives vis-à-vis their coworkers and neighbors.[6] Whether or not they behave in distinctive ways, families subscribing to a conservative Protestant worldview believe that their everyday existence is set apart from the mainstream culture.[7] That perception of difference, then, no doubt impacts on family life and how family conflict is handled.

Hawley and Proudfoot contend that the motifs of otherness and nostalgia encompass conservative religious men in such a way that it "reconstructs an idealized past and attempts to reshape the present along the same lines."[8] Commenting on the role of James Dobson, Randall Balmer argues that in his writing there is a "pining for a halcyon past," failing to take into account that traditional notions of femininity were a nineteenth-century construct, made possible only by the advances of modernity.[9] As we shall see in the brief examination of the Christian family literature to follow, the contemporary gender challenge to conservative church men and women is profound at the point where the feminist struggle asserts that any woman's identity may be found in something other than her family connections.

Yet, we need to be clear that conservative Protestants are not the only religious groups that embrace traditional gender scripts and their associated roles. Fundamentalist movements worldwide, including those linked to Islam and Hinduism, also teach a traditional gender role ideology and informally sanction those members who deviate from the proclaimed pattern.[10] In their studies of women who convert to orthodox Judaism, sociologists Debra Renee Kaufman and Lynn Davidman find that the focus on women's traditional roles and responsibilities are a compelling force in women's decision to return to historic orthodoxy.[11] Home and hearth have a strong appeal, let there be no doubt about it. As the forces of modernity shape men and women in ways they do not like, and as the winds of change shake the foundation stones of religious values and interpersonal connections, the appeal of an all-encompassing, all-enduring gender message gains strength.

Mainstream Christianity, too, celebrates a particular form of family life and family values, to the exclusion of other interpersonal groupings. In the book *Work, Family, and Religion in Contemporary Society,* which they edited, Ammerman and Roof claim that the days when churches could take families for granted are over.[12] Yet, the relationship between religion and family continues to be strong. Penny Long Marler's essay demonstrates how mainline churches have been able to keep their "market share" of both husband-wife-plus-children families and the elderly, losing ground, though, with younger singles and those in nontraditional households.[13] Interestingly, she examines the process by which church programs for children and the youth are "staffed" and supported by older church members who remember with fondness their own participation in the life of the church as a family unit. In such a way, these volunteers have a particular interest in maintaining the link between traditional family forms and their worship of God in a church setting. Seeing other nuclear (and extended) families together reminds them of their younger years when they came to church with their (now deceased) partner and children in tow, everyone "spit-spot," dressed for the occasion.

In contemporary America, Wade Clark Roof and Lyn Gesch demonstrate that attitudes in support of traditional families participating in religion together occur most strongly among those who have the traditional family structure to match.[14] Using U.S. data samples from 1972 to 1990, Bradley Hertel offers a detailed examination of religiosity and labor force participation among men and women.[15] He concludes that by far the most significant challenge to organized religion lies in the declines in membership and attendance attributable to the full-time employment of married women. As women move, then, from more traditional gender role performance in the home to the labor force, this shift is often accompanied by lower levels of observed religious participation.[16]

For our purposes here, it is important to realize that conservative Protestants are not alone in their love for the traditional family or their nostalgia for family life of bygone days. While the language of their discourse may appear somewhat foreign to mainstream Christian ears, the content and its underlying philosophy are recognizable to both. In essence, their argument hinges on the belief that men and women are different, that God designed it that way, and that home and hearth are the center of a woman's being, her raison d'être as it were. If, indeed, the family provides the context of a woman's identity, her purpose, and the associated self-esteem she feels, then the consequences of an abusive family home become even more extreme. As a result, then, the religious woman becomes even more isolated and trapped than her secular sister. Viewed in this way, not even God seems to be on her side.

Conservative Protestantism and the Family

Writing in 1980, W. Peter Blitchington had this to say about family life:

> The strength of a nation can be fairly effectively gauged by the strength
> of its families and the strength of the family can be estimated by the qual-
> ity of its sex roles. . . . There is a specific pattern of family relationships

that "works" the best. This pattern consists of men and women acting out certain roles. It is the pattern that both Greece and Rome followed when they were at the height of their power. But it's even older than these two nations, for it was instituted at the creation. It is the biblical blueprint for marriage.[17]

For the last thirty years, the Christian press has been consumed with producing literature on how families should be structured and how family life ought to be experienced. Claiming that the advances of modernity are attacking the strength and vitality of marital stability and family togetherness, through upward spiraling rates of divorce in particular, many prominent evangelical and populist Christian writers and counselors have argued that family unity is achieved most fully and satisfactorily when couples subscribe to a hierarchical model of family living.[18] In a review of the Christian family literature from the onset of the second wave of feminism (early 1960s) into the 1980s, I have argued elsewhere that hierarchy is considered one of *the* most defining and differentiating features of couples subscribing to a conservative Christian worldview.[19] And, as such, a distinct division of labor permeates the family home, the church, and even the broader culture of which it is a part. Since the family offers the original context for learning and enacting gender roles, what is taught and observed in our families stays with us for life, even if we later reject it.[20]

Tim and Beverly LaHaye have been producing books on *the* Christian family for over two decades, and among our sample of pastors they enjoyed strong name recognition and their work was considered *somewhat influential* in shaping opinions about pastoral counseling. While they are not front-runners in contemporary Christian sales,[21] their conservative stance on the family provides both a backdrop and a springboard for the rise to fame (and publication success) of Christian psychologists like Dr. James Dobson.[22] In *The Spirit-Filled Family,* the LaHayes package in a slightly different way what they have been arguing for many years: that God has a specific design for family living that works the best, and that central to that design is male leadership.[23] For them, as for others writing within this framework, divorce is not an option.[24] The solution to marital unhappiness rests in self-evaluation and deeper Christian commitment. In fact, this husband-wife team writes that "the wife's attitudes and actions of submission are a measure or barometer of her relationship to Christ. . . . Submission is not contingent on the actions of your partner."[25] Gary Smalley in *Making Love Last Forever* is more direct when he suggests that offended partners are to use their "sand storms" for future advantage.[26] The "tool in overcoming anger is to search for 'hidden pearls' in the offense committed against you," writes Smalley.[27] Thus, when problems arise that seek to destroy the family unit, women are to look inside themselves and ask *why:* What has been my contribution to the disharmony we feel? As vice-president of the family charged with domestic affairs, the wife is held responsible to ensure the smooth operation of her domain, the home.

From within the perspective of hierarchy and headship in marriage, Christian writers have proclaimed that men are "aggressive, dominant, logical, independent, active, ambitious and task-oriented" and that women are "submissive, intuitive, dependent, nurturant, supportive, patient and person-oriented."[28] In fact, Blitchington argues that since God created Adam taller and more muscular than Eve his wife, he was to be God's first link in the chain of responsibility and authority. Others warn of the "cult of the aggressive female," and to a lesser extent of the passive or effeminate male.[29] In *Husbands Who Won't Lead and Wives Who Won't Follow,* James Walker, a pastor with the Evangelical Free Church, contends that "the female of the species *is* more deadly than the male" (italics his).[30] Presumably that's why so many of these writers assert that every family needs a strong male leader.

James Hurley, drawing on the analogy of Adam and Eve in the Garden of Eden, claims that Adam was the religious spokesperson and family leader.[31] Reestablishing God's design, then, means returning to the creation-centered relationship pattern of men communing with God and women listening. Within his 1995 book, *Straight Talk: What Men Need to Know; What Women Should Understand,* James Dobson contends that it is a mistake to alter in any fashion the role of "husband as loving protector and wife as recipient of that protection."[32] Gary Smalley redefines the leader-protector role to include almost any behavior a husband performs in good faith toward his wife or children.[33] While abuse is never condoned, it is almost never condemned, because, in fact, it is hardly ever mentioned by any of these authors writing within the best-selling list of the Christian family literature. In essence, the list of conservative religious men writing for a predominately conservative female audience is long and the writings are numerous.[34] Given their tremendous sales (often in the millions), their influence and power should not be underestimated. More recently, Christian authors have turned their efforts to men, and the success of the Promise Keepers Movement is one tangible piece of evidence of this renewed focus on men.

Promise Keepers:
Strengthening Male Dominance in the Family

The brainchild of Bill McCartney (an ex–football coach from Colorado), Promise Keepers is a deliberate attempt to make religion meaningful for men by bringing them together in large rallies to celebrate their love for Christ, their commitment to their families, and their support for their (male) pastors. Established in 1991, Promise Keepers meetings, typically held in a large sports arena or stadium, can attract hundreds of thousands of men; in fact, their goal for 1996 was to attract one million men to their rallies.[35] The movement is posed as a Christian response to the rapidly changing society in which men live.[36] It is clearly both a response to the feminist challenge within contemporary Christianity and a desire to bring the men back to church and family obligations. In a small-scale study completed in one of my undergraduate classes, Danielle Irving interviewed five men who support the Promise Keepers Movement. She argues that men are drawn to it because it blends conservative family ideologies with new definitions of masculinity, including how to be sensitive and nurturing to their families and to each other. In his study of the Promise Keepers, William Lockhart contends that the movement does not display a monolithic return to traditional gender role and family relationships, but rather seeks to highlight the "essence of masculinity," to help men build new relationships and to repair and enhance their family experience and thereby reduce divorce rates.[37]

Influenced in part by the growing Promise Keepers Movement, pastor Gary Inrig, in his book titled *Whole Marriages in a Broken World: God's Design for a Healthy Marriage,* contends that the husband's role is that of servant-leader.[38] Believing that men please God when they are careful to fulfill their duties as husbands and fathers, he argues that servant leadership demands that men support their wives in every way, and in so doing runs counter to the notion that men can use their authority over their wives to implement a self-serving agenda. Women's lives within this model, though, still center around the family home, helping and supporting others as the need arises.

As a men's movement, Promise Keepers has the potential to either reinforce or challenge men's abuse of power in their intimate relationships with women. Given their enthusiastic support for men who are "called by God," Promise Keepers may be fertile ground for clergy to work with abusive men and to garner support among other men to condemn abusive acts in the family. The possibility of peer mentoring among men has not been fully tapped, and this movement offers that possibility.

Christian Marriages in Trouble

So what happens when things go wrong? While it may be easy to say that God has a design for a healthy marriage, what about the scores of marriages—even those with both partners committed Christians—where there is disappointment, pain, conflict, and anguish. What then?

Gary Smalley, who claims to have sold nine million copies of his books and videos, says that marriage partners have "no excuse to be miserable,"[39] for they have a responsibility to stand firm when trouble comes, to look for the good they can glean from disappointments, hurts, and trials, and in so doing become both better developed persons and spouses. Smalley's books and tapes assert that as a marital partner you win respect in the long run if you stake your position and refuse to allow someone to bulldoze you over.[40] Employing principles such as these, Gary Smalley contends that he has never had to suggest divorce to an individual or a couple seeking his help, though temporary separation is sometimes recommended.[41]

President of the American Association of Christian Counselors Gary Collins, in his 1995 book, *Family Shock: Keeping Families Strong in the Midst of Earthshaking Change,* details the changes and crises that encompass all families, including those in the contemporary evangelical church.[42] The challenge for church families, as he sees it, is to remain strong as the winds of change blow and crises erupt in and beyond the family unit. His concluding chapter, aptly titled "Celebrate the Family," is premised on the notion that indeed churched families have an advantage in the secular world. These signs of hope, as it were, are meant to propel families in crises to "hang on"; in fact the chapter ends with the words "Don't quit."

While there are a myriad of Christian authors writing about family life and family problems, no one at present can match the popular appeal of James Dobson.

The Spreading Influence of
Dr. James Dobson and His Focus on the Family

Dr. James Dobson has remarkable influence—let there be no doubt about it. His Focus on the Family series is broadcast in just under two thousand radio stations in the United States and Canada, and as many more around the globe. With a staff of more that one thousand, Focus on the Family publishes ten magazines and an average of fifty books a year, plus the over 125,000 audio-tapes that are distributed each month. It is claimed in some evangelical circles that he alone has the potential to be Billy Graham's successor.

On the dust jacket to his book *Love Must Be Tough: New Hope for Families in Crisis,* we find these words, "Dr. Dobson's strategy, proven successful in hundreds of documented cases, is uniquely valuable because, unlike other approaches, it often works without the willing cooperation of the other person."[43] That same dust jacket claims that at the core of most marital conflicts, including spousal abuse, rests a "kind of indifference that can sabotage a relationship." Dr. Dobson's answer is the concept of *tough love*—a coy phrase and a dynamic concept he coined in 1983—a strategy he believes is able to both rekindle romantic interest and draw the wayward partner back to the home fires.

The words alone conjure up a variety of conflicting images: the teenager who is loved beyond measure despite the harsh words he shouts to his father, a mother's love for her young child that is so intense and all-consuming that at times it can be irrational; a bond between marital partners that sticks it out through "thick and thin." In these images, the toughness of the concept reflects the tenacity of the lovers, their undying commitment to the loved, and their perseverance even in the face of obstacles or opposition. They are loving not because of the love they receive in return, but presumably, as with God's love, they are motivated by their commitment to the loved, a commitment that can be very costly.

Yet as I think about the concept I picture other images too: a teenager who is told to be in on time, hasn't obeyed, and is now facing severe consequences, including corporal punishment; a husband who is showing his wife who is boss, with his mouth and with his fists; the woman who is fighting back, eager to recapture self-esteem she lost years ago. Considered in this way, there are elements of the concept that can appear at face value to be rather difficult to digest or even contradictory. And because of the use of the words "tough love" by others in the secular press, in negotiations, and in our everyday vernacular, they have now been altered in ways perhaps unintended and unwelcomed by their creator. So what does Dr. James Dobson mean by tough love?

Tough love is an action plan or strategy whereby victims of infidelity, abuse, or alcoholic partners exert self-esteem, confidence, and control and through their exercise of this concept win or gain back the respect of their partner, change the behavior of the wayward spouse, and keep the marital bond intact. Tough love is presented as an alternative means of approaching a troubled marriage, though

Dobson in other books has applied this concept to parent-child interactions and conflict as well.

For Dobson, divorce is not an option for ailing marriages. Instead, his *love must be tough* approach is believed to offer the best potential for recovery and healing. Dobson does not claim that this approach will work in every situation; he believes, rather, that it is the best alternative open to victims of marital crises. Through standing firm and then offering forgiveness when the wayward partner confesses and changes, divorce is averted. "Though this kind of forgiveness is difficult to either give or receive, I can assure you," writes Dobson, "that divorce is even more difficult. It leaves scars on its victims that will last a lifetime. This is why God hates divorce."[44]

Within Dobson's framework, a woman is to be loving and devoted as a wife and mother through keeping the home fires burning, by housekeeping activities, living within the family budget, supporting her husband's career aspirations, and doing volunteer work in her children's school and the church. The message is clear: Women achieve their value and self-esteem almost exclusively through the home and their service to their husband and children. A recent issue of *Focus on the Family* ran an article that extolled the virtues of women leaving paid employment and devoting their energies full-time to running the home.

James Dobson has little patience with modern feminism (though he acknowledges that it has won some positive advances for women in the business world), believing that it encourages women to focus primarily on their own needs, rather than on the needs of their husbands and children. In rather strong language, he likens a woman's awakening feminist consciousness to "a computer software package . . . keypunched into her brain,"[45] whereby a traditional gender role ideology is replaced by a radical feminist one. The bottom line is that Dobson does not advocate women's independence apart from their husbands and children, though he does not condemn outright women's temporary participation in the labor market driven by economic necessity (rather than greed or self-expression). Hearth and home provide her system of meaning and opportunity for service to God. Here she will (read *must*) be content.

But unlike some of his predecessors in the Christian family literature field, Dobson does not promote excessively passive women, trying endlessly to win their husband's affection through quiet subservience.[46] He writes, "There is a vast difference between being a confident, spiritually submissive woman and being a doormat. People wipe their feet on doormats, as we know."[47] According to Dobson's principles, then, love sometimes requires toughness, discipline, and accountability. And, accordingly, it is in the victimized partner's demonstration of this *toughness,* that the offending partner is often brought to repentance and behavioral change.[48]

The concept of tough love depends first and foremost on the motivation and ability of the violated spouse to "stand for firmness," perhaps for the first time in her life. Marital unfaithfulness is the example of choice throughout Dobson's book, but part of one chapter is devoted to a letter from an abused wife who has suffered marked physical violence over a period of many years, and Dobson's response to such a crisis. To his credit, Dobson does not underestimate or challenge the woman's story as it is told. In fact, he suggests that wife abuse is a problem reaching "epidemic proportions in today's families."[49] Second, he points out to the readership the four options he believes are available to the abused woman: she can remain silent at home; divorce her husband; remain married but emotionally detached; or adopt the "love-must-be-tough" response. Choosing the last option, he suggests that the abused wife refuse to consent to her husband's unrealistic demands, thereby precipitating a crisis situation. She is to advise friends and relatives that she may need their assistance. Dobson acknowledges that temporary separation may be necessary, and that if reconciliation occurs, a competent Christian counselor has a very important role to play. Dobson firmly and clearly states that women are not required (by God) to live in constant fear, and that to endure such a relationship over time would lead to its demise anyway.

The next case he provides involves a woman whose husband has hit her once, and who is now seeking advice about separation. Dobson's response to this woman is very telling. Here he suggests that sometimes women deliberately bait their husbands until there is a violent act. In this case, Dobson claims that sometimes a "victimized" woman verbally antagonizes her husband until he gives her "the prize" she seeks.[50] After exploring and explaining in some detail his position on women who elicit violence from their husbands, Dobson concludes by arguing that some women are "victims in the true sense of the word"; by implication, others are not.[51]

There are several points I wish to make about Dobson's advice to abused women as it is offered on pages 159–164 of his book *Love Must Be Tough: New Hope for Families in Crisis*. In marriages marked by extreme violence that is repetitive and ongoing, Dr. Dobson's advice includes:

1. Accepting a woman's own story of battery: he questions neither the accuracy of her memory or the severity of what she reports—he believes her story as it is told to him;

2. No suggestion that the woman victim was responsible for that violence: Dobson does not question what the woman did to enrage her husband, nor does he suggest that she change her behavior to please him;

3. The tough love approach is the option of choice: not surprisingly, Dobson suggests that the woman victim put into practice his principle of tough love, which would include her refusal to give in to her husband's unrealistic demands, and the possible precipitation of a major crisis experience;

4. Suggesting to the woman victim that she tell friends and family that she may need to call on their support if a crisis occurs: Dobson encourages such a woman to both prearrange a place to go and alert friends and family whom she can call for assistance;

5. The possibility (but not the promise) of reconciliation: Dobson is quite clear that he cannot guarantee that the tough love approach will always work with a violent husband;

6. Reconciliation (if and when it does occur) should include the services of a competent Christian counselor;
7. Success is defined in terms of keeping the marriage together and averting divorce, while ensuring that the repetitive violent acts stop; and
8. Advising the woman to pray about the entire situation at hand.

In situations involving repetitive, extreme forms of violent activities, James Dobson's advice to abused women is rather straightforward. He accepts their story as told, is empathic to the victim, condemns the abusive events, encourages the *tough love* approach, acknowledges that support from family and friends is imperative, and suggests that if reconciliation is to occur, the services of a trained Christian counselor should be sought. What Dr. Dobson leaves unanswered is how a woman who has been repeatedly battered is to garner up the self-esteem and self-confidence to enact the *tough love* approach, how she is to find family and friend support if she lives in an isolated area or has been geographically mobile for most of her married life, and how her safety and mental health are to be assured during the various stages of the tough love process (as they are outlined in his books).

Moreover, there are a number of troubling aspects to this approach to family crises. Is Dobson actually holding the victim responsible for initiating change in the life of the abusive husband? And if she is unable or unwilling to implement the tough love approach, is she guilty by implication for the continuation of the violence directed against her? Moreover, is there any empirical evidence that victim-focused therapy changes abusive men? And what are some of the (perhaps unintended) consequences of buying into this approach? Does this encourage women to remain indefinitely in marriages that put their physical and emotional health at risk, waiting for the opportunity to implement tough love or for the process to be successful?

I would note in passing that it is disappointing (not to mention inaccurate, uncharitable, and even dangerous) to discuss in such detail a view that some women want physical victimization ("she gets the prize [black eye] she seeks") and to place this discussion immediately following the description and examination of a woman who lived for years in persistent, extreme violence. Why? Because it sets up a false dichotomy: that there are women victims who are repeatedly abused by the extreme measures of their partners; and then there are all the other women (who presumably push their husbands to violence, or want to suffer in this way). As a group, many women victims already feel responsible for failing their marriage, their husbands, and their families; there are no scholarly data that suggest that there is indeed a category of abused women who seek violence from their partners. As a result, it is unhelpful at best and harmful at worst to give almost as much space to a description of women *seeking* abuse as to those who are desperately trying to *flee* it.

While there are a variety of ways to respond to the concept of *tough love* and the concomitant messages Dobson offers about family life, there are four implications I would like to draw to our attention here as we consider the pervasiveness and the nature of wife abuse in faith communities and the response of the Christian church and its leaders to families in conflict and crisis. (1) First, *family life and family relationships are characterized as the sum total of a woman's world.* Clearly, the domain of women is confined almost entirely to the domestic sphere and in a practical way to the schedules and desires of others. Within this framework, women are clearly held accountable for making family life work, through the smooth operation of the home. What happens, then, when family life is torn apart by heartache and abuse? (2) The second implication of this perspective on family life is that *violent marriages can and should be saved.* Dobson writes that God hates divorce, and therefore everything possible must be done to salvage and repair a broken marriage, even a violent one. While the indissolubility of marriage is clearly a major theme in Dobson's approach, it comes with several (perhaps unintended) by-products, such as guilt, shame, and denial, particularly but not exclusively in the life of the victim. Since divorce is not really an option, change is the most obvious alternative. So how is change possible? (3) A third theme within Dobson's writing is that *abusive marriages can be transformed into nonabusive marriages at the initiation of the victim.* While later stages of the tough love approach involve both partners as they seek reconciliation and relationship repair, Dr. James Dobson firmly believes that the change process can be initiated by the victim and her "firm stand." But what happens when a previously "untough" partner now places new demands of firmness on the offending spouse?

That ushers in a fourth building block inherent in Dobson's writing: (4) *the presumption of support from family and friends for victimized women.* To be sure, some women have a circle of friends from which they can draw in times of need; others do not. Some abused wives live close to family members, but others reside far away from their childhood homes or their support networks. It is dangerous to assume that all abused women have at present a strong support system that is both *able* and *willing* to help them in times of crises.

James Dobson in *Love Must Be Tough* never condones violence, but he comes dangerously close to holding the victim rather than the aggressor responsible for changed behavior. As we have observed in chapter 1, for the most part abused women want to remain with their violent partners; they want them to change, but they also want the violence to stop and to begin their own healing journey. Abused women who are religious, or connected with Christian churches, are more likely than their secular sisters to stay longer in violent relationships and to work harder at marriage repair.[52] But the violence does not always stop; temporary remorse does not usually lead to permanent behavioral change; and the healing journey for the victim or abuser is thwarted or at best slow and difficult. What then? As a victim, when can I be sure that I have "stood firm" long enough? During the stages of the cycle of violence when there is temporary penitence on the part of my aggressor for his behavior, is that evidence that "tough love" has worked? Then what happens when he becomes abusive again? How long must I "stand firm," and how will I ever be able to maintain that strength over time?

In the chapters to follow, we will be listening to the stories of women who have been violated by their husbands, families members who are in intense conflict one with the other, and the perspective of clergy and other church people who have sought to give assistance to both victims and perpetrators in the midst of their crisis. We will examine what interventions clergy believe have been most helpful, and what advice abused women themselves have found to augment their journey toward healing and wholeness. Moreover, we will consider whether some of the main assertions of Dobson's model are in fact true to the experiences of abused churchwomen. While this study has not been constructed as a *test* of any specific theory—religious or secular in nature—it is a rigorous examination into the lives of both the violated and those who have cared for them under the umbrella of Christian love and compassion. It offers us a window, as it were, to look at both the help and the harm that spews from the pens of well-meaning Christian authors and the lips of well-meaning pastors and laypeople. But, as we shall see, not everyone has the same story to tell.

Before we consider the response of churches and their leaders to violence in the family context, though, we need to examine briefly how clergy themselves understand marriage and their personal orientation to marital or relationship counseling.

Marital Counseling and the Pastor

In order to ascertain pastors' orientation to marital or relationship counseling, we asked clergy in our interview study a series of questions that enabled them to describe their approach or philosophy to marital counseling, to elaborate on their view of marriage, and to indicate ways in which they felt their view was different from a non-Christian perspective on marriage. Moreover, we attempted to assess which authors or experts in psychotherapy or counseling had influenced their thinking. In this section, we focus on how pastors in our research approached relationship counseling and the various influences that have shaped their counseling strategy.

When asked to describe their marital counseling approach, the majority of clergy in our interview sample talked about factors other than spiritual ones.[53] Fully 56 percent of our interviewees neglected to mention directly any spiritual or religious influences on their counseling approach. As we shall see shortly, this is not an indication of their view of marriage, but rather their *philosophy* of marital counseling. More common responses to the question of marital counseling were process-centered: what to do, when to do it, and whom to involve. The majority view, then, was that this process-centered approach did not involve directly spiritual components, such as prayer, scripture reading, or explicit Christian teaching on marriage. Rather, the average minister described his or her approach in a rather atheoretical or nonepistemological fashion. For the most part, it could not be differentiated from that of a secular counselor, except that an ordained minister was providing the service. As we shall explore more fully at a later point, there are a number of possible implications to arise from this finding, not least of which is clearly the reluctance of clergy to see that they have something *unique* to offer as pastoral counselors.

Clergy were asked to speculate on what enables them personally to be an effective marital counselor. Many responded by smiling, or chuckling that they did not feel they were particularly effective. In George Barna's study of 1,044 senior pastors, he found that only 4 percent listed "counseling" as one of their spiritual gifts.[54] On further probing, the one hundred respondents in our study were able to identify over two hundred reasons for effectiveness. These can be collapsed into six broad categories: friendship or interpersonal skills (n [number] =63), good listener (n=41), compassionate (n=40), spiritual relationship (n=27), family background (n=12), and training (n=7). Three clergy simply noted that they were "available." What is particularly interesting here is the major role clergy believe their personal characteristics play in shaping their counseling and the correspondingly minor role of their formal training. The interview also asked ministers to reflect on how they might be more effective as marital counselors. The overwhelming response was a resounding need for more training; in fact, every single pastor (save two who felt it was too late (!) for them personally) felt more training in pastoral counseling would enable them to be more effective with individuals, couples, and families who seek their help.

When clergy were asked to indicate which particular Christian or secular counselors, psychologists, or psychiatrists have been influential in their thinking and practice of relationship counseling, most respondents referred to individual professors at the university (or seminary) from which they received their highest degree. And, for the most part, these faculty authors had not published particular works in the area of relationship or pastoral counseling. Rather, they were the instructors who had taught the requisite course(s) on counseling as part of the requirements for ordination to ministry.

During the interview, pastors were asked to comment on a list of experts in psychotherapy (or counseling) that we had compiled (and pretested), and to indicate whether any of these people had been influential in the pastors' own counseling approach. While there was a rather wide range of authors who were cited as being of "some influence," there were very few who were regarded as "influential" or "very influential" by more than a handful of clergy. It appears, for the most part, that ministers in our research were either unaware of these experts altogether, or they did not associate their names with the term *counseling*. Having said this, however, I should add that six authors (out of a list of nineteen) were rated as being at least of "some influence" in shaping ministers' marital or relationship counseling approach.

James Dobson emerged as the most influential writer (mean of 3.1 on a 4-point scale, where 4 indicated "very influential"), followed by Charles Swindoll (2.5), H. Norman Wright (2.2), Lawrence Crabb (2.2), Tim LaHaye (2.2), and Gary Smalley (2.0). Carl Rogers received the "highest rating" of any secular counselor at 1.6. What do these results tell us? First and foremost, they document the tremendous support at the grass-roots level for Dr. James Dobson and his Focus on the Family ministry. Second, they suggest that there is a relatively small number of authors who have been able to penetrate into the evangelical market, particularly as it relates to *family issues*. Authors like Tim LaHaye, who began publishing in the area of Christian marriage and the family two decades ago, still have name recognition among clergy. Third, they suggest that while clergy report reading secular material on family violence (see chapter 4), in the interview setting they were unable to cite authors by name; given that most of the interviews took place in the pastor's study, this is a bit surprising, for if these books were part of their library, they could have simply pulled them off the shelf. Fourth, the primacy of the Christian-based authors in the clerical repertoire reveals that, by and large, clergy are not being influenced to any marked extent by secular writing on the subject or, if they are, they are unaware of that influence.

Christian Model for Marriage

There was almost complete unanimity (97 percent among pastors we interviewed) that there is a Christian model for marriage and that they personally subscribe to it. While clergy appeared to have some difficulty articulating what this model was, several features or themes emerged from their comments. First and foremost, clergy noted that the Christian model for marriage is based on a spiritual foundation.

I feel it should be founded on Jesus Christ and what he taught and shared and lived in his ministry, which I feel is totally encompassed by the fruit of the spirit. A lot of people focus on rules and regulations. . . . I focus on the love of Christ.

(Clergy Interview #552)

Second, explicit within the model was a nongendered acceptance of the other, sacrificial love, and undying devotion.

God has put the recipe for marriage together. . . . I have to love my wife, in the morning when she doesn't have her makeup on, I have to love her when she's being pulled [in] 20 different directions by the children, I've got to love her at all times. . . . My responsibility as a husband is to be a protector, to be a provider, to be a helper, to be a friend, to be a guide, and to be a lover to my wife. If I do what I am called to do, I find my wife [has] very little complaint about me, and that's why I find the Bible has got the best recipe for marriage and family.

(Clergy Interview #361)

Third, the model was believed to have been spelled out in scripture.

A Christian model for marriage . . . it's based on scripture . . . seeking the welfare of the other individual before one's self. I think it's of a mutual concern for one another . . . the covenant kind of commitment. I'll stick it through with you for my whole life. . . . It's reflective of the kind of relationship that our Lord has for his church, how he gave himself for each one of us, and how each one of us has made mistakes, we've messed up, we've been very disobedient to God and yet Christ's love for us is one of solid commitment and loyalty to us.

(Clergy Interview #529)

Fourth, the theme of submission as the duty of the wife to her husband was mentioned by one quarter of the clerical sample.

Like Ephesians . . . Paul lays some groundwork for relationships, he talks about the, the dreaded, the dreaded word submission. What does that mean? And I explained to our congregation that submission does not mean he is my Lord and master, my husband, and I am a doormat and I am subservient, but I looked at the model of Adam and Eve. . . . They were copartners, they fulfilled each other's needs and, and requirements. . . . So I think if we, if we incorporate into a model these kinds of components . . . we can build a strong, healthy family relationship.

(Clergy Interview #350)

When they were asked to comment on how their view of marriage differs from a non-Christian perspective, four major themes emerged: the spiritual dimension of marriage (n=52); the undesirability of divorce (n=48); the institution of marriage as God-given (n=42); and the role of love (n=29). Less than ten clergy (out of a hundred) referred to mutuality between husband and wife, the role of biblical absolutes like condemnation of extramarital or premarital sexual relations, a traditional gender role division of labor, or the support of the local church.

While clergy may not see their *philosophy* of marital or relationship counseling as differing markedly from their secular counterparts, they clearly did see their view of marriage as distinct from a non-Christian view. Central to their understanding was: (1) the spiritual foundation on which a Christian marriage is built; (2) the role of scripture in identifying what a Christian marriage is to be; (3) the concept of either *mutual submission* or *the submission of the wife* as a guide to partnership or decision making; and (4) the undesirability of divorce.

Though the particular marital counseling philosophy and procedures of pastors may not be distinct from secular counseling, what sets clergy apart is their model or theory of marriage. As we shall see in later chapters, clergy's interpretation of the Christian model of marriage influences their response and approach to wife abuse.

The remainder of the book will examine how these concepts translate into advice and support for abused women, abusive men, and couples in conflict. Chapter 3 tells the story from the perspective of the abused Christian woman, and chapters 4 and 5 are built on the counseling experiences and counseling advice of pastors. Chapter 6 explores how Christian women themselves respond to the needs of other women in their midst, and the concluding chapter, "From the Steeple to the Shelter," considers the challenge of sacred and secular cooperation in a victim's healing journey.

3

The Abused
Christian Woman

Martha and her husband, Daniel, were key laypeople in First Presbyterian Church of Birch Grove, a picturesque bedroom community to which large numbers of men and women retreat after a long working day in the nearby industrial city. She worked in the denominational headquarters as an office manager, and he held the elected position of Sunday school superintendent in their local church. Together they sang in the choir, and their home served as a comfortable location for many church executive meetings. They were any pastor's dream couple—attractive, talented, relatively affluent, hardworking people who wanted to contribute to the weekly routine of church life. But Martha and Daniel had a secret: he was an abusive husband and she was a battered wife.

The abuse started when Martha was three months pregnant with their first child. They had gone out for a social evening at a friend's home. In the car on the way home Daniel accused Martha of talking to some of the men at the party. Caught by surprise, Martha retorted that they were longtime friends of all these couples and that during the course of the evening she had talked to everyone who was present. When they got home, he called her a whore and hit her across the face.

Martha and Daniel lived the lie for years; eventually they had four young children and resided in a large, two-story house in an enviable neighborhood, but Martha's salary alone could not support food, rent for an apartment, and the children's music and sports activities, let alone money for church projects. She felt trapped, alone and afraid.

Sometimes life was good and Martha was lulled into believing that Daniel had changed. He was often repentant after an abusive episode, and in the early years of their marriage she clung to the hope that someday he would be less abusive and that she would be a better wife. Years passed and the children entered high school. Then an incident occurred that caused Martha to call the police, fearing that Daniel was going to kill her.

They had gone several weeks without speaking to each other, and she broke the silence one evening as she stood at the sink, he at the stove, both preparing the supper meal. Her voice and her words about the vegetables threw him into a rage. Daniel grabbed her and started pounding her head into the kitchen cupboard,

This chapter has been co-authored with Dr. Lori G. Beaman[1]

making an effort not to bruise her face so as to call forth sympathy from others. As Martha told me her story, tears streamed down her face, but then she smiled a little. "My head made so much noise banging those cupboards that Carla, our teenage daughter, came downstairs." Once Carla entered the kitchen, the banging stopped.

It was difficult for Martha to recount exactly what happened in the aftermath of this violent outburst. But the police were called, an arrest was made, and Daniel was escorted temporarily from their home. To her astonishment, the clergyman for whom she worked did not believe her story, despite the fact that Daniel was in jail for the weekend. In a nutshell, Daniel was simply too nice a man—a fine Christian man at that—to ever harm anyone, especially his wife. Martha disclosed the story to no one else.

Her life was now surrounded by a new lie: She and Daniel had irreconcilable differences and they were going to seek a divorce. Her denominational employer was fearful of what people might think about a divorced woman as office manager; her local pastor was fearful of what congregants would think about a divorced Sunday school superintendent. No one seemed to be fearful for the safety of Martha or her children.

The healing process was slow, much slower than Martha had hoped. While the children were supportive, even they did not understand the full extent of Martha's pain or its long history. It was too difficult to tell them; in fact, she wanted them to harbor predominantly pleasant childhood memories, memories where the abuse was still hidden. It was important to Martha that they remember their childhood as one characterized by the words *happy Christian family*. For Martha, though, such a family existed only in her dreams!

❧

For Carol and Joe, life was a struggle just to survive. There was never enough money to pay the bills, never permanent employment, never marital harmony. Moreover, there was always Joe's tendency to drink excessively, school problems with the oldest child, a boy who had been diagnosed with ADD (attention deficit disorder), always a fear that the future would be worse than the present. Because money was so scarce, there were few family outings, few unexpected treats for the children, and very few evenings or weekends of fun. To be sure, Carol and the children had their happy moments when her mother would invite them to her house in the country and the children could run free, or times when Joe would be called in to do mechanic work on the weekend and be able to take their son out to McDonalds and bowling, allowing Carol and the girls a break from all that noise and activity. And there were times when all five of them would go to the park on a Sunday afternoon. But, for the most part, Carol and Joe did not enjoy each other's company and they found the children burdensome.

Carol had been raised in an environment where her father was abusive toward both her mother and one of her brothers. Joe himself was a child victim of abuse, a man who wore the physical and emotional scars of poverty and violence. Both Carol and Joe suffered from low self-esteem and a sense of hopelessness and powerlessness. Joe had "done time" in a local jail, and "time in a rooming house" when he had been given a court order to live apart from Carol.

At the time I became aware of Carol and Joe's story, a particular church community had taken them "under their wing." Carol was participating in a young mother's group, Joe was receiving individual counsel from the pastor, Carol was offered the services of a Christian counselor (paid for by church sources) and the children had been integrated into several age-appropriate programs in the church; moreover, churchwomen were supporting the family through ongoing contact and acts of kindness, such as child care and gifts of food and clothing. According to Carol, Joe had been nonabusive for over a year, and she was working part-time at a garden center. Life was far from easy, but it was looking much better than it ever had in the past.

The violence was condemned, the fear was acknowledged, and the couple were offered choices. According to Carol, most of her church contacts (including the pastoral staff) had encouraged her to leave Joe and to begin a new life free from the violence of the past.

But, because she was reluctant to do that, the faith community were in the process of helping the entire family reach the goal of abuse-free family living. The support had been ongoing for over two years when I first met Carol. By her own account, churchwomen took her places, bought groceries, and came and looked after the children while she was at work, and the missionary group had raised money for her at Christmas. One woman had taken her on a week-long vacation and another *sister in the faith* had cared for the children.

While the story offers no dramatic turnaround or quick solution to the multiple social and economic difficulties Carol and Joe faced, it is clearly an example of support for an abused woman and her children—and the perpetrator of that violence as well—within a local church congregation. And if change is to occur within Carol's family unit, that support from the faith community will need to continue for a very long time!

Abuse against women occurs in every region of the country, among legally married and common-law couples alike, in both rural and urban contexts, in affluence and in poverty. Faith communities are not immune to violence in the family context. Religious as well as secular men hurt and humiliate the women they claim, and have promised, to love. Women who are active in their faith communities are victims of that violence as are women on the fringes of church life. In other words, spiritual commitment, church attendance, personal piety, and religious traditions do not in and of themselves protect a woman from becoming a victim of her husband's rage, nor do they ensure that a husband will always deal with his anger in socially and religiously acceptable ways.

Yet churches as moral communities claim a standard that often exceeds that of the secular world in which they are located. As a result, this discrepancy between teaching and practice highlights for many what they see as the hypocrisy of the Christian church and those who support it. As our examination in chapter 2 showed, there is a close relationship between church and family life. In general,

Christian churches hold *the family* in high regard, teach that the relationship between Christ and the church is analogous to the husband and his bride, and cherish the notion that men and women choose marital partners for life, seeing this as the most desirable context in which to raise and socialize children.

As a result, Christian women who are victims of wife battery have some unique struggles as they attempt to come to grips with and challenge the pain and suffering they have endured at the hands of their husbands. This chapter seeks to understand some of the dimensions to those struggles. Building on our focus group research, and Lori Beaman's doctoral dissertation of in-depth interviews with ninety-four evangelical women, we examine where churchwomen turn when they have family-related problems, the lives of a small group of abused Christian women who were part of our research sample, and some of the features of the healing process.

Sources of Secular and Sacred Help
Sought by Evangelical Women

We asked the women who participated in our focus group research whether they had ever sought the help of secular and sacred resources we listed regarding a problem in their own family. As table 3.1 reveals, two in every three evangelical women in our sample report that they have sought the advice of another woman in their own church for a family-related problem, and likewise two in three claimed to have sought the assistance of a Christian woman in a church other than the one they now attend. A further 59% of women have sought help from their pastor for a family-related matter, 36% consulted a physician, 24% a Christian counselor, 15% a lawyer, and 8% the police.

There are several points which can be drawn to our attention from this data. First, these results offer strong evidence of an informal network of support from within conservative faith communities. Religious women seek out other women of faith when they have family-related problems and need help or advice. Second, most of the over two hundred women who participated in one of our focus groups had also sought help from their pastors for a concern that related to family life. In fact, they were much more likely to seek help from a pastor than from another helping professional, be it a physician or a counselor. In a sense, these data offer corroborating evidence of the demand for pastoral counseling, a subject that will be discussed in chapter 5 from the perspective of clergy.

Third, just under one in four evangelical women had sought help from a Christian counselor, someone trained in counseling within a faith tradition. The growth of professional Christian counseling ministries has been phenomenal over the last decade. Religious bookstores carry dozens of titles relating to marriage, family, and raising children, and magazines like Dr. James Dobson's *Focus on the Family* enter hundreds of thousands of homes across Canada and the United States.

These findings suggest that women within conservative churches seek help for family-related problems within their own faith tradition, first and foremost from other women of faith but also from clergy and specifically trained Christian counselors. Only when these supportive sources are exhausted do they look elsewhere

Table 3.1

Distribution of Sacred and Secular Sources of Help Sought by Evangelical Women

Sources of Sacred and Secular Help Sought by Evangelical Women	%	(N)
Have you ever sought the help of any of the following people regarding a problem in your family?		
Another woman in your church	69.8	(169)
Another Christian woman	66.5	(161)
Pastor	58.7	(142)
Physician	35.5	(86)
Christian counselor	24.0	(58)
Lawyer	14.5	(35)
Police	8.3	(20)

N=242

for help and guidance. As a result, it may be that only the most severely troubled religious women end up on the caseloads of secular service providers, possibly exacerbating those counselors' belief that particular religious persuasions are linked with certain forms of psychopathology or family problems. It would seem that a strong supportive network among women actively involved in their faith community would mitigate against looking for support outside the fold. So what happens when a religious woman looks for help among her sisters in the faith? What types of assistance are offered to battered women by churchwomen? Are victims empowered to make choices and work toward independence, or are they admonished to stay in an abusive marriage whatever the cost?

Within this chapter, we will explore these questions from the perspective of a small sample of abused women with whom in-depth interviews were conducted. Chapter 6 will tell the story from the perspective of the focus group discussions, as groups of churchwomen talked about the support they had individually or collectively offered (or received) from sisters in the faith.

Contextualizing Abuse in the Life of a Christian Woman

The case studies introduced in the following pages provide a glimpse into how evangelical women make sense of their own abuse. Drawing on themes that form a central part of evangelical doctrine such as submission, suffering, and the sanctity of the evangelical family, we will explore the impact of evangelical ideology on abused Christian women. Because of the small number of Christian abused women interviewed, ten in all, it is possible to offer only tentative insight into how evangelical women who suffer abuse use their Christian worldview to both guide and explain the events in their lives.

Life Histories:
Three Stories

What are some of the characteristics of the abused Christian women who were willing to participate in the smaller interview study? Generally, there were three types of situations reflected in this group. In order to give some understanding of their situations without revealing the details of any one woman's life, the text to follow will re-create three conversations with women that are an amalgam of the experiences of the women who were interviewed. The stories reflect three broad categories that emerged from the experiences of the ten women who disclosed current abuse; nevertheless, they cannot be taken to represent the stories of all abused Christian women. They can, however, offer us a basis for understanding several features of the shared experiences of religious women who are victimized by their husbands. The quotations are taken verbatim from the interview transcripts.

Group 1: New Christians

Thirty-six-year-old Angela lives in a basement apartment in an old house in a small town in New Brunswick. As we begin the interview, she explains that she is not sure how much insight about Christian life she can offer, given that she has only been a Christian for about seven months. She attends her church regularly, and has recently become active in trying to establish a committee whose primary purpose will be to raise awareness about family violence. Angela expresses dismay over some of the women she sees in the church who she feels are too submissive. One woman in particular never makes eye contact and seems terrified to speak in the presence of her husband. Angela is committed to raising awareness within the church about healthy Christian family living, a project that has the full support and participation of the church leadership. One year ago, Angela left an abusive relationship. Her husband, a well-educated government consultant, was abusive during their ten-year marriage. When I asked Angela if he was physically abusive, she said:

No, because I never really argued with him. I wouldn't put myself in a position of disagreeing with him and to generate that kind of a response. It was a very conscious decision on my part to tiptoe. I was living on eggshells all the time.

(Church Woman Interview #63)

Since neither of them were Christians during the duration of the marriage, it did not occur to Angela to seek help from a clergyperson, although she has sought the help of a pastor (since she has become a Christian) to deal with the stress caused by the breakdown of her marriage. To some degree, Angela associates her newfound Christian commitment with the breakdown of her marriage, and it certainly has made the pain of the past year more bearable:

Um, I guess I've been able to reconcile what happened by seeing it as a learning experience. Ah, if it hadn't have happened I never would have come to Christ. Ah, and in my marriage I was dying bit by bit. You know, it was just, a marriage is supposed to be a positive experience and encourage you to grow and to improve and to become a better person. My marriage was doing the exact opposite. It was slowly destroying me. Ah, and if it hadn't have happened then I, I would still be in that marriage and it would destroy me at some point. And when I look at where I am now and where I was two-and-a-half years ago, I like where I am now and I like who I am now. And so I reconcile what happened by saying, you know, "Do I want to be there again?" And sometimes women who experience pain grow.

(Church Woman Interview #63)

Now that she is an evangelical Christian, she feels that the church has an important role to play in ending violence against women.

There are a number of important points that emerge from Angela's story. First, like other evangelical women, Angela is using her own experiences as an abused woman as the basis for understanding the pain of other victims of violence. Though only ten women in this interview study were themselves living in abusive relationships at present, over 90 percent had had contact with at least one abused woman—sometimes an acquaintance, but often good friends, sisters, or mothers. Conservative Christian women incorporate this extensive contact in their understanding of and responses to violence against women. In Angela's case, this means lobbying within the church for a better response to victims of violence.

A related point is the sophistication of Angela's understanding of the nature of abuse. In her case, this is grounded in her lived experiences of abuse, but the vast majority of the women interviewed had comprehensive definitions of abuse. Most took the physical aspects of abuse as a given, and then went on to talk about emotional abuse, financial abuse, and even spiritual abuse. Surprisingly, the majority of evangelical women in this study explained violence against women in terms of power and control, an interpretation that is usually associated with feminism.[2]

Though she was not a Christian at the time she was living in the abusive relationship, we see Angela turning to an explanation for her experiences that is Christian-based: "Sometimes women who experience pain grow." The idea that one gains renewal from suffering is a common theme among conservative Protestant women when they think about the pain and suffering experienced by abused women. A number of Christian writers have been critical of the association of suffering with good, particularly in the context of violence against women.[3] The message that suffering is "glorious" or Christlike may have the effect of preventing Christian victims of abuse from leaving their abusers, or may persuade them to suffer in silence, never telling anyone about their suffering. There are two important considerations here: First, Christian churches may need to think more fully about Christ's suffering as it is linked to the everyday lives of Christians; and second, though they may explain suffering in terms of possible growth and ministry opportunities, conservative Christian women do not condone violence against women.

Group 2: I Thought He Was a Christian

Forty-one-year-old Susan was married at the age of nineteen to Hank, a committed Christian from her youth group. In the beginning, they had a "model" Christian home. Over the next few years, however, Susan noticed that Hank had withdrawn from some of his church commitments and seemed less and less willing to participate in family devotions. Susan's life became more difficult too as she tried to juggle the pressures of raising children and Hank's growing criticism of nearly everything she did. While he kept a Christian profile in public, Hank's behavior at home was often abusive—belittling and aggressive, sometimes to the point of physical contact such as pushing and slapping. Susan tried to accommodate Hank by submitting to his demands, but her efforts only attracted more criticism. She describes their relationship:

He's very domineering, always wants his own way, all the time. Like . . . like if you go into a restaurant and just say he's not seated yet, and you go have a seat, he'll want to move to go to another seat, he'll always be like that over everything, so it's kind of like, I never . . . It got to the point like I really didn't have much say on anything, could be like if you want . . . whatever, it got to be like even the smallest little thing, so it was like, you know, so it was like, a kind . . . what it was with me it was just kind of a continuing picking away at me, so . . . so what really happened, the last year and a half, I've been really praying about why I feel always hurt.

(Church Woman Interview #22)

Despite the fact that she regularly attended church, Susan felt isolated and alone; Hank had cut off nearly all contact with friends and family. Susan felt that their marital problems were her fault and that she had nowhere to turn.

I never told anyone. My, my parents came out to visit for six weeks. . . . I never told anyone anything. She [my mother] suspected something was a little strange one time when he said, "I'll see you in the bedroom," and the door was slammed shut and we were there for a rather long time. And I came out in tears, and he came bubbling out as if nothing was the matter, and she didn't like the way he was treating me, but she didn't know anything. And I didn't dare tell anyone; there goes my job, you see my security. He, he, he made good money.

(Church Woman Interview #36)

One day, out of desperation, she talked to the pastor about her frustrations with her marriage. Together with the pastor and his wife, she worked out a plan so that she could leave home in order to let things cool down. She is now doing a Bible study with them that explores the true meaning of Christian submission, not the "doormat" version. They have arranged for an apartment for her, and the pastor is now attempting to counsel Hank. The pastor has told her that while reconciliation is important, if Hank refuses to change, Susan should consider a permanent separation.

Susan's story raises a number of interesting issues. First, though she is a committed Christian whose life is both explained and guided by her religious worldview, as an abused woman she also has much in common with abused women who are not conservative Christians: her financial vulnerability, her feelings of low self-worth, and her tendency to blame herself and to hide the abuse are all elements of many abused women's lives. Though the implications of being an abused *Christian* woman may be quite different when considered in light of evangelical doctrine like the sanctity of the family, Susan shares experiences and feelings with both women of faith and women who do not share a faith perspective.

The second point that emerges from Susan's story is the possibility of a link between the doctrine of submission and the existence of abuse in her marriage. Some scholars have linked the scriptural call for wives to submit to their husbands to the presence of abuse in some Christian families.[4] Susan certainly connects her "misunderstanding" of submission and the pain she is feeling. For the abused Christian woman, submission, like suffering and sacrifice, may form the ideological lens through which she understands her situation. But does Christian submission mean that one must endure abuse at the hands of one's husband? The ninety-four women who participated in the interview study were unwilling to make such a link. In discussing their own understandings of this controversial Christian doctrine, it was clear that most women had interpreted submission to mean mutual submission, equality, and partnership in their own family lives.

Group 3: I'm in Control Now

Sixty-three-year-old Gertrude has been married to John for forty-four years. She is now a grandmother of three, but she rarely sees her grandchildren. John is an alcoholic and is not a Christian. He has physically abused both Gertrude and her children. Gertrude describes the last incident of physical abuse:

It would be three years ago this October, and ah, he just, he lost it, and he come out in the kitchen, it was just over nothing, just, I set the beets down the wrong way— I had four beets in my hand, it was hard to hold them, so I had to flop them over, you know, to get them on the counter—When they hit the counter, that's all he needed, he blew, and, ah . . . I didn't take what he said to me, you know, I just answered back nicely, and he grabbed me right here, around the throat, and picked me up by my head, and carried me over, I mean it was like, when it was used to be when our daughter was a little child, and he just beat my head repeatedly, in the wall. I had a slight concussion, and was very embarrassed, and very, you know, belittled by the whole thing, and astounded, because I hadn't had any of that foolishness, since 19 . . . what . . . 19 . . . 64.

(Church Woman Interview #43)

When asked how she understands her suffering, Gertrude points to her own actions as the precipitating factor. Had she not strayed from God, she would not be in the marriage in the first place.

> You know, the Bible says we reap what we sow, and ah, I was a Christian as a young girl, thirteen, and then when I got in high school I got away, and I didn't . . . I wasn't involved in the church at all. And I started going out with my husband when I was fifteen, and at nineteen we were married, and ah, anyway, I wasn't really followin' the Lord nor was he.
>
> (Church Woman Interview #77)

On two occasions Gertrude has gone to the local transition house for a "time out." Although the transition house workers wanted her to stay longer, and her Christian friends and pastor had suggested that she leave the marriage, Gertrude explains that the pull of love is strong, and she has never left. When asked about her experience with pastors, she tells me that over the years all of them (five in total) have been supportive except one, who did, in fact, tell her that if she prayed about the situation it would be resolved. While Gertrude is resentful about this pastor's approach, she does believe in the power of prayer.

Over the years, the physical abuse has lessened (though it still occurs), and Gertrude has come to feel more and more in control of her life, primarily, she feels, because of God's intervention. She wishes for the day that her husband will share her worldview, but in the meantime she is grateful for the blessings God has provided:

> I get really upset for a few minutes, because I would love our life to be a different way, but it isn't, and I'm thankful to God for what he has provided me with, and I'll just keep on trucking.
>
> (Church Woman Interview #61)

When asked whether she would have left John had she not been a Christian, she responds affirmatively, but goes on to explain that when she was growing up she was taught that a woman stays with her husband no matter what. To Gertrude, leaving is not an answer, and besides, she feels that she is a stronger person now than she has ever been. She reports being in control of the relationship now, and she'll stay with John.

Gertrude's story raises the problem of how to make sense of suffering. Gertrude, like some of the other abused Christian women interviewed, understands her suffering to be a result of her own actions, particularly her choices that, she feels, took her away from what God would have wanted for her or were contrary to "God's will." In interpreting suffering, the ninety-four women interviewed tended to focus either on individual-centered explanations or on God-centered rationalizations (as opposed to social structural ones), the latter being explicated as God's often unknown plan in allowing human suffering. Again, suffering was frequently linked to some ultimate good, such as personal growth or the ability to help others in a similar situation, something that Gertrude herself describes as a benefit of her suffering.

Gertrude also expresses a commitment to the sanctity of the family in her decisions about her marriage. To her, the importance of keeping the family together overrides the pain and suffering she has endured. Though she explicitly links her Christian worldview to her decision to remain in an abusive relationship, she also connects her childhood socialization (in a non-Christian family) to her commitment to marriage. Thus, we see a convergence of sacred and secular (patriarchal) ideology, which together work to emphasize the centrality of a "whole" family and a woman's role as suffering servant keeping the family intact.

But Gertrude as "victim" is not the only story that appears here: Gertrude is, truly, a "survivor" of woman abuse. It is in the picture of the survivor that the image of abused woman as agent emerges most strongly. Interestingly, though her faith community is important to her, Gertrude turned to the secular resource of the transition house for relief and some measure of control over her life. Her deliberate use of the transition house as a tension reliever and safe haven demonstrates her ability to exercise agency within the abusive relationship. She is not a "suffering servant" or "doormat," but a strong woman who is grateful for God's support in her life.

Understanding Abuse

Of the ninety-four women who participated in the interview study, ten were currently living in an abusive relationship at the time they were interviewed. Nine of these women used the "abused woman" label to describe themselves.[5] Among these women, abuse ranged from emotional abuse, controlling behavior, and loss of temper to physical abuse. Four of the men were or had been alcoholics. Only two of the women described their husbands as Christians; although all wished that their husbands shared their commitment to Christ.

Each of these ten abused women described how her faith had enabled her to get through the hard times and inspired hope for the future.[6] In their view, the Lord is on their side:

The Lord showed me in my prayer time in 1980 that I had to take control of my life, so it's still been a constant battle, so it was very often, all the time, before 1980, but still even though I have taken control of my finances and my life he [her husband] still very often tried to take control of mine.

(Church Woman Interview #43)

Another woman, who had occasionally gone to her local transition house for a "time out," described the practical effects of her prayer efforts when asked how being an evangelical Christian had made a difference in her life:

They make a big difference, 'cause He gives me all the strength that I need to get through, and like, and I pray, quite a bit, like especially, at the time, say if my

husband was mentally abusing me, okay, then I tried to discipline myself to start praying for him. And that was it keeps my . . . it keeps my mouth shut, because if . . . if
. . . like I say, if you start . . . saying things back, it's just going to get worse.

(Church Woman Interview #71)

One woman described herself as being bitter about the lack of support she had received from her church community, but distinguished her church attendance from
her commitment to God. Most of the women described their Christian friends as
important resources in their struggle to cope with an abusive marital relationship.
Seven of the ten women's lives could be described as church-centered; to them,
their church-related activities and service were important sources of strength,
which enabled them to cope at home. Three of the women were in a "crisis" situation at the time of the interview in that they felt that their marriages were on
the brink of disaster; two of these women were living apart from their husbands
at the time of the interview. The other seven women, however, were similar to
"Gertrude," described in the third case study we looked at. Like her, they have
endured years of abuse, and have come to a point in their lives where they feel
that they are in control. They are resigned to a marriage that does not match the
Christian model, but they hold hope that someday their husbands will share their
worldview. They see themselves not as suffering servants, but as agents who direct their own lives.

How can we make sense of their reports of being in control? How can we see
abused Christian women as other than suffering servants who have sacrificed their
own happiness for the sake of an ideal of the perfect Christian family? It is useful
to turn to Martha Mahoney's work here.[7] Mahoney argues that we must pay particular attention to individual women's experiences. Further, she points out that
we have tended to dichotomize our characterization of women as either victims or
agents, a dichotomy that does not capture the realities of women's lives. Therefore, to dismiss abused women's reports of being in control as "false consciousness" is, in a sense, forcing a woman to assume the status of victim even if she
herself does not accept that role. Characterizing an abused woman as a victim also
denies the possibility of the existence of both oppression and agency at the same
time. The abused women represented by Gertrude did not deny their abuse (or their
oppression), but they did not report that they felt powerless. It is important also to
recognize that the abused Christian women who were interviewed responded in
diverse ways to their abusive situations, yet each exercised agency in the face of
oppression.

Contrary to the findings of other researchers,[8] those abused women who had
approached clergy about their relationships reported no consistent pattern of being told to "go home and pray about it." Some women reported that despite encouragement by clergy to leave the abusive relationship they had decided to "stick
with" their marriage, and other women were currently working with clergy to salvage their marriages. Only two of these ten women had had negative experiences
in relation to the clergy they had approached for help: one had been told that her
body belonged to her husband and he could do with it as he pleased; the other felt

that her pastor, while he listened, was not providing enough support to her husband, who had been physically abusive in the past. The problem, of course, aside from the individual cases explored here, is that one pastor can have a significant impact on a number of people.

Among those women who had lived in but left abusive relationships, there were few reports of negative experiences with clergy. One woman reported that while her pastor listened to her, she felt that he did not believe her story of abuse. Other women simply did not tell their pastors, or they were not Christians when they were in abusive relationships. The following woman related the tendency to hide her own experiences with an abusive partner:

Um, it's a personal issue, and at the time you're feeling, you're self-esteem is so low that you don't really trust people, and ah . . . I don't know how to put that. I know that when I was in that situation I didn't trust anyone.

[Interviewer: Were you a Christian?]
Yes.

[Interviewer: Do you think Christian women are more likely to hide abuse?]
I think you, um . . . as a Christian you look on it as, you know, suffering for Christ's sake, or a burden you have to bear, and . . . you tend to try to live through it a little bit longer.

(Church Woman Interview #17)

Though most of the women interviewed who were living in abusive relationships had been forthright with their clergy and church community about the existence of abuse in their relationships, a few reported that they had minimized the abuse or had not disclosed it at all.

Religious ideology that glorifies suffering and posits the Christian woman as the suffering servant has implications for Christian women who are abused. Half of the ten women living in abusive relationships explained their suffering in relation to their own choices; from their point of view, if they had listened to God, they wouldn't be in this mess in the first place. Not unlike abused women who do not adhere to a Christian worldview, these women blame themselves for their own suffering. What distinguishes this group from non-Christian women, however, lies in their tendency to relate their own suffering to the will of God. In other words, if one disobeys God, suffering will likely result.

Thirty-three women in this study reported having been abused at some point in their lives, whether by a partner, a parent, or a relative. Each was asked to consider how she makes sense of the suffering she has endured as a result of the abuse. Sixteen of the thirty-three women talked about a higher purpose, or their own move away from God, and their own choices in relation to their suffering.

Well, the way I look at it, I'm afraid, sometimes I think of myself, well, I chose—see, when I met my husband, I kind of backslid and I wasn't going to church, and also too, I didn't know anything about abuse, because I was from a very loving

Christian family, so really you can't blame God. We make choices, but then, there's help, now, at least now there is help, you don't have to stay in a relationship where you can get help, so I don't really blame God, and I don't think that women should blame God.

[Interviewer: So you could talk about your own abuse to God?]

Yah, yah. Sometimes God allows you to go through different things so that you can help somebody else that gets into the same predicament.

(Church Woman Interview #71)

Again, the theme of growth from suffering emerged in relation to women's own experiences of abuse:

Um, I think that God doesn't want these things to happen to me but I think that they happen anyway because, for a whole variety of reasons that we talked about already. Um, I think that, that God gets very upset when these things happen. Um, I don't think he allows them to happen in the sense that he makes them happen, but I think that he allows them to happen in the sense that OK, you're in this situation, let's make it into a positive situation by making it a learning experience and a growing experience. And that, that's been the way I have reconciled, you know, what has happened in my own life, is to look at it from a perspective that OK, you know, God didn't certainly say, "I'm going to make this happen to you because you're a bad person," or whatever. But ah, "This situation has happened to you so let's make, turn it into a positive experience by making it a good growth experience for you."

(Church Woman Interview #63)

While evangelical women may blame their abuse on their own choices, they also see their suffering as having possible positive implications. True to their commitment to service, they understand their own abuse as an opportunity to offer assistance to others who suffer in similar situations. Although Christian understandings of suffering are not directed specifically toward abuse, abused Christian women appropriate it as an interpretative tool in understanding their own lives.

Dimensions to the Healing Journey

Without naming it as such, most of the women in our research felt that the first step in the healing journey related to an awareness of the frequency and pervasiveness of the problem of abuse. As such, churches and their leaders simply needed to recognize that violence against women and their children is a problem of great magnitude, both within and beyond the walls of the local church building. Some women talked in terms of blinders on the eyes of some Christians, not unlike the blinders a horse wears to prevent distraction—they keep the Christians, like the horse, from seeing the full extent of the situation facing them. Other women talked in terms of the masks Christians are prone to wear, masks that hide the pain and humiliation that victims experience and masks that hinder our individual or collective attempts to respond compassionately and fully to the needs of those around us.

Removing the blinders or the masks is a painful process, most painful for those who have been victims of abuse, but also difficult for women, men, or religious leaders who are called on to grapple with the disjuncture between the reality of families in crisis and the high value placed on the intact Christian family. While there are other ways to remove blinders or masks within church life, many felt that one of the most effective means involved simply talking about wife abuse: from the pulpit, in the Sunday school class, in the women's Bible study group, in youth group meetings, among home groups, and during clergy in-service training workshops or seminars.

Raising awareness in the church community of the nature and pervasiveness of violence in the family home encourages victims to come forward for help, even as it sensitizes others to be able to offer that help.

> If the pastor never mentions that women are abused or church never makes any comment on it, then I think women would be less apt to come.
>
> (Woman #5, Focus Group #26)

> But . . . the role of the church and the pastor is to be God's representative and certainly God is not happy with family violence.
>
> (Woman #1, Focus Group #12)

Through our earlier analysis of the Christian women who were currently experiencing abuse, the importance of two religious concepts was identified: the glorification of suffering, and the often-misunderstood doctrine of wives' submission to their husbands. A number of scholars have linked abuse in Christian families to the principle of wifely submission.[9] As we saw in chapter 2, though, the link between hierarchy and violence is indirect, and not as clear as some might contend. We would argue that while contemporary Christian teaching on the family that emphasizes hierarchy offers an environment that may well be fertile for the cycle of violence, failing to condemn that violence as unequivocally as it could and should and failing to respond to victims as fully as it might, it does not in fact produce violence. This is an important distinction. In other words, violence is not inherent in the Christian model of family living, but it clearly develops as a by-product in some families.

Christian women themselves do not understand submission to mean subjection.[10] Rather, not unlike contemporary evangelical feminist writing on the subject,[11] women in our research were more likely to translate submission to mean mutual submission, shared love and partnership, than they were to conceptualize submission as support for unchallenged hierarchical power relations between men and women in marriage. To be sure, there is a certain defensiveness of this doctrine among women, in part because evangelical women themselves are aware of the broader societal criticisms of their willingness to interpret the role of their husbands as "head of the family." Therefore, in the in-depth interviews with these women, it was not uncommon for women to insist that "we are not doormats."[12] Thus, in the minds of churchwomen themselves there is no marked inconsistency between describing one's husband as leader and still interpreting the process of family interaction as partnership.

The glorification of suffering, too, is a doctrine that some have linked to why churchwomen are reluctant to leave abusive partners and begin new lives free from the abuse of the past.[13] The motif of a suffering servant, hanging on a rugged cross for sins that he did not commit, is central to the Christian gospel. For women who have suffered abuse, however, it may in fact serve as a constant reminder that no matter how intense their pain, how long their endurance has been, they can never measure up to the agony of Jesus of Nazareth, God's Son. The issue here is not to downplay the suffering of Christ, but rather to recognize that for some believers the centrality of Jesus' suffering, and by implication the glorification of the suffering of all believers, serves as a deterrent to the exercise of human agency. In other words, if one holds that suffering is central to the life of the Christian, believing that pain and tribulations nurture Christian growth, it is much harder—if not impossible—to ask for and receive spiritual empowerment to leave an abusive family environment.

Closely associated with suffering is the concept of shame. Robert Albers, in *Shame: A Faith Perspective,* believes that men and women within faith communities often exercise the strategy of withdrawal and isolation when it comes to dealing with the shame associated with either substance addiction or violence in the family.[14] In this way, the shame stays hidden as a secret of the family, even as the offending behavior too is a secret. Speaking as a pastoral counselor, Albers contends that one of the goals of church intervention in the lives of victims of abuse is to liberate these persons "from the stranglehold of disgrace shame" and thereby offer them the opportunity to grow and develop.[15]

In a not-dissimilar fashion, some of the women victims in our focus groups talked about the healing quality of sharing their story of pain and its associated disgrace with other women. Shattering the silence becomes an important step in the transition from victim to survivor. But there is also pain associated with telling the story and in coping with the concomitant shame.

> I feel that if, if in the church there are some that have survived it . . . it's in sharing one-on-one the pain and knowing the hope that you have reached or attained a certain place. . . . And sometimes just hearing someone else's story one-on-one shared with them. And sharing the pain as well as the hope, sometimes will lift the burden.
>
> (Woman #13, Focus Group #2)

Another woman reflected on how talking to others about her personal pain was part of the healing journey in her case.

The first time that I shared publicly my testimony . . . that was a healing thing [for me].

(Woman #3, Focus Group #7)

A further theme in the discussion of healing, and one that we will develop at some length, revolves around the controversial subject of forgiveness. As the following dialogue illustrates, forgiveness is a very complicated theological and interpersonal concept. Moreover, its many dimensions touch on aspects of the believer's own forgiveness, the biblical mandate to forgive as we've been forgiven, the pain associated with reliving what is to be forgiven, and possibly the process of either asking for, or offering, forgiveness in a personal encounter between the victim and the perpetrator.

Speaking from her own experience, an older abused woman offered these comments:

I'm almost 51. You don't ever, no matter how much counselling you need, and you can leave it in the hands of the Lord, you can even come to a point you think you've forgiven . . . Because I do fully believe you can forgive to a certain extent, with the Lord's help you can, [but] you can't ever forget a severe trauma.

(Woman #7, Focus Group #7)

[To which another woman responded:]
We have to forgive in order for us to get healed and get on with it, [but] the forgetting part, you never have confidence in that person again.

[At this point another woman chimed in:]
But I think what, what the apostle Paul meant when he talked about forgetting what is behind, he meant not allowing the past to determine how we live today.

(Woman #4, Focus Group #7)

Forgiveness and the
Abused Christian Woman

In their book titled *Shattered and Broken,* the McDills argue that well-intentioned pastors or other church leaders sometimes tell abused women to forgive their husbands and return home.[16] From their perspective, that not only places the victim of wife battery in a situation that is physically dangerous but also has removed her one step further from receiving the help that she needs—through poor advice offered by someone who is in a trusted position within the church. "True forgiveness," they write, "is much more complicated than blind forgiveness."[17] Central to *true* forgiveness is the abuser's repentance, involving not only remorse for the battery but an examination of the motivating factors that turn anger to violence, a renunciation of his violent past behaviors, and movement toward a new way of relating to the wife he once abused. Only then are confession and forgiveness possible.

In an essay titled "Forgiveness the Last Step," Marie Fortune contends that forgiveness is one of the pastoral resources available to assist women and children who have been victimized by the actions of others and, as such, is one aspect of the healing process, one means of the restoration of the victim to wholeness.[18] Yet, pastoral and lay counselors, as well as friends and family members in the faith community, often suggest that a woman victim simply *forgive and forget* what has happened. They are misguided in thinking that words of forgiveness alone reduce the pain and augment the healing process.

Marie Fortune takes another perspective. She argues that forgiveness is the last step in the healing journey, the last rung on the ladder in the victim's struggle to overcome the brokenness of the past. She writes that "forgiveness before justice is 'cheap grace' and cannot contribute to authentic healing and restoration to wholeness for the victim or for the offender."[19] As a result, Fortune believes that premature forgiveness cuts the healing process short and undercuts the redemption of abusers, by making them less than fully accountable for their violent actions. Seen from this perspective, forgiveness that is suggested (or demanded) of the victim too early in the healing journey (by either the perpetrator or the pastor) may actually slow the recovery process for the victim. Premature forgiveness, which of course isn't *really* forgiveness as it is meant in a biblical sense, can be dangerous to the victim, suppress the possibility of reform in the life of the abuser, and perpetuate the abusive cycle in the relationship.

So what is authentic forgiveness? According to Marie Fortune, justice, forgiveness, and healing cannot be dependent on the wishes of the offender and his timetable. These processes become part of the responsibility of the wider society, including the church and the legal system, as well as family and friends who want to support the victim. Fortune believes that the task of the helping professions is to provide the central ingredients necessary for justice, including truth telling and an acknowledgment of the harm done to the victim; breaking the silence of the reality of the abuse; hearing the whole story and thereby refusing to minimize its consequences, and offering protection of the vulnerable (which may include not only the woman victim, but also her children) who might still be at risk.

Within this paradigm, forgiveness for the victim involves the process of letting go of the immediacy of the trauma and the memories associated with it. Fortune contends that, seen in this way, forgiveness is "the choice to no longer allow the memory of the abuse to continue to abuse" one's life.[20] Forgiveness does not involve forgetting, nor does it mean that the victim returns automatically to the abuser. Forgiveness encompasses setting new goals where the memory of abuse is put into perspective so that it no longer dominates one's choices, one's limitations, or one's daily life. Needless to say, forgiveness is a time-consuming and often emotionally difficult process for the victim.

For the Christian, healing is mediated by the work of God's Holy Spirit. As such, the power of God offers the victim strength to forgive and the abuser the strength to repent and to change. Yet, Fortune warns that any attempt by the church, clergy or laypeople, to cut the process of healing short and to offer premature forgiveness means that the possibility of authentic healing is lost. By withholding forgiveness until the justice-making process between victim and abuser is complete, and by waiting patiently with victims until they are ready to offer forgiveness "may be the most charitable and compassionate act the church can offer."[21] By these actions, the church and its leaders take seriously the power and potential of forgiveness to offer hope and healing to victims of violence.

To Conclude

There are clearly areas of overlap between religious and secular women in the journey from victim to survivor. Knowing what wife abuse is, regarding wife abuse as unacceptable behavior, situating oneself as a victim of abuse, disclosing one's personal history of abuse, and initial (and perhaps ongoing) support from the person to whom such disclosures are made are all critical ingredients in the early stages of beginning the healing journey. For conservative religious women, though, there are some unique challenges, not least of which relate to church teaching on the importance of the intact Christian family, a belief in a hierarchical model of family life as God's design for marital harmony, a model of forgiveness that emphasizes "seventy times seven,"[22] the glorification of suffering as part of the process toward spiritual maturity—all compounded by a belief in the separation of the faith community from the secular culture and a concept of an instantaneous, miraculous work of grace in the life of the sinner.

Explorations of the links between these church teachings, such as the glorification of suffering and the celebration of the intact *happy Christian family,* need to be more fully developed if we are to understand how churches can better respond to the needs of abused women within their congregations. This chapter has given a glimpse into how abused Christian women make sense of their suffering, and how, in the context of an abusive relationship, they draw strength from their Christian commitment. For abused Christian women, an evangelical worldview is both liberating and life-giving, while at the same time exacerbating the tendency to blame one's own actions as justification for abuse being suffered.

To evangelical women, their faith is seen not as a liability, but as an asset that has helped them to get through trials with which they might not otherwise have found the strength to cope. They make sense of their abusive situations by seeing them as an impetus to commit their lives to Christ, or as teaching them a lesson that will help them to reach out to others. While many have used secular resources, their Christian communities and friends are of central importance to them. The majority of their experiences with pastors have been positive, but some women have received poor advice from clergy. For the most part, these women see themselves as fully competent agents, who have made choices that are for the benefit of themselves and their families. Paradoxically, while believing God is in control, they take responsibility for their actions and decisions.

4

Evangelical Clergy and Wife Abuse: Knowledge and Response

Celebrating family life, along with its traditional values and patterns, has become a cornerstone of the contemporary Christian message. As a result, pastors—evangelical and liberal alike—have found themselves defining marriage and family patterns, offering advice to enhance marital satisfaction, and counseling those family members whose experience does not match the ideal preached from church pulpits. Parishioner demand for pastoral one-to-one counseling has grown exponentially in recent years, though there is little evidence that clergy themselves are more predisposed—or trained—to offer it. Clearly, the more family life is placed on a sacred pedestal, the wider the gap between the rhetoric and the reality.

The Experience of Conservative Protestant Clergy in Counseling Victims of Abuse

There are several reasons why it is important to explore clergy experience in counseling victims of abuse. First, the celebration of family life and family values exposes a chasm between the ideal of family life that is supposed to characterize men and women in marriage, and the reality of families in pain. For religious women suffering abuse at the hands of their marital partner, such a disjuncture between rhetoric and reality intensifies their suffering. In all probability, it magnifies their guilt, their feelings of personal responsibility for the failure to attain marital bliss, and their lack of self-worth. As a result, one might expect that the gap between how family life is supposed to operate and their personal experience of violence may mitigate against the likelihood of seeking help from their pastor. If this is the case, evangelical clergy may in fact report little experience counseling families in pain. On the other hand, the message of family unity and marital happiness may prompt women who do not experience satisfaction, safety, and self-worth from family life to seek pastoral help. It is clearly an empirical question as to whether the high ideal of family stability and marital harmony drives women to, or away from, seeking guidance from their spiritual leaders.

While the centrality of the message about family life alone would suggest that it is important to examine clerical experience in counseling victims of abuse, there is a second, equally important, reason. Faith communities, especially those that demand a large commitment from their followers, tend to be rather closed entities. As a result, members look inward to others of like faith perspective to assist them in addressing both spiritual and everyday issues and concerns. Thus, churches and clergy that tend to support the idea of distinctiveness from the secular world in terms of both mission and lifestyle may create an environment where members feel uncomfortable sharing their problems "outside the fold."[1] Seeking and receiving help from secular providers, then, may be interpreted as "letting down the standard," thereby providing tangible evidence that the faith perspective cannot protect its members against human frailty, pain, and disappointment. And, furthermore, such help would involve "listening to the world," whereby members might be guilty of blurring the distinction between the sheep and the goats, or the saved and the lost.

Other reasons to investigate clerical experience include the magnitude of the problem of wife abuse,[2] the power of the religious framework in an individual woman's life,[3] and the need to explore multidisciplinary models for coordinating spouse abuse services.[4]

In one of our studies, we investigated the experience of clergy with victims of abuse within two evangelical denominations. A total of 343 evangelical clergy serving in churches across Eastern Canada[5] (a response rate of 70 percent) returned a six-page questionnaire exploring clergy experience with woman and child abuse, knowledge of family violence issues, and referral practices related to violence. The results of the questionnaire project form the basis for this chapter. A second phase of this research involved in-depth, face-to-face interviews with a hundred evangelical clergy, interviews that took place in various churches all across the Atlantic region.

From the survey results, we will explore both the nature and the extent of clergy contact with abused women and their children, abusive men, and clerical understanding of the dynamics that give rise to violence within the family environment. On the other hand, the findings from the interview study will enable us to examine the role of the pastor as a counselor for abused women and abusive men. Here we address the demand for pastoral counseling and the types of problems congregants bring to members of the clergy. We will also consider how ministers conceptualize relationship counseling, and more specifically their own role in providing it. As we explore these results, it is important to consider the implications of the data and the questions they raise for pastors and victimized congregants alike.

Awareness of Violence Issues

Clergy are often criticized for failing to recognize that abuse exists within their churches and the communities their churches serve.[6] Our research suggests, however, that clergy as a group are more informed concerning the problem of violence in the family context than one might at first suspect. But while they may be more knowledgeable than some sources would give them credit for being,[7] there are some glaring inaccuracies and misperceptions in clerical understanding of the nature and extent of violence against women in the homes across the nation, the implications of which may be rather far-reaching for abused women in faith communities.[8]

Ministers were asked to estimate the percentage of married couples—first in Canada and secondly within their own congregations—who have experienced violence as part of their relationship. Table 4.1 illustrates the distribution of re-

Table 4.1

Distribution of Pastors' Perception of the Level of Violence Among Married Couples in Canada and Among Married Couples within Their Own Congregations

Perceived Rate of Violence in Marital Relationships	Married Couples in Canada	Married Couples in the Pastor's Congregation
0–10%	21.9%	55.6%
11–20	19.8	18.2
21–30	26.0	10.9
31–40	13./	5.4
41–50	8.1	3.1
>50	11.1	2.0
Mean	28.8%	18.8

sponses to these two questions and shows that clergy consistently believe the rate of abuse to be higher in the secular world than it is within the families of their own congregations.

As one can see from these results, pastors consider that more than one in four married couples (28.8%) in Canada are violent, as compared to under one in five (18.8%) in their own congregations. While clergy estimates of violence are pretty much on target as it relates to society at large, they appear to underestimate violent behavior within their own pastoral charge.

Researchers in the field of violence have consistently argued that the rate of male violence against women (as well as other forms of family violence) knows no religious boundaries.[9] If this is so, then the percentage of church families experiencing violence would be equal to the level of abuse found within the general society. So why do pastors consider that the rates of abuse are so much lower among families of faith? Where do clergy derive their view that violence is more rampant outside than inside the church walls?

Clergy Knowledge of Abuse against Women

Clergy Understanding of Abuse in General Society

Generally speaking, clergy in our research point to reasons consistent with social scientific findings to explain the existence of abuse in marriage, why men are abusive toward their partners, why women remain in abusive relationships, why women hide the abuse they have suffered, and the long-term consequences of physical or sexual aggression. To be more specific, we found that the majority of ministers listed male anger/male desire to control (62%), intrapersonal problems of the abusive man (61%), and the intergenerational transmission of violence (47%) as the three most important reasons to explain why men are abusive toward their wives/girlfriends. Cited less frequently were difficulties the abusive man had relating to women (25%), the stress level of the abuser (21%), and prevalent role models within the general society (17%). Less than one in ten ministers considered the influence of spiritual forces or an "unchristian worldview" as part of their explanation for male violence against women, and just 3% noted "provocation" on the part of the wife.

While not all clergy are cognizant of the plethora of factors related to why men abuse the women they claim to love, it is striking to note that, as a group, clergy are not generally ill informed about abuse. Rather than claiming that clergy are misguided in their understanding of why men abuse women, it would be more accurate to say that they hold an incomplete picture. And, as we shall see shortly, there are also traces of incompleteness as we consider clerical perceptions about abuse victims and the resultant long-term impact of the violence women have suffered.

When asked to comment on what they believe are the reasons women remain in abusive relationships, clergy highlighted four factors: women's commitment to family stability (73.5%), women's lack of options (65.3%), women's intrapersonal problems (52.7%) such as low self-esteem, and fear (45.8%). By comparison, fewer clergy noted social pressure on the woman to remain in the marriage (17.4%), the influence of the church (11.4%), or family background (6.9%). Clearly, pastors perceive that women are so committed to family stability that they are willing to risk their own physical and emotional safety in order to preserve the family unit, but they fail to appreciate that there are subtle (and not so subtle) pressures on women from both church and society to stay in the relationship.

In fact, "commitment to keeping the family together" is understood by pastors to be one of the major reasons why women hide the abuse they have suffered. When asked to report what they believe are the reasons women are reluctant to disclose their experiences of abuse, embarrassment or shame emerged as the number-one factor. Fully 69% of clergy mentioned embarrassment, followed by fear (54%), personal problems including low self-esteem (27.1%), and a commitment to family stability (27%). Factors reported less frequently included guilt (19%), lacking viable alternatives (5%), and the influence of family background (2%).

Clergy were also asked to indicate what they believe to be the long-term effects of physical or sexual abuse on victims. There was fairly unanimous agreement (84%) that victims experience intrapersonal problems, such as psychological distress or emotional scars, as a result of abuse; some referred to self-injurious behavior or "complete devastation" as examples of the types of emotional problems survivors face. A majority of clergy also mentioned "ongoing relationship problems" (54%) and "low self-esteem" (52%); a much smaller proportion noted physical effects (12%), persistent fear (9%), the marring of one's relationship with God (7%), shame (5%), or a low view of women (4%).

There are several points that we can draw out from this data on clerical understandings of victims' responses to the abuse they have suffered. First, clergy appear to be appropriating general social scientific knowledge into their personal understandings of why violence occurs in homes across the nation. And while we will discuss some of the implications of this result a little later, we can state here that it is clear that clergy as a group are not lacking in basic knowledge about either the prevalence of violence or the major dynamics that undergird it. Their understanding may be incomplete (as in the rate of violence in families of faith), but for the most part it is not rooted in perceptions lacking a scientific basis.

Second, like their secular counterparts, clergy appear to be reluctant to employ any spiritual or religious reasons to account for victims' reluctance to report abuse, women's response to it, or the long-term implications emanating from having experienced violence within one's home environment. This apparent lack of a spiritual connection is noteworthy. Is a religious framework unable to account in any way for the persistence of wife and child abuse in our social world? Are religious leaders devoid of any unique perspective on this major issue affecting millions of families?

As we shall see, it is not that clergy have failed to incorporate their religious worldview into their understanding of abuse, but that such an incorporation of spiritual values and principles appears to be reserved solely for why *Christian* families are violent, rather than being part of the overall explanation for violence against women in our neighborhoods and indeed across North America.

Third, while clergy responses are certainly consistent with emerging notions concerning why family violence occurs in individual homes, and continues to be a major social issue in the society in which we live, there are some ways in which ministers as a group are unique. In particular, clergy appear to be less likely to recognize the role of fear and financial vulnerability in the lives of battered wives, while they are very likely to consider the impact of women's commitment to family stability. There may be several reasons for this, not least of which is the extremely high value Christianity has placed on *the family*. Also, suggesting that women's commitment to family stability keeps them in the abusive home, rather than fear or financial dependence, roots the explanation for women's failure to leave firmly with the abused woman, rather than as a function of a social structural system that disadvantages women.

For the most part, then, these clerical responses take into account the mounting scholarly evidence as to the nature, extent, and consequences of wife battery across the country and indeed around the globe that we examined in chapter 1. Moreover, our discussion of the literature on Christian families in chapter 2 helps us to contextualize clerical views about why women remain in violent homes that threaten their safety and self-esteem.

In a related question about the role of alcohol, almost two thirds of pastors felt that substance abuse played an extensive role in creating an abusive environment within the home, though most did not regard it as a causal factor. One in five ministers noted that alcohol reduces a person's inhibitions, and as a result may act as an accelerator for performing abusive behavior. Given that evangelical clergy as a group prohibit both the nonmedical use of drugs and the consumption of alcohol,[10] one might have anticipated that they would have exaggerated the role that substance abuse may have in accounting for aggressive behavior in the family unit. On the contrary, the majority of pastors in our research responded to this issue in a way that could be considered consistent with the general social scientific literature on this subject. Researchers have pointed to the link between alcohol and violence, but argue that men who batter their wives while drinking (to excess) also abuse her when sober.

To summarize, then, clergy appropriate many of the findings of social science and feminist writings on male violence against women into their personal understanding of why abuse occurs within the communities where they live and work. First, their estimates of the prevalence of violence among couples do not deviate substantially from that reported by Canadian and American studies of violence. This clearly indicates that clergy—especially conservative clergy who receive the lion's share of criticism—do not have their heads buried in the sand as some would have us believe. As we shall see shortly, though, their misinformation on the prevalence of violence is rooted in their underestimation of the prevalence of violence within their own faith communities. Thus, while clergy are cognizant of the rates of violence in the secular world, they seem to be unaware of its prevalence within their own churches.

Second, when asked why men are abusive to their partners, why women remain in violent relationships, why women hide the abuse they have suffered and the long-term consequences of life in an abusive relationship, the majority of clergy (not all) in our research were cognizant of the male desire to control women (especially within the family unit), of the intergenerational transmission of violence, and of intrapersonal problems of the abusive man. As we have discussed earlier, in chapter 1, there is an emerging literature expounding these questions. And while there is no consensus of opinion as to why any specific man exhibits violent behavior toward his wife or girlfriend, the role of patriarchal societal attitudes and structures, past childhood experiences of abuse (or witnessing abuse), and selected intrapersonal problems like low self-esteem feature prominently in the writing. It is important not to exaggerate ministerial knowledge of these issues, but it is clear from this research that clergy have had exposure (from some source) to information about violence against women perpetrated by the men who claim to love them. Obviously, individual ministers differ in the level of sophistication of their knowledge base, but what remains true is that the majority of clergy are, at the very least, aware that violence is linked to men's anger and their concomitant desire to control the women in their lives.

Third, where there seems to be less widespread knowledge among clergy is the impact of male violence on women victims. Clergy appear to be aware of women's commitment to family stability—and perhaps overstate the importance of this factor in their reluctance to report or leave violent relationships. Nevertheless, ministers seem less informed about the economic and social pressures on them to remain married despite the abuse. In part, this may be a reflection of conservative clergy's overemphasis on personal responsibility for life events, coupled with a reluctance to see the role of structural inequities in the system that impact on women's lives. In particular, financial exigency was mentioned by less than 30 percent of clergy; a more popular clerical response simply stated that women "lacked options." I would argue that this difference is not just a matter of semantics. If clergy fail to understand women's economic vulnerability in the family, coupled with a reluctance to see the degree to which women are economically disadvantaged in the labor market, that faulty belief has rather far-reaching implications in terms of their potential advice to an abused woman who might seek clerical help. For example: If ministers fail to appreciate that women who have been full-time homemakers for many years are unable to make the transition to paid worker easily[11] (or receive any credit for their volunteer experience in the home environment), and if ministers fail to understand that in Canada women on average receive about 70¢ for every $1.00 that a man earns,[12] they may overlook a woman's economic vulnerability and exaggerate the ease with which she can "leave an abusive relationship and begin to support her children on her own."

Fourth, and somewhat surprisingly, clergy in our study are reluctant to employ spiritual or religious reasons to account for violent men or violated women. Contrary to what one might anticipate from a cursory reading of writings by prolific evangelical writers, sin, selfishness, and separation from God do not appear to be part of the clerical repertoire in understanding family violence in homes across the nation. But just as clergy are reluctant to suggest any religious or spiritual explanation for violence in the secular world, as we shall see, these same clergy are equally reluctant to appropriate social scientific discourse on abuse to explain why Christian couples are violent. Do clergy really assume that the social scientific research speaks only to those outside the household of faith?

Clergy Understanding of Abuse in Christian Families

Abuse as Spiritual Struggle

Without exception, evangelical clergy in Canada understand abuse within Christian families as a *spiritual* issue. First and foremost, they regard abusive behavior on the part of the man as a sign of his struggle with spiritual issues.[13] From this perspective, abusive behavior reflects a man's lack of spiritual growth, or his lack of maturity in the faith. Many conservative clergy explained the occurrence of male battering among churchmen as a prime example that "Christianity does not erase a man's human nature." They seemed to suggest that the spiritual man passes through a series of stages, or battlefields, in his struggle to *contain the old man* and *put on the new man,* fashioned in likeness to Christ. Violent behavior toward one's wife or girlfriend was taken as evidence that the man was not far along in his spiritual pilgrimage, from darkness to light or sin to newness of life. The predominant explanation offered by ministers as to why some Christian families were abusive corresponds to the position that Christianity involves a process of renewal and growth. Yet such thinking deviates, in part, from the more predominant "crisis experience" emphasized in many evangelical circles, where the crisis is coupled with a rather dramatic change in attitude and behavior. Later, in chapter 5, we will consider how clergy as a group are overly optimistic about the possibility of change and transformation in the life of an abusive man. At that point we will see that clergy acknowledge, much more fully than they do here, the centrality and impact of a life-changing "crisis experience." Nevertheless, in response to why some Christian men are abusive, ministers tended to rely on the notion that spiritual maturity takes time and patience.

On the other hand, one in six clergy felt that an abusive Christian man was not *really* Christian at all. While to some this would appear to be a clear-cut example of tautologous thinking, I would not want to dismiss the importance of this point of view too quickly. For a minority of clergy, anyway, there is a striking incompatibility between the notion of the Christian man and the violent man. Perhaps in part a reflection of the enthusiastic support that churches offer to the twin concepts of *family life* and *family values,* for this group of ministers one was either violent at home, or one was Christian. Some may want to argue that this was simply a clever way for many clerical respondents to reconcile a difficult, and challenging, issue: violence in families of faith. Yet, for the nearly fifty clergy who offered this as a response, my interpretation is that they simply were unable to acknowledge that: (1) Christian men are violent; (2) the Christian worldview does not eradicate violent behavior in all its followers; and (3) many Christian families diverge sharply from the common notion of "happy family living." In essence, they were engaging in a form of denial.

Evangelical clergy also reported a second strand to this spiritual struggle. Here they raised questions about the effectiveness of the local church and minister to assist abusive church families. As we shall see later in this chapter, clergy are fairly unanimous in their call for additional training to help them respond more effectively to what they perceive as increasing demands for pastoral counseling of abusive relationships and family units. As a result, many clergy are caught between attempting to offer counseling with limited training or experience, and their reluctance to refer parishioners to secular agencies or professionals for help. They feel they *should* be able to help women, children, and men who seek their help, yet they feel inadequately equipped for the task, and, moreover, they appear somewhat resistant to involving other church or secular resources in responding to the crises at hand. With a predominant viewpoint that violence among families of faith is a spiritual issue, clergy believe that they alone *should* be able to offer help, yet they also experience a marked degree of anxiety in so doing. Their dilemma is captured in the following question: Since violence among Christian men is a specific example of a spiritual struggle, isn't the minister as a spiritual guardian in the best position to offer help?

Abuse as Linked to
Hierarchical Family Relations

A further reason that clergy cited for violence in Christian couples related to the enthusiastic acceptance of the hierarchical model of marriage. Here pastors acknowledged a distortion of the true Christian message on family living (13 percent). These ministers hinted that the message of hierarchical positions of responsibility in the family may be responsible in part for male aggression. In other words, the emphasis on men's leadership rights and responsibilities within the family unit may lead some men to excessive control (including aggression) toward other family members. A few clergy felt that the church in some instances had been guilty of exacerbating the problem of abuse in families by its enthusiastic endorsement of male headship and female submission.

Abuse as a Combination of Sacred and Secular Influences

Not to detract from the centrality of spiritual factors in the explanations the majority of clergy offered for why some Christian families are abusive, others pointed to the twin influences of the spiritual and the secular. In our sample of evangelical clergy, one in four regarded abusive Christian families to be evidence of the belief that Christians experience all of life's problems. The thinking here went something like this: Christians are not immune to the forces at work in the secular world. Those reporting this viewpoint saw the explanation of violence among Christian men and women to have both religious and nonreligious components. In a sense, clergy espousing a "secular/sacred" combination of influences in the lives of abusive Christian families were attempting to incorporate both their spiritual worldview and their secular knowledge, but it was a minority of clerical respondents who adopted this approach.

Abuse Due to Life Stressors

Of all the factors highlighted to account for why Christian families are abusive, only 29.5 percent of clergy responses could be clearly considered nonspiritual in origin. Here, the clerical thinking paralleled what these same clergy mentioned in response to why abuse is prevalent in general society. Factors such as personal psychopathology of the abuser, the intergenerational transmission of violence, the pressures of life, and interpersonal relationship problems were noted. Interestingly, there was not a single mention of the male desire to control women, or men's anger toward others. Thus, while over 60 percent of clergy (n=204) reported the influence of male anger and desire to control as part of their explanation for why some secular men are abusive toward their wives, not one pastor suggested that a Christian man who was violent was acting in response to uncontrolled anger, aggression, or the desire to control.

Understanding the Clerical Viewpoint

As we will discuss at a later point in this chapter, there is a marked uneasiness among conservative clergy about identifying hierarchical family relations as partly responsible for violence in families of faith. Moreover, this is accompanied by a rather uncritical acceptance of the view that men who act as leaders of their family unit do so out of love and service to all (ensuring that the needs of their wives and children take precedence over their own needs). If men are to love their wives as Christ loved the church, what does this mean in practice? From the point of view of clergy, a man must be willing to give up his life for his wife, and to put her needs first; service must become the hallmark of the marital relationship. To be quite blunt: Christian men who are abusing their wives and children pose a direct challenge to this position of selfless male leadership. Rather, abusive Christian men offer evidence that male leadership and power can be motivated by a desire to *control*, rather than a desire to *serve*, as the model suggests. As I have argued earlier, violent Christian families explode the myth of the all-pervasive "happy" Christian family. And given that so much of the model depends on a hierarchical style of family dynamics, are violent families an example of the model gone awry?

Clearly, among this sample of evangelical pastors there is divided thinking as to the origins of abuse within "secular" versus "church" families. While cognizant of the major social scientific explanations of abuse and a willingness to see the explanatory power of such findings among families in the mainstream society, they seemed oblivious to the power of these same explanations to account for the behavior of families connected with their church or faith community. In essence, their vision of violence was bifurcated: secular explanations for secular families, spiritual explanations for church families. The implications of this are obvious: since the "origin" of the problem of violence in Christian families is spiritual in nature, the "cure" must be spiritual too; church families in crisis need the support and counsel of clergy, not advice and support from secular agencies; secular knowledge does not *really* enhance the church in dealing with its own internal problems or the problems of its members and adherents, and so secular counselors do not *really* understand and cannot therefore *really* be effective or even appropriate for abused Christian women.[14]

Linked to their bifurcated vision of violence in the secular world and among families of faith is the finding that clergy estimate that 29 percent of married couples in Canada have experienced violence in their relationship, while they regard the proportion of violent families within their congregation to be 17 percent. So why do pastors perceive the rate to be so much lower among the families within their local church? Several possibilities come to mind.

First, it may be that clergy are aware of the violence in the secular world through secular sources like the media. They have watched television programs where violent men and violated women have been interviewed, they have heard "experts" refer to the statistics on the radio, or they have read in a newsmagazine an article about violence against women. Within the church world, however, they may have had little or no exposure to teaching on violence. In a content analysis of two evangelical magazines, Lori Beaman reported that over a ten-year period from 1985 to 1995 there were only a few issues that even mentioned the problem of family violence, and in only a couple of cases was violence the main focus of a feature article.[15] While clergy do attend workshops and other forms of in-service training, here the occurrence of violence is often hidden in a discussion of "family life" or within a more general focus on "counseling" techniques. Even though a growing number of religious scholars and counselors have prepared workshop curricula on these issues, most clergy are either unable or unwilling to take advantage of them.[16]

My personal experience of offering workshops on issues of male violence against women or other forms of family violence suggests that most often the group that assembles in the workshop is made up of those clergy who are both most knowledgeable and most experienced in dealing with pastoral responses to abuse. As a group they lament that their colleagues most in need of sensitization to these issues are not present when the training opportunities are available. Interestingly, when I am asked to offer a keynote address at a clergy retreat or at regional meetings where attendance is all but mandatory, the question period following my remarks differs greatly from workshops where participants are self-selected. Allow me to elaborate on this point.

Many clergy—conservative and liberal alike—are resistant to the notion that family life can be dangerous. Regardless of the denominational stripe of the clerical participants, there is considerable resistance to the notion that religious families can be violent. Moreover, the greatest challenge I find in addressing clerical audiences is that ministers become quite agitated when evidence is presented that men of faith sometimes have a desire to control their wives, and may even use force to ensure that control. Any challenge to the "happy family living" motif so prevalent in Christian circles stirs the ire of many. My point here is quite straightforward: in my experience, clerical audiences are distinct from either lay church or secular audiences in that they are very reluctant to question the nuclear family unit or the sacredness of family togetherness.

Second, as we shall see later in this chapter, many clergy report limited experience counseling women, men, or children who live in unhealthy, violent relationships. As a result, they may be inclined to interpret their experience as an indication that violence within their local congregation occurs at a rate lower than that reported by secular sources in the community where their church is located. This point, of course, prompts a number of questions: Do churches exert a strong but subtle pressure on families to maintain the appearance of tranquillity, even when the home is a pressure cooker of tension and abuse? When families of faith experience violent episodes, do they turn to their clerical leader for help? If so, what help are they looking for? If not, where do they go instead?

There are a number of competing explanations for the lack of clerical experience in counseling victims of abuse, which we will explore later in this chapter. In part this represents a question of the chicken or the egg. Is there, in fact, less violence in families of faith? Or in families of faith is the violence hidden even more fully than in the secular world? Irrespective of which side of the argument you take, what is clear is that violent men and violated women represent a stark contrast to the burgeoning Christian literature that celebrates the virtues of the family.

Third, it may be that church families as well as clergy have a bifurcated vision of violence and the role of the faith community. More specifically, they may feel reluctant to seek out a spiritual leader to assist them in dealing with the practical matters of daily life when those daily occurrences seem so contrary to the pulpit message of family bliss. Just as clergy appear reluctant to see secular forces at work in the lives of Christian families, so those very families may be reluctant to see the role of spiritual forces in reducing the violence from which they suffer. As a result, they may actually seek out pastoral help for other problems, but refrain from disclosing the problem of conflict and abuse. It may simply be perceived as too stark a contrast, beyond clerical sympathy or help.

Fourth, it may be that clergy have substantial experience in counseling abusive families but fail to recognize or acknowledge that those families are indeed abusive. In other words, clergy may be less likely than other counselors to *ask* women or men seeking marital repair whether or not violence has been present in the relationship. To be sure, many women and men present themselves for counseling without a complete understanding of the dynamics or causes of the malaise they feel. Moreover, many couples come for help without a lot of insight into why "they don't feel love anymore." It takes a skilled and perceptive counselor to conduct a thorough and comprehensive personal or relationship assessment, to determine the role of conflict or abuse in the person's life (or the dysfunctional marriage), and to empower and assist those seeking help to decide on an appropriate course of action. In other words, clergy may be less likely than secular counselors to ask about violence,[17] because they minimize the probability that it exists, they are too uncomfortable to ask the question, or they don't want the responsibility of responding to the answer. For others, it may simply never occur to them.

As we will see in chapter 5, many of the clergy we have interviewed do not ask about violence unless such information is volunteered. So what is the relationship between clerical knowledge about violence and their experience counseling couples in distress? Are clergy actually asked to respond to the needs of abused women? violent men? or adults suffering the long-term effects of childhood abuse? As we shall see, clergy have regular, but limited, experience dealing with violence in the family home.

Clergy Experience in Counseling Victims of Abuse

As table 4.2 demonstrates, two in every three evangelical pastors in our research have counseled a woman with an abusive partner, a couple where violence is common in their relationship, a woman who was abused in childhood by a parent, a man who is abusive toward his wife, and children who have been abused by their father. Moreover, two in every five conservative pastors in the region have counseled the following situations: a father who is abusive toward his children, a man who was abused in childhood by a parent, a woman whose husband is abusing the children, children who have been abused by their mother, a mother who is abusive toward her children, a teenager who has an abusive boyfriend and a woman planning to marry a man who has been abusive to her in the past.

Looking more closely at the data reveals that the most common counseling scenario for conservative pastors is a woman who has an abusive partner. Eight out of every ten pastors (81%) have counseled this type of situation, with just under 10% of the evangelical clergy reporting that 5 or more women with abusive partners seek their help each year. While most clergy report ongoing (but limited)

Table 4.2

Distribution of Evangelical Clergy in Atlantic Canada
by Experience Counseling Situations
Involving Violence within the Family Setting

Have Counseled the Following Situations:	5+ Times per Year	2–4 Times per Year	1 or Less per Year	Never
A woman who has an abusive husband or partner	9.3%	33.5%	40.4%	16.8%
A woman who was abused in childhood by a parent	12.0	29.4	35.8	22.8
A man who is abusive toward his wife or partner	6.1	23.2	41.1	29.6
A couple where violence is common in their relationship	6.0	22.3	45.8	26.0
A child/youth who has been abused by his/her father	6.7	21.4	39.6	32.3
A man who was abused in childhood by a parent	6.3	14.6	32.4	46.7
A father who is abusive toward his children	3.5	14.6	38.9	43.0
A woman whose husband is abusing the children	2.4	11.5	35.8	50.3
A child/youth who has been abused by his/her mother	2.6	10.7	34.4	52.3
A mother who is abusive toward her children	1.3	11.6	33.4	53.7
A woman who is being abused by her son or daughter	1.0	10.0	19.9	69.1
A teenager who has an abusive boyfriend	0.6	10.2	33.2	55.9
A man who has an abusive wife or partner	0.6	9.1	30.1	60.2
A woman who is abusive toward her husband/partner	1.6	8.1	28.6	61.7
A woman who is planning to marry an abusive boyfriend	1.0	6.1	36.6	56.4
A man who is planning to marry an abusive girlfriend	0.0	0.6	11.9	87.5

N=332

Table adapted from Nason-Clark *Conservative Protestants and Violence Against Women: Exploring the Rhetoric and the Response*, Mary Jo Neitz and Marion Goldman, eds, *Religion and the Social Order*, vol 5: 109–30, 1995 JAI Press.

experience in counseling abused women and children, it is easy to overlook the fact that many clergy also report experience counseling abusive men. As table 4.2 documents, 57% of evangelical ministers have counseled a man who is abusive toward his children, and 70% have worked with a man who abuses his wife. While few clergy report extensive experience counseling abusive men, a significant minority do have regular contact with such men. This finding is particularly important, given that services and self-help support for abusive men are relatively rare and poorly funded.[18] Clergy, then, may be one of the few community-based resources for perpetrators of abuse.[19]

In sum, our research data collected from over three hundred pastors in eastern Canada reveal that a minority of evangelical clergy have substantial experience counseling victims of abuse, while the majority report limited, but ongoing, pastoral experience in this area. Yet it is important not to exaggerate clergy involvement in responding to the needs of abused women and their children, since the level of abuse prevalent in Canadian society indicates that clergy experience does not in any measure match the need.[20] But, clearly and unequivocally, clergy are one important form of resource for women suffering the trauma of violence contextualized in the family home.[21]

How clergy respond to those victims of abuse who seek their counsel is an issue on which there are strong sentiments[22] but very little empirical research.[23] While we will consider more fully the results of our interview study with one hundred evangelical clergy in chapter 5, it is important to note at this point that counseling means something quite different to the majority of clergy than it does to therapists trained in the social work or psychology professions. Yet, contrary to what some have argued, we are finding little evidence that clergy tell battered women to return to their unchanged abusive environment or to suffer in silence;[24] it is more likely that clergy cling to excessive optimism that abusive men *want to stop* and *can stop* their violence with help, and consequently that violent relationships can be transformed into healthy family living. The clergy in our research are reluctant to see even a violent marital relationship terminated permanently and a divorce sought; what appears to most differentiate clerical from secular counselors is the speed with which a counselor advises that course of action.[25]

Pastoral Experience in Relationship Counseling

The average pastor in our sample spent 16% of his or her professional time providing relationship or marital counseling. In terms of the weekly routine of church life, this translates into two afternoons or one day each week, with two or three different individuals or couples seeking the help. One minister in every six, however, reported that over 25% of their pastoral work involved counseling.

Of those persons seeking pastoral assistance, we learned that 37% are seen on an ongoing basis (of three or more sessions), though 30% of ministers claimed that over half of the individuals who approach them for relationship or marital problems are offered (and come to) more than three sessions of counseling. Youth pastors, as a group, were less likely to be involved in ongoing counseling than those in senior positions or solo pastorates.[26]

While ministers differ, of course, in the number of years they have helped individuals and couples through pastoral counseling, the overwhelming majority (85%) report that the demand for relationship counseling from the pastor has been—and continues to be—a growth area. In fact, several ministers spoke of the increased pressure they are under to direct more and more of their time to pastoral counseling. The provision of pastoral counseling services is for many ministers one of the greatest stresses of their current work.

So what are some of the myriad of problems that are presented in these counseling contexts to pastors? When we asked ministers to identify in an open-ended question what particular issues are frequently mentioned to them in counseling, "communication" and "financial problems" were at the top of the list. Within the interview setting, however, we listed in a more structured way a number of areas in which marital or relationship problems are experienced and asked clergy to estimate how often they see each of these problems in the couples that they have counseled. Table 4.3 documents the range and nature of the problems presented to the pastoral counselor. Within this format, as well, communication problems (such as difficulty expressing one's view or listening) and money and work (controlling money, budgeting expenses, working too many hours, debts, and excessive spending) are frequently presented as problems to the pastor counselor. Other frequently presenting relationship problems include children and parenting issues (for example, problems with the children, differences over parenting style or standards), role conflict (such as decision-making conflicts, differences in familial duties and responsibilities, and power issues in the relationship), and spiritual issues (different church backgrounds, marriage to an unbeliever, or different spiritual expectations).

Of particular importance to our discussion is the frequency with which clergy are presented with marital conflict, and so this issue was subdivided into three categories: marital conflict involving verbal put-downs (such as accusations or name calling); marital conflict involving physical responses (such as pushing, slapping, or pinning against the wall); and marital conflict involving injury (for example, broken ribs, severe bruising, or sustaining a concussion). While 39% of clergy reported that they are often or very often presented with marital conflict involving verbal put-downs, far fewer clergy reported that they often or very often deal with marital conflict involving physical responses (7%) or injury (2%).

Looking more closely at these data, we see that while very few clergy report *frequent* experience with these presenting problems, a majority of clergy report *some* experience dealing with these issues. Take marital conflict involving physical responses (like slapping) as an example. While 7% of clergy reported that individuals or couples who seek their help "often" or "very often" present with marital conflict involving physical responses, 25% of these clergy noted that "sometimes" physical responses are presented, 49% indicated "seldom," and 19% "never." We find a smaller, but similar, pattern for responses of clergy to the presenting problem of marital conflict involving injury. Whereas 2% of clergy reported that they "often" or "very often" have couples or individuals present with

Table 4.3

Distribution of Marital or Relationship Problems
Presented by Individuals or Couples to the Pastoral Counselor

Problems/Issues	Mean	% Often/ Very Often
Communication	3.88	75.0
Money and Work	3.47	55.0
Children and Parenting	3.26	44.2
Role Conflict	3.22	43.0
Spiritual Issues	3.21	42.4
Marital Conflict: Verbal Put-downs	3.09	39.0
Sexual Issues	3.01	30.0
Personal/Emotional	3.00	33.0
Parents/In-laws	2.63	18.8
Marital Conflict: Physical Responses	2.23	7.0
Leisure and Recreation	2.14	12.0
Marital Conflict: Injury	1.69	2.0

Note: A response of 4 denotes "very often," a response of 1 "never"

this issue, 9% said "sometimes," 45% indicated "seldom," and 44% "never." We will discuss the implications of these results more fully at a later point, but suffice it to say here that among the problems that individuals or couples bring to the pastoral counselor, marital conflict (even involving direct physical responses) is clearly part of the repertoire of marital issues clergy face on an ongoing basis.

Other presenting problems clergy deal with include sexual problems (lack of affection, frequency of sexual intimacy, sexual dissatisfaction, and unfaithfulness), personal or emotional issues (such as psychiatric problems of one spouse), and parent or in-law problems (including interference from parents, looking after parents, or too much dependence on parents).

Referral patterns related to cases of abuse will be discussed more fully in a later section. It is important to note here that most clergy do not refer with regularity to other, nonclerical counselors the individuals or couples who approach them about marital problems. Fully 15% of the clergy we interviewed noted that they *never* have referred an individual to a nonclerical counselor. Looking only at those ministers who have at some point made a referral to a nonclerical counselor, 39% report referrals in less than one in ten of their marital counseling cases. At the other end of the spectrum, 14% of clergy report that they refer to nonclerical counselors half or more of the individuals or couples who seek their help for marital or relationship issues.

We asked clergy to reflect on what factors would lead them to refer an individual or couple to a nonclerical counselor. The most frequently cited reason was that a case might be too difficult for them to deal with singlehandedly. Here pastors talked about their lack of counseling expertise and bemoaned the fact that their training in counseling had not prepared them for the demands of pastoral ministry. A recurring theme of our interviews with one hundred pastors revolved around the disjuncture between congregational expectations for counseling availability and expertise from clergy, and the pastor's own perception of inadequacy to provide these services.

Other ministers (less than 25%) mentioned that when longer-term counseling is needed they refer cases to a secular counselor, in light of the fact that, as pastors, they are simply too busy to provide ongoing counseling. Eighteen (out of 100) pastors specifically mentioned referring cases that involved marked conflict or abuse. A few pastors (less than 10%) noted that sometimes the lack of secular resources makes a referral impossible. Having noted these tendencies, however, 80% of the ministers in our study indicated that they have a specific network (or identified individuals) to whom they could make a referral. The reluctance of clergy to use these referral networks in cases involving abuse will be explored in chapter 7, but it is important to mention here that the overwhelming majority of pastoral counselors report that they have been satisfied with the counsel parishioners received when they followed through on clerical advice to seek the help of a secular counselor. Perhaps surprisingly, only 8% of clergy noted that they have generally been dissatisfied with the advice offered by secular sources in cases where they have referred individuals or couples for nonclerical counsel. So why the reluctance to refer?

We asked clergy to indicate what factors have shaped their counseling strategy. The number (n) of clergy indicating the various factors showed that seminary or college training (n=63), pastoral experience (n=36), ongoing professional training such as reading (n=28), spiritual life (n=23), personal family crises (n=21), and one's personal suitability as a clergy counselor (n=20) were the six major themes to arise in the discussion. A few others noted the influence of a mentor (n=12) or their personal level of compassion (n=6). Though most clergy felt that their professional ministerial training had not equipped them well for pastoral counseling, nevertheless they felt that what little training they had was valuable in shaping their counseling orientation. Ministers here spoke fondly of one or more of their seminary or Bible college professors. They lamented the fact that they had only one or two courses dealing with counseling issues, but were especially grateful for the dedication and expertise of the faculty who had taught them. Unfortunately, the courses in counseling that many of the ministers had experienced were rather narrow in their focus—prison counseling or psychiatric inpatient counseling, for example. As a result, clergy had received some exposure to counseling, but its contents were related more specifically to the interests and expertise of one or two seminary professors than they were to the range and breadth of pastoral counseling demands.

Experience, though, for many was the most valuable teacher, as the following comment illustrates.

My personal experience has been, um, very interesting because I've had both a sister and a brother that found themselves in violent situations. . . . I realize that it can happen, and it can happen to anybody at any time. . . . My training has shaped me, [but] . . . I guess experience more than anything.

(Clergy Interview #543)

Others spoke of their ongoing attempts at keeping up-to-date on the pastoral counseling front through the reading of relevant books or magazine articles, with several noting the influence of James Dobson's *Focus on the Family* periodical. A few mentioned the role of their own spiritual relationship with God as shaping their counseling strategy.

Interestingly, twenty-one clergy commented on the influence of personal family crisis as one of the major contributors to their orientation to counseling others.

Like I was saying before, about sometimes seeing my pie-in-the-sky approach to counseling when the rubber hit the road in the real world, wasn't cutting it. . . . I know what it's like to be three mortgage payments behind and I know what it was like to have practically no food in the cupboards, and if it wasn't for my wife's extreme love for me, I would have been just another statistic, another clergy marriage breakup. . . . I got some counseling and it was really, really good.

(Clergy Interview #373)

Another pastor talked about his wife's trauma as a significant influence on his counseling style.

I think that . . . the major [factor] that influenced my counseling was, and I have my wife's permission to say this to you, about four years ago she began to remember incidents of abuse when she was a child. . . . And then these memories started to come, which I can almost cry when I think about it, 'cause it really hit us both like a ton of, and for the last four years we've been living in hell with these, with these memories. . . . I encountered in my caseload a number of people who had been abused and who were remembering the abuse. So as I say, that has been, the last 4 years or so the primary thing that, that has shaped my, my counseling. . . . I've joined a spouse's support group and it's been an interesting concept too, as a counselor to go for counseling. . . . We've had a couple of very good counselors . . . whose knowledge of marital counseling were always far beyond what mine was.

(Clergy Interview #480)

Some other clergy noted that you cannot really help others in counseling until you "work on your own recovery, your own healing" (Clergy Interview #552).

Finally, many pastors reflected on their own personality or personal suitability for the role of counselor. Many referred to themselves as a "people-person," while others spoke of a level of self-understanding that they believed helped them to understand others. Here they tended to reflect on themselves as "down-to-earth" people, easy to talk to, chatty and outgoing, nonthreatening in interpersonal encounters. Since they made people feel at ease, they were sought out during times of trouble. For these clergy, their primary skill as a counselor was their personal warmth and empathy. And for the most part this was regarded as an inherited quality, not one that you could enhance through training or experience.

It is interesting that while only a handful of clergy mentioned their personal warmth at this point in the interview, *friendship* became a key word when discussing why people seek out a pastoral counselor. Regarding the pastor as their friend, was believed by clergy to be integral to a person's seeking out their help. As we shall see later, this view put pastors under rather intense pressure. Not only were they responsible to befriend parishioners, but when couples in crisis sought their help it was virtually impossible to remain the friend of both victim and abuser. As a result, many ministers felt caught between the needs of the abused woman for support (often including the advice to leave an abusive environment) and the needs of the abusive man intent on keeping the family intact.

Clerical Counseling Experience

Three particular groups of clergy emerged from our in-depth interview sample of 100 evangelical pastors based on their experience of pastoral counseling. A total of 15 pastors reported that they had extensive experience in offering marriage or relationship counseling to men, women, and couples. In fact, this group of ministers revealed that at least 30% of their pastoral work involved relationship or marital counseling. In a typical week, at least five individuals or couples would seek their counsel, and many of their counseling relationships extended over a rather long period of time. A second group of clergy (n=15) included those for whom counseling occupied about 20–25% of their pastoral responsibilities. For these clergy, one or two relationship counseling situations would arise each week. A third group of ministers (n=33) included those for whom relationship counseling was a less central component of their pastoral work but nonetheless an ongoing responsibility, occupying 10–15% or less of their time. A final group (n=34) was comprised of ministers for whom relationship counseling occupied less than 10% of their workweek.[27] Several of this group reported that in a typical week they were not involved in any counseling situations, though most did report at least one experience of relationship counseling per week.

Clergy differed markedly in their conception of the role and purpose of counseling and in their level of preparedness for offering it. As we shall see, those ministers who reported extensive counseling experience tended to have views about the efficacy and nature of both pastoral and secular counseling that set them apart from colleagues who had less relationship counseling experience. In many ways, it was their attitudes about counseling rather than their level of training that distinguished these four groups of ministers from one another.

Clergy Reporting
Extensive Counseling Experience

Generally speaking, the clergy who reported extensive counseling experience also reported fairly extensive referral patterns. As a group, they were less pessimistic about the difficulties associated with referring a parishioner to a secular counselor for help, and they were far more knowledgeable about what resources were actually available in their local area. As one pastor reported:

> When I move into an area, one of the first things I do is . . . to make contact with other helping agencies. . . . I don't refer people to . . . secular counselors very often unless I know the individual very well, their type and style of counseling service.
>
> (Clergy Interview #350)

Other clergy within this group reported that there are many different agencies, including transition houses, hospitals, and mental health clinics that are useful resources in the community. One pastor—who had six years' counseling experience—felt that many of the community agencies were particularly open to the outreach of the clergy. He concluded that there was "quite a bit of networking" going on between clergy and others in the local area where he was ministering. Many of the clergy who reported extensive counseling experience had rather formalized links with community agencies or the professionals in their community. A pastor who had been offering relationship counseling for about five years told us:

> I am in connection with the [name] Psychiatric Hospital in [small city] and I'm in connection, communication with a number of psychiatrists who are there. I meet with the head of psychiatry in the [small city] area, I would say, maybe once a month.
>
> (Clergy Interview #552)

For the most part, clergy with the more extensive counseling experience did not differentiate in their referrals between those counselors or professionals in the community who were explicitly *Christian* and others. They made their referrals based on a knowledge of the person and their counseling or professional skills. And, for the most part, they were satisfied with the support and counsel their parishioners received when they followed through on their advice about referral.

Clearly clergy who were among the more experienced counselors had far less difficulty explaining their marital counseling approach or philosophy and seemed far less puzzled about any response to how their pastoral counseling was similar to or different from that offered by secular professionals. This is not particularly surprising since they were in contact more often with these community professionals, had established at least some networking opportunities with them, and were no doubt challenged as a result to think about the specific role of the pastoral counselor.

Each of the more experienced pastoral counselors offered us a fairly detailed overview of their counseling approach. Although these philosophies differed markedly from one another, what became clear was that clergy with extensive counseling experience had formulated what they offered to individuals and couples and understood what was unique about the pastoral counselor. What might appear to be rather ironic at first glance is that those clergy with extensive experience talked more frankly about the explicitly spiritual emphasis of their counseling. They showed little anxiety with our questions about either their approach to relationship counseling or the role of the pastoral counselor.

One pastor, living in a coastal community of Nova Scotia, described his marital counseling approach this way:

Biblically based . . . I use the Bible I suppose as my groundwork and base of operations. But I'm not opposed to using some good solid, you know, concepts, the psychological and sociological concepts for . . . where the family is and where the marriage is too.

(Clergy Interview #350)

Another pastor with extensive experience talked more in terms of process:

I try to do . . . indirect, client-centered approach, helping the individuals, couples, or families to bring their stories, their traumas, their pain, their heartaches, their breakdown, the dysfunction to me in letting them share their story. Being an active listener using empathy, caring, sensitivity, gentleness in my approach to help them share their story. . . . I use workbooks all the time . . . that I have gotten through Minirtz Meier Counselling Centre. . . . I feel that they are just great, they are Christian but they are also very psychologically sound and person-based.

(Clergy Interview #552)

Clergy with extensive counseling experience were rather unanimous that the main reason for referral rested with understanding their own limitations as a counselor. Referring when the presenting problem was "beyond their area of expertise," these pastors had a high degree of self-awareness that led them to accept and celebrate the uniqueness that various professionals brought to helping to alleviate a family or personal crisis. Moreover, these clergy revealed the level of contact they actually had with secular counselors by referring to other therapists or health care workers with whom they were cooperating.

Several of the pastors with extensive experience in relationship counseling had personal family experience dealing with the impact and longer-term implications of abuse. In two cases, the clergymen had sisters who were living in abusive marriages. Here, they learned firsthand, as it were, the pain and despair that battery brings into a woman's life, her lack of choices, and the stigma that she feels. One pastor summed up his reaction this way:

I realize that it can happen and it can happen to anybody at any time, and it's wrong, abuse is wrong and that's all there is to it.

(Clergy Interview #543)

This younger clergyman reported that his personal exposure to violence (in the life of his sister) assisted him most in understanding the suffering of other women, and thereby enabled him to become an effective pastoral counselor. Another minister, reflecting on his own sister's abuse, reported :

I don't think that she had any choice. I would never . . . say to a couple or to a woman or to a man "You've got to stay in this relationship because God says you've got to stay in this relationship"—I think that's hogwash. . . . I am not a miracle worker, uh, I work for the miracle worker. Unless [God] intervenes in a dramatic way, some relationships dissolve, and all I can do is apologize for that, but I can't change it.

(Clergy Interview #350)

Clergy with rather extensive counseling experience have a more fully developed understanding of their unique role as pastoral counselors, are far more optimistic about collaborating and cooperating with secular professionals, and report some rather innovative measures in attempting to respond to the inter- and intrapersonal needs of men, women, and children who seek their help.

Clergy Reporting
Moderate Counseling Experience

Those pastors who reported that about 20–25 percent of their pastoral work involves relationship or marital counseling seemed much more concerned about locating the services of a *Christian* counselor when they deemed a referral necessary. Several of these clergy talked of *Christian* counseling centers in or near their regional location. Others had specific *Christian* contacts who worked within secular mental health agencies, so that when they placed a referral to one of these agencies they asked for a specific worker there.

Relative to their colleagues with more extensive counseling experience, these pastors seemed less optimistic about the advantages of the secular and sacred working together in relationship or marital counseling. Moreover, they appeared to have greater difficulty articulating their unique role as a pastoral counselor. Still, like their more experienced colleagues, reasons for referrals tended to be based on a recognition of one's own limitations, coupled with a knowledge of the sources available in the community. Clearly one of the differentiating characteristics of those pastors who had substantial experience in relationship or marital counseling in contrast to those with a moderate amount related to the ease with which they were able to discuss the role of the pastoral counselor and the unique contribution they believed pastoral counseling could offer to individuals and couples.

Clergy with Less Experience
in Relationship Counseling

Interestingly, those with limited experience in relationship counseling were the most reluctant to refer those individuals or couples who did seek their advice. In a sense, referrals were most unlikely to occur where they were perhaps needed most. Clergy with less experience seemed to have little knowledge of what secular resources were available and little faith in those with which they were familiar. They tended to feel that secular and sacred counselors would be likely to work at cross-purposes, yet they were unable for the most part to explain exactly what a pastoral counselor could offer to a damaged or hurting person or marital relationship.

Although our transcripts from experienced pastoral counselors would often record thirty to fifty typed lines of text describing their marital counseling approach, those ministers with limited experience tended to give one-sentence answers. While educationally these pastors did not differ from their more experienced counterparts, their answers indicated that their ministry style set them apart. For example, in reference to how their advice or intervention might differ from what a nonclerical counselor outside of an explicitly Christian ministry might offer, one clergyman reported that he was concerned with the witness implications of a Christian marriage in trouble. He reported a concern for "the way they [the couple] projected themselves to the rest of the community." These clergy were adamant that their counseling approach was very different from the secular world, yet they were unable to articulate how this was so.

Clergy Referral Patterns

Having explored some of the issues surrounding referral from the interview data, we turn now to consider the referral practices among the 343 pastors who completed our survey. As table 4.4 documents, the majority of clergy have referred at some point individuals, couples, or families to a counselor or social worker, to a psychiatrist or psychologist, and to a mental health community agency. Two in every five pastors reported that they have also made referrals to another pastor in their local area, a layperson in the church, the pastor's wife, and to a transition house. The most frequent referral pattern, though, involves a social worker: 5.7% of the pastors in our research referred 5 or more cases per year; 30.3% two to four cases per year; and 39.4% one referral a year or less; while only 24.6% have never made such a referral.

Although most pastors in our research do not make referrals often, they do refer individuals, couples, or families to other community or church resources occasionally. Further analysis of this data revealed that 31.4% of clergy had made a referral to a church-related resource at least twice a year, and 23.9% had made as frequent a referral to a secular professional; 44.7% of ministers had referred people to other secular agencies two or more times per year. In one of our Team's reports to the churches, we argued that pastors who make relatively few referrals are slightly more likely to seek out church-affiliated services.[28]

Table 4.4

Distribution of Evangelical Clergy in Atlantic Canada Regarding Referral Practices in Counseling Situations Involving Violence within the Family Setting

Have Referred the Following Situations:	5+ Times per Year	2–4 Times per Year	1 or Less per Year	Never
The person/couple to a counselor or social worker	5.7%	30.0%	39.4%	24.6%
The person/couple to a psychiatrist or psychologist	2.9	21.3	36.8	39.0
The person/couple to a self-help group	3.9	12.3	32.4	51.5
The person/couple to a mental health service	1.3	14.4	36.2	48.1
The person/couple to another pastor on my team	2.6	12.9	20.5	63.9
The abuser to a counselor or social worker	2.9	11.4	32.7	52.9
The person/couple to another pastor in my local area	1.3	12.0	32.1	54.5
The abuser to a psychiatrist or psychologist	2.3	10.3	25.2	62.3
The abused woman to a pastor's wife	1.3	10.9	28.1	59.7
The abuser to a self-help group	3.0	8.5	20.0	68.5
The abused woman to a laywoman in the church	1.6	9.4	29.5	59.4
The abused woman to a woman's ministry of my church	1.3	8.8	20.5	69.5
The person/couple to a layperson in my church	1.6	8.2	33.8	56.4
The abused woman to a transition house	1.3	7.4	32.0	59.2
The abused woman to a medical doctor	1.3	6.8	22.7	69.3
The abused woman to a lawyer	1.0	6.5	23.4	69.2
The person/couple to the emergency department of the local hospital	0.6	6.5	22.7	70.1
The abused woman to a female pastor	0.3	3.9	10.2	85.6
The person/couple to a denominational staff person	0.0	2.0	11.8	86.3
The abused woman to a police officer	0.3	3.6	19.9	76.1
The abuser to a lawyer	0.0	2.3	12.0	85.7

N=332

While it is clear that most clergy do not make frequent use of community resources in terms of referring individuals, couples, or families, from time to time referrals are made by clergy to secular professionals, community agencies, or other church personnel. What we are unable to resolve here is whether or not pastors would *like* to make more use of referral networks but either find that such are nonexistent in their local area or are unaware of what resources do exist. Moreover, we do not know what happens after a minister suggests a referral source to an individual or family. Do pastors know whether parishioners follow up on their referral suggestions?[29] Do clergy continue their counseling relationship with an individual or family after a referral has been made?[30] Are pastors satisfied with the counsel offered their parishioners by mental health professionals in the community?[31] Do ministers also receive referrals from secular professionals or agencies in the community?[32] We will explore some of these questions as we turn in chapter 5 to examine the role and efficacy of the pastoral counselor in cases involving wife abuse.

5

The Pastor
as Counselor

On a typical Sunday morning in Canada and the United States millions of women attend a religious service that could be considered Christian in perspective.[1] Within this gathering of religious followers are more than one million victims of wife abuse, women who know firsthand the pain and suffering violence has brought into their lives, their homes, and their spiritual journeys.[2] The numbers alone should convince us of the pervasiveness of the hurt and the potential for healing. Yet, translating the rhetoric about "happy family living" and "human wholeness" into concrete help for women, men, and children in crisis is a difficult and time-consuming challenge.

This chapter explores that challenge from the perspective of the pastor, the person whom we might refer to as the church's front-line crisis worker. What are pastors able to offer to abused women, abusive men, and couples seeking marital help? Do they have a unique role to play in assisting families in crisis? How does the sacred counselor differ from a therapist working in a mental health clinic or a transition house? What advice do pastoral counselors offer to women living in violent homes? And does that advice have the potential to empower Christian women to take control over their lives and destinies? Or are clergy guilty of minimizing the pain and consequences of abuse?

Advice to Families in Crisis:
Counseling Scenarios and the Pastor

One of the central criticisms of the involvement of clergy in the lives of abused women is the perception that clergy tell women to "go home and pray" that the abuse will end and that they will become better, more loving, and more spiritual wives and mothers.[3] Others have suggested that the motifs of the suffering servant, or "no pain, no gain," are used to remind Christian women that glorification comes from suffering and that if women endure, they will be rewarded in the life to come.[4]

As a result, the advice clergy offer abused women, abusive men, and couples in conflict is a central feature of our research program. There are a number of ways that one might assess the advice clergy offer. First, how do clergy understand violence against women and other forms of family violence? As we have seen in chapter 4, clergy appropriate social science models and concepts into their views about violence among families in the community, but cling to spiritual factors to explain violence among families connected to the church. Second, we could ask women who have experienced clergy counsel to discuss the advice they received. The stories of Christian women form the basis of chapters 3 and 6. A third way to assess the advice clergy offer is to ask clergy to recount particular counseling cases and discuss their intervention strategies, referral patterns, and perceived outcomes. It is this third approach that will be our focus here.

Case Scenarios

A large portion of our clerical interview was directed toward a discussion of pastoral contact and counseling with individuals, couples, or families who had sought their help for issues related to marital conflict. We asked clergy to reflect on some of the people who had come to them over the years for counseling, noting that the questions we would be asking related to specific cases and explaining that it was the nature of the problems that families experience and the clergy's advice to them that were of most interest to us.

Following this brief introduction of purpose, clergy were presented with the first of three specific case scenarios. The first case described a woman who was experiencing marital distress, in which she was being blamed for all the marital problems. The second case involved a woman who had just experienced her husband's pinning her against the wall, following years of intense verbal arguments. The third case revolved around a woman who had been hit and punched repeatedly by her husband and who was very frightened of his anger. After each of the case scenarios was read, clergy were asked whether they had ever counseled a situation like the one in the scenario. If they had, they were asked to describe some of the details of that case, without revealing the identity of the family members. Once the case had been described, there were a series of questions probing the presenting problems in the family, the choice of pastor as counselor, the involvement level of the pastor as counselor, the pastor's interpretation of the problems and issues involved, and the pastor's professional response to the woman/man/couple, including intervention, referral, and follow-up. For pastors who had *not* experienced counseling a case similar to the one presented in the scenario, the ensuing questions were asked as hypothetical—*IF* this case presented itself to you for pastoral counsel, how *would* you respond?

Clergy Experience in Cases
Involving Marital Discord

For clarity of presentation, we will focus on each of the case scenarios separately, and then analyze some of the patterns to emerge from the pastors' answers. Within the pastoral interview, the following case was read.

CASE 1 The first type of counseling situation I want you to think about is a woman from your congregation who comes to you for advice about marital problems. She indicates that over the last few years, her marriage has become less satisfying and the number of arguments between her and her husband has increased. During disagreements, the husband becomes frustrated, criticizing and blaming his wife for all their marital problems. She wonders whether there is any hope for the marriage.

Ninety-eight out of one hundred clergy in our interview sample had experienced a counseling situation like the one just described. One pastor serving in a rural area offered this case.

> The couple are . . . the woman is Christian, man is non-Christian. . . . The woman is very dedicated and committed and the husband's, uh, useless, slobbish. . . . The number one problem is the fact the man's an alcoholic and he won't admit it. . . . The number two problem in their family is that he's more often unemployed than employed. . . . Regarding responsibilities . . . he just doesn't do anything around the house. When the lawn needs mowed, she does it; the garden needs planting, she does it . . . the house needs painting, she does it. He, all he does is sits around and complains. . . . There's a lot of verbal abuse from him . . . there has been some physical abuse, but mainly to my knowledge it's in the area of pushing as opposed to hitting. . . . He just won't accept any responsibility that he's part of the problem. . . . Everything's dumped on the wife, you know, who is one, she is one of the strong Christian leaders in the church here.
>
> (Clergy Interview #490)

The pastor reporting this counseling situation went on to explain that his intervention with the husband was as a *friend* more than a clergyperson: "I told him . . . whenever the need comes to . . . turn to the bottle, call me. I'll sit down with you and we'll go for a drive, we'll talk, we'll do anything you want to do, just you need . . . the alternative to . . . buying a bottle." With regard to his intervention with the wife, the pastor replied, "I have given her tons of advice, most of which she does not take." The interview probed whether pastoral intervention was successful in this case. "Not very," replied the pastor.

Another pastor described the following case:

> [They were] in their mid-forties, twenty years of marriage . . . The main problem is that they don't see eye to eye, they argue a lot, quite a bit, and he is very irresponsible financially, doesn't provide for them at all. . . . He's very irresponsible . . . she is a person that is very shy. . . . If she gets upset she's quite verbal and she's insecure in some ways . . . he flips out very easy. . . . The marriage itself was an imposed one . . . she was not ready . . . [and]she has regretted it until today.
>
> (Clergy Interview #216)

The pastor telling this case story went on to explain that the husband is very controlling, he doesn't consult her on any decisions, including the purchase of the car or house, and she doesn't respond any more to him sexually. The relationship, as the pastor sees it, is at an impasse. When asked to describe how he intervened in this case, the minister talked about taking the husband fishing and hunting, during which times he tries to get the husband to discuss problems, and makes suggestions about offering the wife more freedom and more money. "I even told him, she might leave you," said the pastor, recounting one of their fishing expeditions. "One week later he's great and then he's back again," said the minister with a sigh.

The pastor encouraged the woman in this case to update her nursing degree and credentials, allowed his address to be used for correspondence about possible employment (so that the husband wouldn't find out she was job hunting), and tried to help her to begin to establish some financial independence. Was the intervention successful from the pastor's perspective? "Somewhat successful" was the reply.

These two cases illustrate the complexity, and sometimes the ambiguity, of the role of the pastoral counselor. What do pastors mean by counseling? Why do people seek their help? What types of assistance are they looking for? What intervention strategies do clergy try? How is success evaluated? What is unique about the role of pastors in responding to pain and crisis?

Each of the ninety-eight ministers who reported a counseling situation similar to the first-case scenario offered us a description of the issues that led the individual(s) or couple to seek pastoral help. We now turn to a more general discussion of the results of the analysis of these case stories.

When asked to indicate what they believed were some of the problems in the case they recounted, relationship-related problems featured most prominently (n=73), followed by husband-related problems (n=56), wife-related problems (n=26), external forces (n=24), and problems related to the children (n=17). The presence of abuse was noted as well: verbal abuse (n=21), sexual or physical abuse (n=12), and substance abuse (n=2). In a minority of cases, the presence of spiritual problems were identified also (n=12).

In order to try to capture how clergy conceptualized the issues within the family they identified for case 1, we asked them to comment on how the husband— and then the wife—was contributing to the problems being presented in the counseling situation. Out of a total of 209 responses concerning the contribution of the husband to marital discord, 14% (n=29) related to the husband's desire to control or bully other family members, including almost always the wife. Other reoccurring pastoral comments related to the husband's "being financially irresponsible" (n=23) or "not communicating" (n=20). We asked clergy to attach a percentage to their assessment of the husband's influence on the marital problems. While there was a broad range in the responses, a mean of 60% was found.

In a similar fashion, clergy then were asked to report how they felt the wife was contributing to these marital problems. Eight out of 178 responses (4%) related to the wife's desire to control or bully other family members, 8 responses mentioned "not communicating," and one pastor noted that the woman was "financially irresponsible." More common responses related to the wife's "expecting too much from her husband," having unrealistic standards for the relationship, denying the existence of problems in the marriage, or "failing to confront the husband when problems arose." In essence, clergy were holding women responsible for either setting unrealistic goals for the husband and the marital relationship, or failing to recognize or deal with problems that did exist.

When they were asked to attached a percentage to the wife's influence on these problems, a mean of 38% was attained.[5]

To summarize to this point, almost all of the clergy in our interview sample had experience counseling a situation like the one described in case 1. For the most part, clergy articulated the problem as being first and foremost a relationship issue, followed by husband- and then wife-related factors. The presence of abuse was clearly evident in many of the cases, but spiritual factors were less likely to be mentioned. While a myriad of issues emerged with regard to the husband's— and then the wife's—contribution to the problems presented, there was greater similarity in the responses of clergy as to the involvement of the man in the ensuing problems. A lack of communication, financial irresponsibility, and controlling behavior were mentioned by a significant number of clerical respondents as the contribution of the husband to marital difficulties. Although a large number of issues emerged with regard to the involvement of the wife, there was less overlap in the responses given. Expecting too much from the relationship was one issue on which there were several responses, as well as a denial that marriage problems existed. In general, clergy saw the contribution of the husband and then the wife to the problems in the case along the lines of a 60/38 split. In essence, while both parties were believed responsible for the difficulties that called for counseling, the contribution of husbands was believed to exceed that of their wives.

Once the case had been described in some degree of detail, clergy were asked to indicate why they believed that the individual or couple came to them for pastoral help. A total of 16 clergy (out of 100) mentioned specifically spiritual reasons for the choice of a pastoral counselor. But for the most part the responses reflected a fairly widespread view that the pastor was chosen because of prior trust or respect (n=22), because as pastor he or she was a friend (n=15), or the pastor was perceived as someone who would listen (n=11). Others, perhaps unwilling (or unable) to think of their own personal qualifications for pastoral counseling, noted that there was a paucity of other referral sources available or that the individual or couple had experienced some dissatisfaction with other (predominantly secular) agencies or professionals.

We asked clergy to indicate the nature and duration of their intervention in the case. Within the interview sample, it was reported that the individual(s) or couple were seen an average of 14 times, over a period of 19 months, for sessions that averaged 65 minutes. Most of the clerical discussion of their own intervention in the case focused on process issues: whom they saw; how they determined the problems; and how they assessed the needs. There was less discussion about what might be called explicitly spiritual intervention (e.g., praying with the couple, looking up relevant biblical passages). One in every four clergy (24.7%) described something about their intervention in spiritual or religious terms. While some clergy talked about themselves as "listener" and others as a "referral source," the predominant pattern was for the discussion to focus on issues related to whom they saw, how they met, where they met, and how the issues were formulated. We asked clergy to comment specifically on the extent to which they felt that the individual's or couple's conflict was a reflection of spiritual, emotional, or relationship problems. While there was obvious overlap in their responses, what was clear in the data was that clergy formulated the opinion that first and foremost it was a relationship issue, followed by a combination of emotional and spiritual factors, with little emphasis given to outside factors (such as unemployment, poverty, etc.).

Clergy reported that in most of the cases they were describing the conflict and marital discord continued (82%), but that it did not escalate over time (30% reported that it did escalate). We were particularly interested in how clergy assessed the issue of personal risk for the wife — and then for the husband — in the case they had described. The prevailing pattern of responses was for clergy to conclude that there was "moderate" risk for the wife and "low" risk for the husband.[6]

On a scale of 1 to 10, where 1 is "not at all serious" and 10 is "extremely serious," clergy rated the conflict in the case as being 7.4. We asked them how they came to that conclusion. Three prevalent themes emerged within their responses. A total of 43 mentioned that the relationship was experiencing serious problems (or in danger), 37 clergy noted that the home was being destroyed, and 27 referred to tension building or abuse. Risk, then, was more clearly aligned with risk to the marital relationship or permanence of the family unit, rather than as specific risk to the woman's physical or emotional health, though her safety and security sometimes were included in the response.

The final set of questions related to their assessment of the uniqueness and efficacy of pastoral intervention in this case and the referral process and resultant follow-up. The overriding opinion of clergy in our sample was that pastoral counseling in the case described was "somewhat successful"; 12% saw it as "extremely successful," 23% as "successful," and 12% "not at all successful." On the whole, pastors viewed that their intervention was successful to the degree that it helped the relationship (n=64; of which 13 specifically stated that they "kept the couple together"), while others noted that they had assisted the wife (n=25), the husband (n=9) or the children (n=4). Five ministers reported that their intervention averted further violence in the relationship. On the other hand, clergy were quite forthcoming about what they perceived as the shortcomings to their intervention. While a myriad of factors were raised, several pointed to the persistence of conflict in the relationship, the lack of reconciliation between husband and wife, their failure as pastor to engage the husband in counseling, and the persistence of spiritual problems in one or both parties. In spite of this, looking back on the case, 47% of our clerical sample reported that they would not do anything differently now than they had at the time the individual(s) or couple sought their help.

In total, 51 pastors referred the case to someone else for further assistance. The most common referral source was a *Christian* counselor (n=18), a *secular* counselor (n=14), or a psychologist/psychiatrist, with no attending spiritual or secular designation (n=5). Four pastors mentioned the transition house in the local area to the woman, and four others referred to a local support group that the woman might attend.[7] In 29 cases, the pastoral counselor had further contact with the individual or couple once a referral had been made, and in 13 cases they were involved (in some capacity) with that referral source. Of the 29 clergy who followed up the case after a referral had been made, 19 reported that they were satisfied or extremely satisfied with the counsel the individual or couple had received, 7 reported being "somewhat satisfied," and 3 were "not at all satisfied."

Finally, we asked clergy to indicate how they believed their intervention/advice/assistance was similar to—or different from—the advice the case might have received from a nonclerical counselor (outside of an explicitly Christian ministry). An interesting pattern of responses emerged. In terms of *perspective,* most clergy (54%) felt that they differed *greatly* from a nonclerical counselor. In terms of *process,* most clergy (42%) felt they differed *moderately* from a nonclerical counselor. And in terms of *outcome,* most clergy (67%) felt they differed *little* from a nonclerical counselor.[8] On the whole, pastors felt that their worldview or perspective was notably different from those professionals operating outside an explicitly Christian framework. As we examined in chapter 2, clergy believe that their views on marriage and family set them apart from others within the secular world. Central within their perspective of the Christian family is the important role of religious belief and practice, creating a marriage triangle between husband, wife, and God. A second integral strand within their framework is the undesirability of divorce, or the view that marriage is for life. As we shall see later in this chapter, while clergy did not oppose divorce under all circumstances, they clearly see it as a last resort to resolving conflict between husband and wife. And for most clergy in our sample, divorce implies not only that the relationship has failed, and that the husband and wife separately have failed, but that their intervention as pastoral counselors has failed as well. In essence, then, divorce is viewed as failure all around.

Our examination of clerical counseling in cases involving intense arguments and verbal put-downs (as in scenario 1) reveals a number of interesting points of clerical intervention. First, almost all (98 out of 100) of the clergy we interviewed had experience counseling a woman who had been blamed by her husband for all their marital problems and who sought help from her pastor when she finally began to question whether there was any hope for the marital relationship. Without question, then, clergy are engaged in ongoing experience responding to the needs of couples in crisis. While there may be disagreements as to the supportive role they play, there can be little argument that this is an area involving almost all ordained clergy. Counseling skills, then, are central to the performance of the clerical role. We will pick up some of the implications of this at a later point in the book, but suffice it to note here that surely this has implications for seminary training programs.

Second, clergy perceive that their credibility in the counseling sphere is related to their ability to befriend people, to make people feel comfortable, and to support them in a nonthreatening and nondirective way. Unlike professional counselors, who are credentialed through advanced education and practitioner examinations, clergy do not believe that their training per se is what equips them to be successful in the counseling arena. As a group, clergy are indeed desirous of more training and bemoan their lack of academic preparation for counseling, yet clearly even those with more training see personal qualities of warmth and friendliness as more important than academic preparation for counseling. They believe parishioners and community members alike seek them out not because of their skills as relationship counselors, but because of their integrity and their friendship.

Third, in cases involving verbal aggression, clergy in our study understand the conflict primarily as a relationship issue, with husbands holding responsibility for their desire to control other family members, for failing to communicate effectively (or at all), and for their failure to be financially prudent. On the other hand, wives were regarded as being unrealistic in their relationship demands and as failing to recognize and confront problems when they do exist. On average, they felt the responsibility for the conflict was split 60/38 husband/wife. Clearly, pastors regarded those cases involving verbal arguments and blaming to be firmly rooted in relationship problems, though they tended to see the husband as contributing more fully than the wife to the discord that developed. Given that it was more often wives than husbands (or couples) who sought pastoral assistance, clergy were left to sort out relationship problems with only one partner, the partner who they believed was less responsible for the ensuing difficulties.

Fourth, many clergy were very practical in the assistance they offered women and men in cases involving blaming and verbal put-downs. Although great differences surfaced between clergy in terms of the nature and level of their support, it is clear that many clergy believed that women needed to have their self-esteem raised and that men needed to be more in tune with (and able to control) their own emotions and better equipped to meet the needs of their wives and children. As a result, some clergy suggested that women seek paid employment or engage in interests outside the domestic area. For men, clergy frequently advised what they perceived to be relationship-building activities: dinner out, gifts, and emotional closeness. It is noteworthy that our interviews provide myriad examples of how clergy tried to put their "advice" into action: some clergy offered to help the woman locate a job; some clergy invited the man on outdoor excursions, like fishing trips; some clergy offered their home for baby-sitting so that the husband and wife could have time alone together. While these examples do not relate to all ministers, they are clearly indicative of a pattern among our interviewees to attempt to implement their advice to couples experiencing relationship problems.

Fifth, clergy tended to see their intervention with cases like that described in scenario 1 as "somewhat successful." Its success tended to be defined in terms of whether the couple was still together and experiencing less conflict. Clergy were fairly hard on themselves for what they regarded as their inability to engage husbands in the relationship counseling they offered the wife. Rather than blaming the husbands for failure to cooperate in relationship repair, clergy tended to blame themselves as pastoral counselors. Clearly, hooking in the husbands was viewed as the responsibility of the clerical counselor.

Sixth, almost half of the ministers suggested a referral source to the woman/man/couple, but it was only a minority of individuals or couples with whom the pastor had continuing contact after the referral had been suggested. For most, then, referral was the last effort on the part of the minister to bring restoration or repair to a damaged relationship. In the minds of several clergy, referrals were made only when they believed they had nothing further to offer the woman or couple. As a result, once the referral was made, the minister figuratively "washed his or her hands" of any further involvement with the case. Clearly, though, that was not the pattern for everyone. Among those clergy who were most experienced at counseling, referrals tended to be a more regular part of their counseling repertoire, and they continued their contact with the man/woman/couple even as they sought assistance from other sources. For these clergy, *pastoral counseling* did not duplicate the services a woman or couple would receive from a secular agency or professional. As we saw in chapter 4, those clergy most experienced at pastoral counseling (who were also those most willing to refer parishioners to other sources) held fairly firm ideas about what the pastoral counselor provided and why. As a result, they showed far less reluctance to cooperate or collaborate with secular professionals; since they provided *sacred* counseling, working within a team setting was very appealing to them.

Clergy Experience in Cases Involving
Physical Responses to Marital Discord

We turn from a discussion of pastoral experience responding to cases involving verbal put-downs and intense arguments to cases involving a physical response to marital discord. Clergy were asked to consider the following scenario.

CASE 2　The second type of counseling situation I want you to think about is a Christian woman from your congregation who comes to you as a result of escalating conflict in her marriage. She confides in you that she has been getting into some very intense verbal arguments with her husband, whom you know as a fine Christian leader in your church. To your surprise, she indicates that the arguments can last for days and cloud the entire family life. Last week they got into another fight, and this time it ended with her husband pinning her against the wall. She had never seen him so angry and frustrated before. This frightened her and she now feels they must go for help.

Fifty-three of the 100 clergy in the interview sample had experience responding to a counseling scenario similar to the one just identified. One pastor offered the following example:

Well, they were quite young. They were young when they were married. And he'd had a serious drinking problem, and I tried really to discourage against marrying him, I really did. I said, "You know, you are going to have a very hard life," and I said, "Unless he straightens up for a while. . . ." I went ahead and married them eventually. . . . He was pretty rough with her. It was fine for about two months and after that things just seemed to get worse and worse. . . . The greatest problem was . . . his drinking . . . he was really nasty with her and would hit her and everything, and slap her.

(Clergy Interview #532)

Like many pastors, the one reported in this case story made the initial contact with the couple during premarital counseling, and the wife made contact with the pastor when the marriage was in trouble. According to the pastor, the husband was a carpenter, who worked with a group of men with whom he liked to socialize and drink, sometimes to excess. According to the pastor, the wife was frustrated by her husband's inattentiveness and began "harping at him" about his whereabouts after work. Tension built from there. She used words to vent her anger, he used his fists. The pastor intervened by "dropping in" to their home (after having been tipped off to conflict by the wife's phone call). Though the minister continued to see the couple, to "reason with him," the problems continued and the pastor reported growing somewhat impatient with the husband. Then an industrial accident sent the husband to the hospital for several weeks. In the pastor's mind, this "scare" helped him to "straighten up his life." At this point, pastoral counsel made an impact. The husband credited the minister for "helping us to get our life together again." Perseverance on the part of the pastor led to reduced marital conflict and eventual marital reconciliation.

A second pastor described the following case.

Well, I was involved in a situation where the husband, as it turned out, was abusing prescription drugs. . . . He treats women as second-rate and inferior, and [with a] very, very defined domestic role. Her unwillingness to fit into this role made her a square peg. . . . He got aggressive and my antenna, as I say, was really shooting one Sunday at noon, when I had a call from her that was interrupted, so I felt that there was something terribly amiss, so I went to the house, and got no answer, and called him by name, and heard him punching her. . . . My voice interrupted what was going on. . . . You could tell by looking at her that she needed to go to the hospital, so at that point I had to decide how to cope with all this. . . . [In my car] I got her to the hospital, she was severely beaten about the face and head. . . . [Once in hospital] I coreferred because there is a community chaplain. . . . We got involved with the psychiatrist as well, to follow up . . . and the family doctor.

(Clergy Interview #488)

According to this pastor, the husband had "an old-world view, in which the woman . . . [has] a very clearly defined role within the four walls of the house. It is not a role many modern women want. And this wife wouldn't accept it."

In response to this woman's abuse, a team of people including the police and justice system, the physician and psychiatrist, as well as the pastor worked with particular aspects of the case. The husband was sentenced to the county correctional center, where he received counseling and became involved in the support group AA. As a couple they received therapy from the psychiatrist, and the pastor kept contact with both the woman and the man. The relationship with the abuser was delicate for the pastor, because the investigating police had taken a statement from the pastor which had been read in court, prior to the man's conviction. As a result, the abuser felt betrayed by the minister and the minister felt caught between the need to ensure the woman's safety (and the abuser's conviction) and an interest in rehabilitation for the abuser.

In this case, the pastor became part of a team. In his words, "That situation was so loaded with dynamics that it was beyond me." When the wife was in the hospital, this minister suggested the transition house as a possible temporary refuge from the violence of her husband. But, according to his words, "she staunchly refused to abandon the family home." The family doctor treated her physical wounds, the psychiatrist dealt with the emotional problems and the husband's addiction. Despite this, this minister saw himself as the "principal therapist." Defining counseling as holistic health, the pastor perceived his role to be one of ensuring that the woman was attending to her various physical, emotional, and spiritual needs, routinely checking up on her and monitoring progress. Once her physical wounds had been attended to, she went home.

There are a number of observations that we can draw from the two case illustrations presented above. First, in both cases the pastor arrives at the family home during a violent episode, after having received a "call for help" from the wife. Clearly the pastor is acting as a crisis intervener. While the wives in these cases could have called the police, they chose to ask the pastor to respond to their family crisis. And it appears that their confidence in the skills of the pastor developed, in large measure, during the planning stages of their respective weddings.

Second, in both cases the husbands were involved in substance abuse. And according to the pastors' interview transcripts, their overuse of alcohol or prescription drugs acted as a disinhibitor for the husbands' anger or aggression. Third, in both cases the husbands employed physical acts to demonstrate their displeasure with their wives, yet in neither case did pastors report that these men used physical means to deal with disappointment on the job or in other contexts. They were selective, in other words, in their use of force, and it was their wives who suffered the pain of their violent acts. Fourth, in both cases pastors put themselves at risk by their involvement with the couple. In the second illustration, where the minister carries the battered woman to his car, his intervention raises the level of anger and hostility of the violent man. In fact, during his interview the pastor reported that the abusive husband did not want him to take his hurt wife to the hospital, preferring to take her himself. Yet, the pastor persisted in offering support despite the level of personal danger involved. My point is not to minimize the suffering of the abused woman in either case, but it is important to realize that ministers do place themselves at considerable risk when they intervene *alone* to a crisis call.[9] While neither of these cases involved any overt act by the abusive man toward the clergy, other pastors reported that they had experienced an abusive man's anger, his threats, or his violence.

And finally, both cases reveal the long-term nature of support to abused women and abusive men. During the interviews, these pastors reported that their involvement with the cases just considered extended over several years; in one case the pastor saw them once a month for approximately four years; in the other case, the contact continued for a long period of time, but it went through cycles of intense contact (weekly) and then months with no contact.

General Issues That Arise When Dealing
with Conflict Involving Physical Responses

We now turn our focus to consider the emerging themes in the responses of clergy to the case they chose to discuss as an example of their involvement with a woman or couple where there was a physical response to marital discord. When clergy were asked to indicate what they considered the problems in the family to be, husband-related difficulties came to the foreground (n=42), followed by relationship problems (n=22), external forces (n=17), problems related to the wife (n=7), and children-related issues (n=7). Verbal abuse (n=17) and sexual or physical abuse (n=26) were also believed to be integral to the problems presenting in this case. Also, eight clergy noted the presence of problems linked to spiritual factors.

Clergy were asked to comment on how the husband—and then the wife—was contributing to the presence of problems represented by this case. Excessive control, coupled with force, emerged as the most frequent response of clergy (n=66) as to the husband's contribution to marital discord. Communication issues, which had been central in clergy's thinking about men's contribution in case 1, were much less frequently cited in case 2. Moreover, financial irresponsibility on the part of the man (reported frequently for case 1) was mentioned by only one clerical respondent. On average, clergy attributed to the husband 68% of the responsibility for the problems that were presented, though the percentages were scattered among clerical respondents from a low of 43% to a high of 100%.

When clergy discussed the wife's contribution in a situation similar to case 2, "nagging" emerged as a factor (n=21), followed by control or violence (n=13), failure to understand the husband (n=10), and expecting too much from her partner or the relationship (n=8). They attached a figure of 30% to the wife's influence on the problems in the case, though there was quite a range of responses, from 5% to 60%.

In sum, just over half of the clerical sample we interviewed had direct counseling experience with a woman (or man or couple) presenting with marital discord like that described in our second-case illustration. Generally speaking, clergy held that the problems in this case were more fully related to the husband than to the wife or the relationship per se, and that there were clear signs of an excessive use of control or force. They tended to see the wife as contributing to the marital discord through unrealistic expectations placed on either her husband or the relationship, coupled with "nagging" and, less frequently, excessive control or force. While case 1 was assessed by clergy to hold a 60/38 male/female responsibility breakdown for the problems presented to the clerical counselor, case 2 was assessed as 68/30.

As with our questioning about case 1, clergy were asked to indicate for the second counseling situation why they believed that the individual or couple sought the counseling services of the pastor. In total, 17 clergy reported they believed specifically spiritual reasons were behind the individual's choosing to see them personally. While trust in and respect for them as pastor (n=16) were believed important, the major clerical response to this question had to do with the perception that the pastor *was a friend* (n=51). Others reported that they were viewed as a listener (n=19) or someone who could bring resolution to the conflict (n=10). Just as with the first scenario, many pastors (n=27) mentioned that people sometimes seek their help because other services are simply not available.

Interview questions probed the nature and duration of the pastoral intervention in case 2. The individual(s) involved were seen an average of 15 times, over a 21-month time period, for an average of 60 minutes per session. Pastors reported their intervention mainly in terms of process (n=83), whom they saw, how they assessed the problems, and in 14 cases noted the use of their referral network. A total of 14 clergy mentioned that they intervened in some specific spiritual or religious manner (e.g., praying with one or more individuals, direct *spiritual* counsel in terms of God's will or plan for family life). Most clergy noted that the conflict and marital discord continued over time (82%) and 63% said that it did in fact escalate.

We asked clergy to assess how much personal risk was involved in the relationship for the wife, and then for the husband. A total of 58% of clerical respondents said that they believed there was "high" risk for the wife in case 2, while 22% reported that there was "high" risk for the man as well. On a scale of 1 to 10, where 1 represents "not at all serious" and 10 means "extremely serious," the conflict in case 2 was assessed as 8.1. Several factors were reported as informing this assessment. First and foremost was the issue of tension building and abuse (n=44), followed by the marriage's being in danger (n=26), the role of alcohol (n=16), relationship problems (n=13), problems in the husband (n=13) or wife (n=2), destroying the home (n=3), the role of external forces (n=2), and spiritual issues (n=1). A small number of clergy (n=7) noted that despite the evidence they had reported to the contrary, they still believed that change was possible.

The final set of questions concerning case 2 revolved around the uniqueness and efficacy of pastoral intervention in this case, and the ensuing process of referral and follow-up. Clergy were very divided in terms of how successful they believed pastoral counseling was in the particular case they had described: 20% reported "extremely successful," 26% "successful," 35% "somewhat successful," and 19% "not at all successful." As a group, pastors reported that they believed that their intervention was successful in terms of helping the relationship (n=29, of which 2 noted that they had "kept them together"), helping the wife (n=9, of which 4 noted that they had "helped her leave the relationship altogether"), helping the husband (n=7) or the children (n=1). Thirteen pastors believed that their intervention in this case averted further violence, and 6 noted an increased interest in spiritual or religious matters as a result of their contact with the individual(s) or couple. A few also mentioned their ongoing relationship with the persons involved, as a listener (n=5), a friend (n=4), or a referral source (n=3).

How did clergy feel that their intervention with this couple was less than fully successful? Well, first of all, 10 of the 53 clergy who reported this experience were of the opinion that indeed their intervention was fully successful. Of the remainder, 12 said they were unable to help the husband to admit to any problems (a further 3 said the couple would not admit to problems, and 1 noted the wife would not admit to problems), 11 reported the ongoing presence of conflict with the couple, and 7 said that the lack of reconciliation between the partners was evidence that their intervention was not successful. A total of 13 pastors cited their lack of clerical training. "Looking back on it now, would you do things differently?" we asked in the interview. The majority of clergy responded "no" (53%), while 15% mentioned they should have referred one or both individuals to other sources for help.

The majority of pastors (65%) indicated that they had referred the individual(s) involved to someone else for further assistance. In a fashion similar to case 1, the most common referral source was a *Christian* counselor (n=21), a *secular* counselor (n=16), a psychologist/psychiatrist (n=9), a physician (n=5), or a lawyer (n=1). Eleven clergy suggested the use of a support group, and 19 mentioned the local transition house. A further 5 pastoral counselors suggested contact with another member of the clergy, and 1 referred the individual(s) to a couple in the church.

In 45 cases, the pastoral counselor had further contact with the individual or couple after the referral suggestion, and in 37 cases clergy had contact with the person to whom the referral had been made. Of the 19 clergy who commented on their perceptions of the counsel received by the referral source, 5 clergy reported being "extremely satisfied," 10 were "satisfied," 2 were "somewhat satisfied," and 2 "not at all satisfied."

Finally, we asked clergy to indicate how they felt their pastoral intervention/advice/assistance differed from—or was similar to—the counsel the case might have received from a nonclerical counselor (outside of an explicitly Christian ministry). As with case 1, most clergy (52%) felt their *perspective* differed *greatly* from a nonclerical counselor, most clergy (74%) felt that the *process* of their intervention did *not differ greatly,* and most clergy (80%) felt that the *outcome* of their intervention differed *little* from a nonclerical counselor.[10] In essence, pastoral counselors reported that it was the way they conceptualized the family and the world that set them apart from secular counselors. Conversely, though, they saw little difference between themselves and secular professionals in terms of the style or methodology of their counsel or its impact.

We can draw a number of interesting observations from clergy experience counseling men, women, and couples where there have been physical responses to marital discord. First, over half of the pastors (n=53) in our interview sample had direct experience assisting a woman who had been the recipient of her husband's physical reaction to his displeasure with her behavior. Clearly, then, clergy are involved in responding to the needs of abused women. While their involvement has come under intense criticism from both church and secular sources, and may not in any measure match the level of need, a majority of pastors have been called on to assist a woman who has been the object of her husband's frustrations and anger.

Second, despite the level of clerical exposure to cases involving physical acts of aggression by husbands, the proportion of pastors with experience in this area is far less than pastoral experience dealing with verbal aggression, blaming, and intense arguments. While almost all (n=98) pastors reported assisting women or couples where there was marked verbal conflict, just over half (n=53) of our sample had experience responding to the needs of women who had been the object of their husband's physical aggression. We will draw out some of the implications of this finding more fully at a later point; suffice it to note here that there is undoubtedly an interplay between the *level* of conflict and the *reason* pastoral help is sought. For the most part, clergy report that parishioners and others seek their pastoral counsel because of their interpersonal warmth and appearance of friendship. For situations involving modest levels of conflict, seeking out a pastor who is also a *friend* may be perceived as the option of choice. As the intensity of the conflict increases, though, the pastor as friend may appear a less obvious choice.

Third, unlike case 1, clergy were less likely to report *relationship issues* as paramount in the explanation of cases involving physical responses to marital discord. Instead, pastors were more likely to see the husband's excessive control as the problem, coupled with unrealistic expectations or excessive demands on the husband as women's contribution. As shown by our data presented in chapter 4, pastoral counselors are not unaware of some of the major features of social scientific discourse on wife abuse, such as male control. The 68/30 breakdown for male/female responsibility for marital discord is further corroborating evidence that while clergy see men as the aggressors (and responsible for their violent acts), clergy are committed to interpreting marital breakdown as a two-way street. They simply do not want to place the *blame* for violent acts firmly at the hands of men.

Fourth, while clergy reported rather extensive contact with the cases they used as an illustration of their experience, very few pastors (n=14) indicated that they had intervened with the woman, man, or couple in some specific spiritual or religious way. One might be tempted to conclude that clergy simply *assumed* that we (as researchers) would understand that they prayed for people, or read scripture verses when such was appropriate, or offered explicit spiritual counsel when there was confusion about God's design for family living. But, clergy did not *assume* other, far more taken-for-granted issues. They told us that they set up appointments, that they offered people coffee, that they listened to the wife first and then the husband, and so on. In other words, it is hard to make a case to suggest that clergy are engaged in some form of direct spiritual counsel they neglected to mention to researchers who were interviewing them about how they respond as clergy to abused women, abusive men, and couples in crisis.

Rather, I think it is fair to conclude that there is a very limited amount of direct spiritual counsel occurring within the office of the pastoral counselor. *Why* that is the case is really beyond the scope of this research. In fact, we expected to find far more explicit references to spiritual issues, spiritual insight, and spiritual counsel. As we saw in chapter 2, clergy were not hesitant to talk about the role of an explicitly religious framework when dealing with marriage and the family in an ideological or theoretical way. On the contrary, their understanding of the dynamics, nature, and purpose of family living is firmly rooted in a theological discourse and religious worldview. Yet, their counsel to families in crisis seems divorced from theological underpinnings. As we shall discuss in a later chapter, in part this may be a reflection of a fair degree of discomfort on the part of clergy with responding to families whose lives do not match the ideal of "happy family living." Moreover, given that their training for pastoral counseling is very limited, it appears that in many ways they are attempting to replicate in the church office what they believe secular counselors provide to their clients, with two exceptions: (1) they do not have the background, as they have not received the secular training in counseling;

and (2) they resist any notion that would "water down" their explicitly Christian worldview, a worldview they do not believe secular counselors share.

Within this context, then, it is hardly surprising that clergy believe that people seek their counsel because of the performance of the role of friend par excellence. To be fair, clergy are caught in a very difficult bind: the requests for pastoral counsel keep increasing, but are not matched by their perceived level of training to provide it. In a sense, the demand is ever present, but so too are their own personal feelings of inadequacy.

Fourth, pastors were not particularly optimistic about the efficacy or longer-term impact of their own pastoral intervention. Over half of the clergy we interviewed felt that their intervention was at best "somewhat successful." The desire to keep couples together and at the same time avert further violence meant that many clergy simply had unrealistic expectations about what they could accomplish with the family in the case they described. Engaging the husband in counseling (or even helping him to admit to a problem) proved for many pastors to be an immense challenge, one at which they felt they had failed. Still, a not-insignificant number (n=13) believed that their intervention had averted further violence, and four pastors described how they had assisted the wife to leave her abusive environment. These factors notwithstanding, many clergy claimed to have been only mildly successful if the couple were no longer together. With such high expectations for their own performance, coupled with the difficulties of the presenting problems people bring, it is easy to see why many clergy feel discouraged about their role as pastoral counselors.

Clergy Experience in Cases Involving Persistent Physical Abuse

We turn now to consider pastoral advice to women who have been victims of repeated physical abuse by their husbands. In the interview setting clergy were asked whether they had ever counseled a woman who presented with problems similar to the following case scenario.

> CASE 3 The third and final type of counseling situation I want you to think about involves a woman from your congregation who asks to see you about a crisis in her life. Through tears, she tells you that she has been caught in a very unhappy marital relationship for several years. The marriage is frought with conflicts that often escalate into yelling and screaming matches. On several occasions her husband, a well-respected member of your congregation, has lost control, hitting and punching her repeatedly. She is now very frightened of his anger. After the last fight he was particularly remorseful and promised never to harm her again. Despite his plea, she wonders whether it is finally time to leave.

Twenty-nine out of 100 clergy in our interview sample had experienced a counseling situation like the one just described. The following two case illustrations reveal both the complexity and the pain involved.

They were both older than I was—second marriage they'd been through and they knew what had failed before. . . . I did the wedding against my better judgment and later learned not to go against my better judgment; if I don't feel good about it, I won't do it.

One night . . . I just pointed out that I'm 6'2" and he's 5'2" and if he hit her again I'd visit him in the hospital, 'cause that's where I'd put him. Now that's not professional counseling—this is a case of, you know, your health is on the line. His father who was one of the pastors supported me in that 100 percent.

They weren't members of my congregation, but they were both active in a church. And my wife and I met them at a denominational convention. . . . Her first husband she had divorced because he had moved out on her, he was living with another woman. . . . In the fella's case, his divorce was on the grounds of mental and physical cruelty. And I wouldn't have touched this with a ten-foot pole, but he made a straight statement, claimed up and down that that was before his conversion, that he'd been saved, this was all taken care of; 2 Corinthians 5 says, "If anyone be in Christ, he is a new creature, old things have passed away, all things have become new" . . . so even though I didn't feel that confident, I took that at face value. . . .

I'd been doing some Christmas shopping and I dropped in on my way back to my home, just a social call. Got there, oh, I don't know how long before the fight had been, probably half an hour. She'd gone back to work, he was in the middle of feeling very remorseful. . . . And I just walked in at a time when he was willing to say what had happened and told me the whole story. . . . We were up until 2 in the morning before we finally wrapped up.

(Clergy Interview #277)

There are a number of important details about this story to consider. First, the violence was initially disclosed to the pastor during his unplanned social call to their home. Unlike most professionals, who have no opportunity to arrive unannounced at their clients' homes, clergy—especially those who work in rural contexts—are expected to engage in pastoral visitation on a rather routine basis. During our interview, many ministers reported casually "dropping into" homes where they suspected conflict and tension. And often the timing of such a social visit coincided with a violent outburst. It was at this point that clergy were able to assist as crisis interveners. Sometimes their arrival actually stopped aggressive acts, but more often they were simply there to hear the anguish of the victim and the confession of the aggressor. Sometimes they transported the wife and children to a medical facility or to safety. Sometimes they took the violent man out of the house in order to offer respite to the family. Many times, they simply stayed for several hours with the couple until the immediate crisis was averted.

A second observation about this pastor's case illustration involves the role of the clergy in premarital counseling. Many of the one hundred clergy we interviewed mentioned that pastoral contact with a couple during the planning stages of their wedding laid a foundation of openness and support. Later in the relationship, at a time of crisis, the pastor was perceived by either the wife or the husband as a "friend" who could be called on, someone who understood them, someone who would be able to remember that at one point they had experienced happiness in the relationship. What would typically happen was that a couple would be involved in relationship building with a pastor during premarital counseling, and in so doing develop trust in the pastor's counseling and interpersonal skills. Then when trouble began the pastor was regarded as a friend, one who understood about marriage and the problems that can occur. Most often it was the woman who sought out the pastor for both premarital counseling and postmarital conflict.

A third observation involves the primacy of spiritual issues. According to the pastor, the man in this case had a marital history of violence, with his first marriage ending because of his physical and emotional cruelty. Yet, intertwined with this intragenerational pattern of aggression were spiritual overtones. In fact, during premarital counseling the man quoted scripture to the minister, indicating the role of behavioral transformation in the believer's life. It appears that when the pastor revealed some reluctance to marry the couple, the abusive man engaged in a spiritual discourse with the pastor. The pastor was caught "off guard" as it were, not completely understanding the dynamics of abuse or the manipulative power of an abuser. Furthermore, he was not able to articulate fully the interdependence of "faith and works" in the life of a new convert. As a result, the pastor interpreted his awkward situation as having one of three alternatives: (1) having to renounce the power of Christian transformation, something he was unwilling to do; (2) denying the abusive man's conversion experience, something he was frightened of doing; or (3) accepting the transformation and hence agreeing to marry the couple. Later in the interview, the pastor reported that his own lack of training and experience led him to accept at face value the integrity and sincerity of an abusive man's desire for and probability of change.

A fourth observation about this case involves the pastor's personal admonition to the abusive man, *"I'm 6'2" and you're 5'8"."* Several of our clerical interviewees reported that they were explicit about their height and weight to abusive men. Offered as a potential deterrent to the abusive man's future violence, the pastor perceived that a bigger or taller man could "frighten" an abusive man (who was shorter or lighter) into nonviolent behavior. Failing other rational or spiritual means to cope with violent outbursts, several pastors resorted to *"I am bigger than you and if you hurt your wife again, I will come after you."* Needless to say, ministers of smaller stature did not make such claims. Interestingly, though, a significant proportion of clergy felt that by condemning an abusive man's violent behavior he would stop. Integral to this perception was the clergy's belief that a violent man did not *really* understand that his violent behavior was unacceptable. One pastor put it this way: "The guy was an abuser, period. . . . He needed to be told in a very firm, yet loving, way that what he was doing was very abusive and he needed help right away" (Clergy Interview #552). Ministers, then, saw themselves as messengers of that news.

A final observation about clerical involvement relates to scheduling issues. In the case illustration, the pastor stayed with the couple for six or seven hours, until the time that the anger had subsided and the talking had ceased; when everyone was exhausted and the immediate danger was averted, the minister left and returned home. Over and over again, clergy reported that they "counseled" into the early morning hours with victims and abusers. Like the emergency ward of the local hospital or the city police, pastors were "on call" twenty-four hours a day.[11] Although such emergency responses were infrequent for clergy, it is important to understand that for those pastors who reported much experience in relationship counseling, they were not uncommon. As several ministers noted, their personal availability was a prime factor in being called on to help families in crisis.

In the case illustration, the pastor responded by trying to help the woman see that she had options other than remaining with the abusive man. He attempted to show her that the children were at risk. Eventually she left and sought a divorce. Reflecting on his involvement the pastor reported:

Personally, I almost think that's a success solution. No kid got hurt and, and the wife got out without getting beat to pieces. . . . I don't think that marriage is to be preserved at any cost. . . . God doesn't call us to be stupid—faithful yes, try it yes, stupid no. . . . A divorce is a failure, but it's not the person necessarily who has failed, it's, it's the relationship that failed. And maybe what failed, and I fully, you know, would say this in this case that we've been talking about, maybe what failed is whoever did the wedding and did the premarital counseling didn't do the job right, and I didn't. If I had, if I had done my homework with these two . . . there's no way in God's green earth I could have that wedding. . . . That was one of the questions that was asked to me when I was on the witness stand on her behalf. You know, his lawyer was really trying to put me on the spot. He said . . . "You're testifying in favor of divorce and you did the wedding." And I told him, I'm testifying that what she told the court was the truth [about the abuse]. . . . I feel far more awkward having done that wedding than I do about being [in court] today.

(Clergy Interview #277)

This case highlights many of the features common to other pastors' experience: the severity of the violence; the fear of the woman victim; the level of pastoral involvement; the ambiguity of the pastoral role; the high expectations pastors place on themselves for marital reconciliation; the manipulative power of abusers; the way spiritual issues arise in violent religious families, and the need for temporary separation and/or divorce as the only option to ensure a woman's safety (and that of her children).

A second case illustration from a pastor went like this:

I've had a lady who has come to me out of, out of fear for her own life and her children's lives, with a husband who, again has come from an abusive home. They have had eighteen years together, it has not been a happy relationship. . . . He has pushed and shoved her from time to time. But his scare tactic is to take his hunting rifle out and lay it on the bed and say, "OK, I'm gonna shoot myself, I'm gonna shoot myself and somebody else." She has endured this kind of abuse for . . . years and he always comes back, in tears himself, with being remorseful and says I'll never do it again . . . only to repeat it.

(Clergy Interview #350)

The pastor goes on to explain that the husband engages in a variety of activities to cover over his behavior, like taking his wife out to supper. She has grown tired of his cycles, reporting that her heart is cold and that "she has no feeling left for this man." The man is modeling his childhood home where his father was abusive to his mother; he is a moderate drinker, and he works the "graveyard shift," meaning midnight until eight in the morning. According to the pastor, his church attendance is "C and E," Christmas and Easter, and "on those special occasions when she can drag him out."

The wife sought out pastoral help after eighteen years of agony. The pastor advised her to leave the abuse. Feeling overloaded by the dynamics involved, and judging his own limitations, this minister referred the abused woman to secular counselors for more in-depth therapy. Yet he was very apologetic about his advice:

> Because I counseled her, which, you know, it's kind of strange that a pastor would do this, but I, I uh, if the situation is abusive like that I don't counsel the woman to go back, unless he is willing to secure some good counseling, but he wasn't.
>
> (Clergy Interview #350)

There was a general reluctance on the part of clergy to believe that their intervention had been successful if the relationship ended in divorce. This is unfortunate, and produced a lot of anxiety and insecurity among pastoral counselors. They feel a pressure to keep families intact, a pressure reinforced by the Christian family literature and a theology that emphasizes reconciliation and dramatic change in a believer's life. By their own accounts they are stalwart supporters of *the family,* yet they need help to realize that some families cannot be repaired in such a way as to match the Christian ideal of marital and family bliss. In a sense, pastoral counselors find themselves in a very difficult double bind: they preach their undying support for the family, yet many of the families who seek their help are in the advanced stages of marital dissolution.

This observation is not to downplay the assistance that clergy can and do offer. Quite the contrary. It is simply to point out that pastoral counselors themselves are under enormous internal pressure to "keep families together." Added to this pressure is the expectation of many women and men who seek their help that clerical intervention will be a "quick fix" for ongoing family difficulties. Not surprisingly, pastors feel caught. If they have received training in relationship counseling (and many have not), it tends to focus on strategies for reducing conflict that keep the family together and enrich the family experience. In a sense, they are best prepared to deal with rather modest levels of conflict, like communication problems, differences in parenting styles or philosophies, or issues involving marital intimacy. Pastors report that they feel more comfortable helping to *enhance* the marital experience or promote happy family living for those whose problems are less severe. But they report feeling very poorly trained to deal with issues involving intense conflict or abuse, where keeping the family intact may be neither desirable nor possible.

General Issues to Arise
in Dealing with Persistent Intense Conflict

From these two case illustrations, we now turn to consider the features, similarities, and differences in the experiences of the twenty-nine clergy in our interview sample who reported involvement in counseling a situation like the one
described in the scenario.

When asked to indicate what they believed some of the presenting issues in this
family were, clergy were not hesitant to refer to the problem as "husband-related";
in fact all 29 clergy cited the husband as the major source of the problem. Furthermore, 67% of the responses named the violence per se as one of the major presenting problems in this case. A total of 2 clergy mentioned wife-related problems,
and 1 noted problems with the children. Three cited external forces. No one mentioned spiritual problems.

A total of 73 responses were given as to the contribution of the husband to the
problems presented in their case description. First and foremost, many pastors
(38.7%) felt that the husband was contributing to the problems in this case through
his use of excessive control and force. Unlike the previous two case scenarios reported earlier in this chapter, pastors did not see communication issues or financial irresponsibility as even modestly contributing to the unhealthy relationship,
though some clergy mentioned that the husband had grown up in an abusive environment. Overall, clergy attributed 78% of the influence for the family problems
to the husband, though responses ranged from 30% to 100%.

Clergy cited a total of 40 factors in response to how the wife was contributing
to the problems represented in this case. These items ranged from "emotional baggage from her past" (n=6), to being "too passive" (n=6), "avoiding problems"
(n=6), or a tendency to "blame herself" (n=3). Perhaps ironically, the largest
number of responses could be collapsed under the heading "Her biggest mistake
was that she married him in the first place" (n=7). A further three respondents
noted that the wife was "too aggressive," and two mentioned substance abuse.
Though responses ranged from 1% to 70%, the average pastoral counselor felt that
in the case they described the influence of the wife was 23%.

To sum up, the third-case scenario revealed that 30% of the clergy in our study
have had counseling contact with a woman (or couple) where intense physical violence is a recurring pattern in the marital relationship. These clergy were not reluctant to see the husband as primarily responsible for the aggression and marital
discord. They tended to see the wife's contribution in terms of her childhood past
(emotional baggage) or her decision to marry the abuser (who may or may not have
been abusive to her at the time of marriage). If anything, it was her passivity or
avoidance of conflict that was cited as the contributing factor of the wife to the presenting case, much more so than other factors (such as verbal put-downs or ag-
gressiveness). Overall, clergy saw the husband/wife responsibility for the ensuing
conflict as a 78/23 split. In essence, the husbands were viewed as primarily responsible for the problems in cases like that described in scenario 3.

Of the 29 respondents in the interview sample with experience in counseling a case of repeated physical abuse of the wife, 22 clergy reported that their

intervention tended to revolve around support for the wife (of which 14 noted that they advised her to leave). A total of 15 pastors had contact with the husband, and 8 saw the couple together. Eight clergy reported intervention that involved some activity that was spiritual in nature. And 5 clergy mentioned that they actually took the woman to the local transition house. Others described "process-related" information concerning the parameters of the counseling setting. Clergy were less likely to see the conflict as a result of a relationship problem than they had been with earlier case scenarios; rather, they conceptualized it primarily as an emotional problem on the part of the abusive man.

Ministers we interviewed were fairly unanimous in their interpretation of the conflict in this case as being "extremely serious," when they rated it 9.1 on a 10 point scale. Pastors reported that the violent actions and the aggressive behavior led them to conclude that the level of conflict was very serious. Twenty clergy (69% of respondents in this case) referred the individual or couple to someone else for assistance. Unlike earlier cases, common referral sources here were the transition house (n=7), a *Christian* counselor (n=7), a physician (n=5), a secular counselor (n=4), or a psychologist/psychiatrist (n=3). At least one (out of 29) pastor mentioned the following referral sources: support group; lawyer; police; social assistance; prison chaplain; or other pastor.

There are a number of observations that one can draw from the clerical experience involving women suffering repeated abuse. First, while almost all clergy have contact with verbal aggression, and about half the clergy have experience with physical responses like shoving and pushing, only a minority of the clergy (n=29) report assisting women who have been the victims of ongoing, intense physical battery from their husbands. Many of these clergy reported that the women they were assisting were in life-threatening home environments. Some of the clergy feared retaliation against themselves[12] or against the women they were attempting to assist.

Second, there was fairly unanimous agreement among clergy that in cases involving repeated violence (like hitting), male aggression was primarily responsible for the marital discord. Whereas ability to communicate or to provide financially were common responses of clergy to the contributions of men to marital discord in earlier scenarios involving less physical forms of violence, in case 3 pastors were not hesitant to name the acts of aggression. Interestingly, it was women's passivity and avoidance of family problems that clergy perceived to be the contribution of wives in these cases. Ultimately, women were held responsible for marrying the abuser in the first place, though clergy also felt a degree of responsibility for the marriage if they had in fact performed the wedding or conducted premarital counseling with the couple. Clergy were quick to condemn the violence in this case; in no instance did we interview a pastor who minimized or reinterpreted the level of aggression. Contrary to what some secular sources might suggest, we found no evidence in cases involving ongoing physical battery of wives that clergy suggested that women return to an unchanged abusive environment, or that they should simply endure the suffering, or that they should work harder at being better wives or mothers. Rather, we found that clergy rated the violence as extremely serious, that they were very concerned about the woman's and her children's safety, that it was not uncommon for the pastor (and church members such as the pastor's wife or other lay leaders) to assist an abused woman to leave her home or to offer her temporary lodging and/or financial assistance.

Clergy are still reluctant, however, to see a marriage terminated until all sources of help have been exhausted. They prefer that a woman seek temporary shelter apart from her abusive husband (in a transition house or other facility) and for the abusive man to obtain counseling. Only when it becomes clear to the pastor that the abusive man will not cooperate with counseling or has not changed as a result of counseling will the possibility of divorce be discussed. To be sure, in the minds of the pastoral counselors divorce is a last option. But it is important to recognize that even though they are reluctant to see abusive couples divorce, they do not oppose it in principle or in practice. In fact, 14 of the 29 clergy with experience in responding to cases of repeated violence suggested that a battered woman leave her abusive husband.

A couple of other observations warrant mention here, though they have been developed more fully in other chapters. Though clergy are far more likely to have contact with abused women than they are with abusive men, it is noteworthy that in approximately half of the cases involving extreme physical violence the pastors had contact with the violent man. From the interview transcripts we learned that clergy were often discouraged about their lack of progress in helping male batterers stop their violence, and often the violent men stopped coming to the "marital" counseling when they realized that their violence would not be tolerated. Clergy are not alone in finding it difficult to engage violent men in counseling. In fact, one of the persistent challenges for men who run programs for batterers is to keep the men in the program[13] if they are not court-ordered to attend, and if their attendance is court-ordered, the challenge is to engage them in the therapeutic process.[14]

Pastoral Counseling and Advice to Abused Women and Couples in Conflict: A Summary

This chapter has explored how clergy respond to the suffering created by violence in the family context. We have sought to tell that story from the perspective of the church's frontline crisis worker, the pastor as counselor. Through in-depth interviews with one hundred clergy serving in rural as well as urban contexts, we have been able to capture some of the dynamics and challenges for ministers as they strive to respond to the needs that are presented to them. Translating the evangelical rhetoric of "happy family living" and "human wholeness" into practical help for women, men, and couples in crisis is no easy task. It is time-consuming and emotionally draining; it is ongoing and often discouraging, and the rewards can seem few and far between. Without a doubt, abused women, abusive men, and conflict-ridden homes pose a direct threat to the message of marital and family harmony proclaimed from pulpits from the Atlantic Coast to the Pacific Ocean. In fact, providing safety for a woman victim is sometimes at cross-purposes with maintaining the continuity of the family unit. Reluctant to see even a violent couple divorce, clergy find themselves caught in the cross fire between the ideology of the family the churches hold dear and the reality and persistence of male aggression and abuse.

While the average pastor spends two afternoons a week providing relationship or marital counseling, one in every six ministers directs fully 25 percent of his or her work load to counseling-related activities. With the demand for counseling services on the increase, many pastors feel stretched beyond their limit to provide pastoral counsel to needy individuals and families on the basis of very little prior training. The range and nature of the problems frequently presented to the pastoral counselor include communication issues, financial problems, difficulties with children and parenting duties, spiritual issues like church attendance, and marital conflict involving verbal aggression, sexual issues, and emotional difficulties. Less frequent problems include difficulties with parents or in-laws, incompatibility regarding leisure, and marital conflicts involving some form of physical response or injury. While some clergy refer a large proportion of the individuals or couples who seek their help to nonclerical counselors, most pastors attempt to deal singlehandedly with the problems that are presented to them. Those clergy who are most experienced in counseling are the ones who have established referral networks and make such referrals on a more regular basis.

Through a presentation of three case scenarios, each involving a woman seeking pastoral help for marital discord, we learned that almost all (98%) clergy have experienced counseling a woman who has been the object of her husband's verbal aggression, 53% of pastors have assisted a woman who has experienced a mild form (e.g., shoving) of physical aggression from her husband, and 29% of clergy have been called on to respond to a woman who has been repeatedly battered by her partner. While pastors believe that it is their interpersonal qualities or friendship ties that encourage people to seek them out for help, our data reveal that many couples who later seek pastoral help first have contact with the minister at the time of their wedding preparation, including the sessions of premarital counseling. Often it is here that the pastor's credibility is established. Later on, when conflict erupts, that initial link with the pastor is reestablished, most often by the woman, but not until well on in the cycle of violence.

We have explored the myriad of ways pastoral counselors attempt to bring support, reconciliation, and healing to those who seek their help. While ministers differ greatly in their counseling experience and the advice they offer, the data reported in this chapter offer *no* evidence that clergy deliberately or directly dismiss a battered woman's call for help. In fact, among those clergy reporting experience in responding to the needs of abused women, offering practical help and support far outweighs what might be considered specifically spiritual advice or religious activities, like prayer. Contrary to what some might think, clergy appear rather reluctant to offer direct spiritual counsel to abused women. Nevertheless, clergy are very slow to suggest dissolution of even a violent marriage, preferring instead a temporary separation, followed by counseling and eventual reconciliation. Pastoral counselors are quite optimistic about the possibility of reform and renewal in an abusive man's life, but their optimism is frequently tempered by the unwillingness of such men to engage in the therapeutic process or to change their behavior. Under these conditions, many clergy advise permanent separation and divorce.

In cases involving less direct examples of physical force, as in the example of shoving or pushing, clergy are much less likely to understand that behavior as an illustration of unrestrained male aggression. Here they are far more likely to look at the presenting difficulties as relational in nature and to see both husband and wife contributing to marital disharmony. Although there is no evidence to suggest that clergy support or encourage men to respond to their wives through these behaviors, as a group they appear less likely to single out the aggressive behavior for condemnation. Rather they focus much of their attention on helping these men to be attentive to their wives and to be involved in caring behaviors toward her (like dinner out or gifts). Here too, they attempt to help wives take on more responsibility for the ownership and solution of problems, which some may be tempted to see as blaming the victim. Yet our transcripts of clerical interviews would suggest otherwise. Clergy are committed to enhancing the marital experience for men and women within their faith community and within the neighborhood where the church is located. Except for cases of extreme violence, clergy appear somewhat uncomfortable laying sole blame at the hands of men; this should not surprise us, since in large measure marital restoration and reconciliation are dependent on both husband and wife assessing their contribution to marital disharmony and working toward enhancing the relationship they share.

Finally, when clergy were asked to respond to a case involving verbal aggression, there was a much wider disparity in the responses. While some pastors clearly felt that verbal aggression can be as damaging to a woman's sense of self-esteem as physical abuse, others were far more likely to see the blaming and name-calling as examples of marital discord for which both parties were responsible. Here pastors tended to think that men's contribution centered around issues of financial irresponsibility and communication, while women held unrealistic expectations for the marital relationship or their male partners. Within this context, altering discrete behaviors (such as learning how to communicate better) was believed to result in a decrease in the verbal aggression. In other words, pastors felt that a lack of skill and self-understanding was at the heart of the discord, rather than a desire to control or destroy the other person.

To conclude, the story of the pastor as counselor involves a myriad of relationships, with men, women, and children living in distressing and often conflict-ridden environments. Sometimes the pain is obvious, and in those cases clergy appear desirous to bring safety and healing. Sometimes the pain is obscured by other presenting problems; here clergy appear to have greater difficulty seeing the need for safety or healing. While clergy themselves are the first to admit that they lack sufficient training in pastoral counseling, the need of parishioners has taken precedence over their feelings of personal inadequacy. Given the level and nature of violence in relationships both within and beyond faith communities, the task facing the pastoral counselor is immense.

But if one out of every four families are being abused, the minister, if everybody came to the minister like that, he would never get home for supper. I mean he, he wouldn't have the time. . . . I don't think we can leave it up to the pastor, I think it's impossible.

(Woman #5, Focus Group #1)[1]

The pastor would never be able to respond to all that pain, individual by individual.

(Woman #5, Focus Group #26)

The chance of [abused women] coming the first time it happens are probably slim and by the time they're out searching for help, it's probably pretty desperate.

(Woman #3, Focus Group #17)

And I think that . . . a woman, you know, that's been abused will come to probably a woman in the church first even before the pastor.

(Woman #4, Focus Group #17)

The first time that I shared publicly my testimony . . . that was a healing thing. . . . You feel shamed to have been abused. . . . I think women need to become healed enough that they can share so that they can help others but it, it takes time. I mean, it took me eight or nine years.

(Woman #3, Focus Group #7)

In reference to someone talking about an abused woman sleeping on her couch, another woman who herself had been battered replied:

I know for myself, I couldn't even admit it to myself for years and years. . . . Who do I go to? There was no one with a couch . . . you see.

(Woman #2, Focus Group #28)

6

Women-Helping-Women

Transforming Victims into Survivors

Celebrating the rhetoric of happy family living is one thing that appears to unite Christian clergy and laypeople, men and women alike. The emphasis on family values and family unity stands in rather stark contrast to the reality of families whose existence does not match the ideal of bliss and togetherness. As we saw in chapter 2, a review of the conservative religious literature on families underscores the importance that this sector of Christianity has placed on both family harmony and a gendered family experience for all members. A distinct division of labor in the family, the church, and the broader society is believed to be the biblical blueprint for family living.[2]

Historians who have studied fundamentalist thinking on the family argue that this brand of religious thought idealizes woman as the self-sacrificing wife and mother, content to run the home rather than the business world.[3] As conservative Protestantism has flourished, its most powerful message has been one of solid, secure, changeless familial relationships.[4] In this way, sacredness has been attributed to a particular family constellation or pattern of family life.[5] However, as social scientific research has documented, there is far more latitude in how conservative faith communities interpret and make gender messages operational than one might expect by listening to their rhetoric.[6] Despite this, the contemporary gender challenge to the conservative family framework is profound at the point where the feminist struggle asserts that a woman's deepest identity—and indeed her safety and security—may be found in something other than her family connections.

However much conservative Protestants extol the virtues of home and hearth, they are far from unique in their celebration of happy family living. In fact, across the contemporary Christian landscape (Protestant and Catholic alike) there is persistent and overwhelming nostalgia for "the family"[7] and a pining for a bygone era when families were believed to stick it out through "thick and thin," with death the only divide.[8] One of the by-products of this fascination with family togetherness is the failure family members feel—wives and children in particular—when they participate in a family characterized by unhappiness, conflict, or abuse. Since women are expected to set the "tone" that pervades the family home, they are particularly sensitive to failure and guilt when family life or their marital relationship is marked by tension, fear, and physical battery. While women not connected with religious communities also experience feelings of failure at the dissolution of marriage,[9] the focus on the *sacredness of the family unit* serves to exacerbate this experience for religious women. As a result, women connected to churches, and especially conservative faith traditions, stay in abusive marriages longer and work harder at marriage repair.[10]

Given the focus on strong families united in purpose, it is not unrealistic to expect that this sector of Christianity would have given more thought—and developed more programs—for families in crises. With all the emphasis on family values and family unity, however, the pressure to stay together may simply create greater guilt in the lives of women, and hence greater reluctance to leave a violent home. As a result, it is important to ask if abused women can find support in an environment that places the intact family on such a high pedestal?

As we have been considering in the preceding chapters, the answers to these questions are multifaceted and sometimes contradictory. To be sure, there is not as much church-sponsored, concrete help for divided families in the weekly routine of church life as there is ongoing support for healthy families. Most church programs are geared to intact, nuclear families with children, despite the fact that growing numbers of the membership do not experience family life in this way.[11] Moreover, the communities that churches serve are far less likely to be populated with traditional two-parent, one-income family constellations than they are with the myriad of other family forms, such as single-parent families, blended families, senior adults on their own, families divided by divorce or abuse, and so on. The assistance, then, that hurting, fearful abused women need may not be as forthcoming from the institutional church, or even the clergy, as one might expect or hope. But do women of faith themselves look out for other women?

This chapter tells the story of the response of faith communities to abused women and their children from the perspective of churchwomen, almost all of whom believe the church has a critical role to play in the fight to end violence against women in homes across our land. Some of these women have been abused themselves, and many of them have sought to support another woman in her struggle for safety and survival. For clarity of presentation, this chapter is divided into three sections: how evangelical women conceptualize wife abuse; then, the nature of support that evangelical women have given to other women who are or have been victims of battery; and two case illustrations of how faith communities have responded to the needs of women in their own backyard.

Themes in Understanding Abuse

It's like mom saying back two or three years ago. She was up here and we were sittin' at the table Saturday night playing a game of Scrabble and she said, "You know, I just don't understand these transition houses." She said, "People lived for years without them, and any woman is a fool that lets a man abuse her!" And I said, "Mom, how many times do you think you come to the hospital to see me when my eyes were black and blue, my teeth were droven through my lip, and my throat was cut, that I fell down the stairs or tripped on a sled?" . . . They will die with it inside them, because they have nobody that will listen.

(Woman #7, Focus Group #7)

Later on, in the focus group, she commented:

And he was the most perfect human being. And everybody said, "Oh, he's a sweetheart, and he's a Christian and he's a deacon of the church." And you go with him for two years and he treats you like a queen and you marry them and within thirty days they'll beat the crap outta ya.

(Woman #7, Focus Group #7)

There's a good many men out there that mentally abuse their wife but he'd never touch them. But mentally they, they've got them in the chopping block.

(Woman #12, Focus Group #4)

Several strands appear in the tapestry of churchwomen's discussion of abuse. In large measure they conceptualize violence against women by reference to their own personal experience, or it is framed by the pain and humiliation of the women they know who have been victims. In this way, the issue of wife abuse is contextualized out of the experiences of women they trust, love, and relate to in a personal way rather than by an intellectual definition shaped by the news media, family violence researchers, or even church sources. Because it is so personal, it strikes an emotional chord; for the women in our study, it was virtually impossible to discuss violence from any perspective but the victim's. In fact, it is noteworthy how sensitive nonvictimized women were to friends, neighbors, or family members who were abused by the men in their lives. As we shall see, however, the context from which most women conceptualized violence was their service or support to other women in need. As a group, then, the religious women in our study were far more sympathetic to women victims and far less condemning of their choices than one might have hypothesized.

Over the years evangelical women in Eastern Canada have become impatient with their churches and religious leaders when it comes to addressing the level and severity of family violence. Partly because evangelical women's knowledge of family violence issues is so rooted in their own personal experience or that of their sisters and friends, they are far more sympathetic to victims than one might expect. In fact, a study of 287 Wesleyans revealed that these women used their personal life circumstances and everyday experiences to filter the religious dogma and teaching on the family they received from their faith community.[12] Clearly, they were appropriating selected feminist principles into their conservative Protestant ideology, at least in their understanding of wife abuse.[13]

The focus group study on which this chapter is based asked women to estimate what proportion of married couples in Canada have experienced violence in their relationship, and then to rate the level of violence among married couples in their congregation. As table 6.1 reveals, the mean level of perceived violence for married couples in Canadian society was 43.3%, or two in every five couples. Yet when they were asked about their faith community, that percentage dropped to 18.0%, or less than one in every five couples—less than half the estimated rate of secular society.

Table 6.1

Perception of Evangelical Women of the Level
of Violence Among Married Couples in Canada and
Among Married Couples within Their Own Congregations

Violence in Marital Relationships	Married Couples in Canada	Married Couples in the Congregation
1–10%	9.7%	56.9%
11–20	10.2	14.9
21–30	14.8	12.6
31–40	18.9	3.4
41–50	18.9	5.2
>50	27.6	6.9
Mean	43.3%	18.0%

N=196

I would like to draw our attention to four observations about this data. First, it is clear that evangelical women are informed about the frequency of violence in relationships across the country. The recent Violence against Women survey found that three in every ten Canadian women had experienced at least one violent episode from a live-in partner. The religious women in our study, then, are not unaware of the extent of male violence against wives. In fact, their estimates of violence exceed that reported by Statistics Canada. Why might this be so? In large measure, religious women have learned about the frequency and severity of violence perpetrated against women through the lives of their mothers, sisters, and friends. In a fashion not unlike their secular sisters, religious women's *ways of knowing* about violence is experientially based, not gleaned from the pages of the newspaper or TV reports.[14] They *know* about wife abuse because friends and family members have disclosed their own personal pain and turmoil to them. And that personal *knowing* has been filtered through a lens of secular society that now dares to talk about wife abuse and acknowledge both its prevalence and its pain. This broader secular context for understanding violence, then, both contributes to women's willingness to disclose their personal abuse to others and helps to ensure that women to whom such disclosures are made will see them as parts of a broader pattern of violence rather than the particular experiences of one hurting woman.

Second, clergy consistently rate the level of violence between married partners lower than the churchwomen. In chapter 4, we examined results from over three hundred pastors and found that their perception of violence in the secular community was lower than the Statistics Canada report. There is considerable disagreement in the scholarly community on just how frequent wife abuse is in families across the nation. Some features of that debate were highlighted in chapter 1. Suffice it to point out here that ministers estimated that 28.8% of married couples in Canada are violent, almost 15% lower than the women of their churches.

Third, religious women believe there is less violence in couples associated with their own congregation than within the broader society of which their church is a part. In fact, they rate the violence as being less than half as prevalent in church families as in secular neighborhoods. As we will see throughout this chapter, religious women, not unlike their clerical leaders, have a bifurcated vision of both the frequency and explanation for violence in sacred as opposed to secular families. This is one place where we can see very clearly the impact of the burgeoning literature on *Christian* families. On one level, religious women *know* about the nature and severity of violence through their own experience or the lives of other women: as a result, they are extremely sensitive to the magnitude of the problem, its cycles, and its persistence. On another level, however, religious women are very influenced by the church's celebration of family life and family values. In a sense, they *believe* the family is sacred, but they *know* it is not always safe.

Fourth, and finally, religious women and their clerical leaders estimate an almost identical level of violence within families connected with their churches. Women report that 18.0% of families in their church are violent, while the clergy estimate the proportion to be 18.8%. One possible explanation for the discrepancy between perceptions of the level of violence in secular families of clergy and of women and the close agreement between these groups when it comes to the level of violence in church families may be related to the fact that both women and clergy turn to similar sources for their knowledge of church families, but have divergent frames of reference concerning the world outside the church. It is quite likely that concerning the sacred world, religious women turn to church sources for their knowledge, taught by clergy who themselves believe that violence in families of faith is lower than national levels.

While researchers in the area of family violence argue that abusive behavior has no faith boundaries,[15] there has been little attempt to measure incidence rates. Those writing on the family for a populist Christian audience generally ignore altogether the issue of wife battery, or mention it only very briefly.[16] As we saw in both chapters 1 and 2, there are several authors, representing numerous faith traditions, who have drawn attention to the plight of abused women,[17] but their books have not had nearly the widespread distribution or reading audience of people like Dr. James Dobson or the LaHayes, even among the clergy. It is not surprising, then, that clergy and church women alike underestimate the prevalence of violence in families connected with their faith community, even as they are knowledgeable about incidence rates in secular society.

Explaining Violence in Christian Families

When it happens within the church I think it's very difficult because it's one of those things that you expect should happen in the outside world. But none of us like to believe that it would happen in the church, especially with people that we would consider good Christian people. And the first time that I encountered physical abuse in terms of a wife who was being battered, her husband was the church treasurer and they were very active in the church and it was an extremely difficult thing to comprehend. I mean, I saw the black eyes, I saw the variety of things that had happened, I got the "I walked into the door at work." . . . And knowing what I know now about wife abuse I probably would have questioned. But back then I didn't, I never asked a question, I mean I just, I didn't expect that it would happen. And when we found out I was devastated.

(Woman #4, Focus Group #7)

Later on she said:

I think sometimes in the church it almost makes it worse, because not only do we have to have the societal cover-up but we've got the religious cover-up. . . . And we wear masks too much of the time, it's hard to let, let the mask drop to tell somebody you're having a problem of any kind. But if you're having a problem with abuse, it makes it that much more difficult.

(Woman #4, Focus Group #7)

In this section, we turn to consider how evangelical women explain the fact that some Christian families are violent. As table 6.2 demonstrates, they tend to rely on spiritual explanations to account for battery within families of faith. Fully 50.9% of the responses of individual evangelical women as to why some Christian families are violent rely on a spiritual-based factor, and an additional 11.5% of their responses combine a spiritual and a secular component. Only 37.3% of evangelical women's responses to violence in faith families considered the role of nonspiritual factors, like controlling behavior, the pressures of life, the intergenerational transmission of violence, issues of low self-esteem, or personal psychopathology on the part of the abuser.

Looking more closely at these data, we observe that the primary response of evangelical women as to why Christian families have been found be abusive rests in their belief that Christianity as a life-changing experience has not erased all the negative aspects of humanness among its followers. As a result, there continues a struggle between the human nature (which they see as sinful) and the Christian experience (which they see as purifying). Seen from this perspective, then, violence is a specific example of the continuing war between good and evil.

Violence represents the "old nature" and marital harmony the "renewed nature." A response related to this position is that a lack of spiritual maturity is believed to characterize the life of an abusive Christian man. While the emphasis at this point is similarly lodged on the spiritual plane, it is much more directed to the followers' lack of progress in the faith. As a result, the focus rests more fully on the believer than on the forces of good and evil operating in the world in which we all live. A small proportion of women (5.4%) claimed that any abusive man was not really Christian at all, a perfect example of a tautologous stance.

Table 6.2

Distribution of Evangelical Women's Opinions Concerning
Why Some Christian Families Are Abusive

Viewpoints Concerning Why Some Christian Families Are Abusive	%	(N)	Total %	(N)
Spiritual Factors			50.9	(168)
Struggle over Spiritual Growth				
Christianity has not erased humanness	36.3	(74)		
Lack of spiritual maturity	26.9	(55)		
Not *really* Christian	5.4	(11)		
Struggle over Church's Effectiveness				
Distortion of *true* Christian message	9.8	(20)		
Church inability to deal with problem/				
exacerbates problems	3.9	(8)		
Spiritual/Secular Combination			11.5	(38)
Nonspiritual Factors			37.3	(123)
Personal psychopathology	20.6	(42)		
Intergenerational transmission of abuse	10.3	(21)		
Pressures of life	22.1	(45)		
Interpersonal relationship problems	3.4	(7)		
Lack of opportunities/support	2.5	(5)		
Minimized the reality of the violence	1.5	(3)		

N=330 responses from 204 women

To place this discussion in context, it is important to understand that these same women used social scientific explanations to account for violence in families not identified by faith perspective. When asked why men are violent, why women remain in violent marriages, and why women sometimes hide the abuse they have suffered, evangelical women were not slow to point to power abuses in marriage, male anger and men's desire to control women, the intergenerational cycle of violence, intrapersonal problems of the abuser (like low self-esteem), the role of stress, and societal influences. When they considered families of faith, however, evangelical women's knowledge of social science findings did not seem to impact their interpretation of abuse in a specific faith context. In other words, their understanding of the dynamics of abuse was compartmentalized according to the religious convictions of the family involved. As we noted above when considering prevalence rates, evangelical women have a bifurcated vision of wife abuse:

secular explanations for families outside the faith community; sacred explanations for religious families.

As we noted in chapter 4, our research has documented this same divided thinking of sacred/secular explanations for violence among clergy samples. Consistently, evangelical clergy understand abuse within Christian families as a spiritual issue, and they regard abusive behavior on the part of the religious man as a sign of his lack of spiritual growth. In fact, clergy were even less likely than the evangelical women to report the role of nonspiritual factors to explain why Christian families can be violent too. While cognizant of the major social scientific explanations of abuse, and willing to see the explanatory power of such findings among families in the mainstream society, they seemed oblivious to the power of these same explanations to account for the behavior of families connected with their church.

The implications of this thinking are rather obvious: since the "origin" of the problem of violence in Christian families is spiritual in nature, the "cure" must be spiritual too. Thus, given their orientation to spiritualize wife abuse, it is not surprising to find that many evangelical clergy are reluctant to refer parishioners suffering the pain and despair of violence to secular counselors and government-funded agencies, such as transition houses.

Level of Support to Abused Women

Before we discuss in detail the various ways churchwomen have responded to the needs of abused women both within and beyond their faith community, it is important to examine the overall nature and frequency of the assistance they are offering. The majority of evangelical women (55.1%) in our sample of almost 250 women indicated that they had been personally involved in supporting an abused woman, offering a total of 314 examples of that support.[18] As table 6.3 reveals, the types of support could be categorized as "emotional support," "physical support," "spiritual support," "referral," and "advice/counseling." By far the most common type of assistance evangelical women claim to offer abused women relates to emotional support. Fully 56.4% of the responses came under the umbrella of emotional support to the abused woman through friendship, a listening ear, or sharing one's own personal story of abuse. Being a "listening ear" for another woman was the most frequent response; in fact, 92% of the women who reported personal support for a woman suffering the pain and humiliation of abuse mentioned that they were simply available to listen to her story and to support her in making decisions about her life that would reduce her risk of further abuse. A smaller proportion of women (5.9%) noted that they had been involved in accompanying an abused woman to court.

A second type of support noted by evangelical women I have termed "physical support." A total of 25.8% of the responses fell within this category. Here, evangelical women recalled their involvement in providing child care for an abused woman, taking food or other material resources to her, or offering a battered wife transportation to a shelter or to appointments with counselors or social assistance

Table 6.3

Distribution of Evangelical Women by Their Support to Women Who Have Been Abused by Their Husbands*

Types of Support to Abused Women	136 Women Who Offered Support (55.1%)	
Emotional Support	%	(N=177)
Listening Ear	91.9	(125)
Friend/showed kindness	27.2	(37)
Accompanied places (e.g., court)	5.9	(8)
Shared my personal story	3.7	(5)
Helped with support group	0.7	(1)
Helped a relative	0.7	(1)
Physical Support	%	(N=81)
Lodging	22.8	(31)
Child care	12.5	(17)
Financial	10.3	(14)
Transportation	5.9	(8)
Food	3.7	(5)
Furniture	2.9	(4)
Financial (indirect)	1.5	(2)
Spiritual Support	%	(N=17)
Prayer, Bible reading	12.5	(17)
Referral	%	(N=19)
Referral to a secular agency (e.g., transition house)	12.5	(17)
Referral to a minister	1.5	(2)
Advice/Counseling	%	(N=20)
Advice as a friend	12.5	(17)
Advice in a professional context (e.g., nurse, social worker)	2.2	(3)

*Note: There was not always a perfect relationship between what women reported in the focus group session and what they included on their individual survey form. In one case, over a dozen women present in a focus group reported involvement in a church-based support group, but only one woman actually mentioned it on her survey form. As a result, women's personal recollection of their own social action as recorded on the individual survey form may well be an underrepresentation of their actual activities.

offices. One in five churchwomen noted that they had provided lodging to a battered woman and her children, whereas 10.3% had given direct financial help.

While the categories of emotional support and physical support encompass most of what evangelical women reported as their assistance to abused women, spiritual support, referral suggestions, and counseling were also noted by some. Spiritual support included praying together or reading verses from the Bible to a woman victim. Those who noted they had referred an abused woman to someone else for help tended to mention the transition house in their local area. Finally, a few women (20 in all) reported that they had been involved in counseling or offering advice; three of these evangelical women noted that such advice had occurred within a professional work relationship.

One of the purposes of collecting individual data from each woman at the end of the focus group was to ensure that we would not assume to speak to the experiences of individual women as if the focus group dialogue was equally representative of everyone. For sure, some women were more forthcoming than others in the group setting, particularly as it related to sharing information that might be perceived to bring them praise. We wished to neither overestimate nor underestimate churchwomen's assistance to abused women. To that end, the focus group discussions gave us rich insight into how churchwomen respond to the needs of abused women both within their own faith community and within the neighborhoods where their churches are located. The individual survey forms, on the other hand, served as a reality check about the level and nature of that support.

It will become obvious, no doubt, in the pages that follow that it was a deeply moving experience to hear women talk about how they had offered another woman shelter, child care, money, or "just tea." The words on a survey form alone would have been completely inadequate as a way to capture the intensity of their care and their concern. Moreover, the stories of support tended to be offered as one woman in the group recounted *another* woman's loving acts. Often the scenario went something like this: "Mary, didn't you help that woman who lives out in the trailer park, whose husband had such a violent temper?" Mary would then respond by saying, "All I did was take her children for the weekend when she needed a rest herself." At that point another woman in the group would pipe up and say, "Ethel, what about that woman who lives in an apartment at the end of Circle Boulevard; didn't you go with her to court?" After a few minutes, all seven or eight women in the group would be talking at once, priding themselves in the care offered by some other woman.

At first, I was inclined to see this from the perspective of women not wishing to boast about their own service to others. But later I realized that for many Christian women service to others is such a large part of their very existence that they did not even consider it noteworthy. It was part of living the Christian life, and because it was so ordinary, women tended to forget about what they had actually done. An example from focus group 1 makes the point. After a rather lengthy discussion, an older woman said, "Well, now that I think of it, there was a woman being verbally abused and I took in her daughter for eight to ten months." "Is that all?" another woman in the group teased. That exchange prompted a story about a woman who had become a foster mother; was sent a child "temporarily," and the little girl "ended up staying for seven years."

Before discussing more fully the themes that emerged in our focus group discussions, I would like to make three brief comments about the level of support individual women reported on the questionnaire format. First, contrary to what many feminist activists might claim, religious women appear to have substantial experience in offering some form of support to an abused woman and her children. Second, the nature of the support that churchwomen offered to other women is not defined primarily in spiritual terms. On the contrary, religious women reported that most of their support to other women could be classified as showing kindness to a friend and offering a listening ear to someone who is in pain. Finally, practical help featured prominently in the types of support evangelical women offered one to another. Particularly impressive—and yes, even surprising—is the number of religious women who had offered temporary lodging to an abused woman and her children.

Responding to the Needs of Abused Women and Their Children

I don't think that we personally have had to suffer abuse to be empathetic to somebody else who's been abused. . . . And I think the other thing is, women have a wonderful networking system that men just don't seem to share, from what I've perceived. Women are able to emotionally share themselves with other women and men just don't do that. . . . You put two or three perfectly strange women together in a room for an hour and and, and you know, you'll know about their kids and their family. . . . And so women within the church, I think, have a wonderful way of being able to minister to other women, because we're able to put ourselves often in other people's shoes and . . . be supportive emotionally. . . . We have the emotional reserves to be able to share.

(Woman #4, Focus Group #7)

If I'm being abused by a man, would I go to a man minister? I mean like [get real!].

(Woman #5, Focus Group #1)

Four particular themes emerged in the focus group discussion related to the response of churches and churchwomen to women victims and their children: issues of urgency and safety; women as friends; spiritual support; and sacred/secular partnerships.

Urgency of Response

The issue of safety was raised at several intervals as groups of women discussed the problem of violence against women. Not surprisingly, safety included a concern for the physical, emotional, and spiritual well-being of the individual woman and her children. But, interestingly, safety also included the provision of a response setting that was attuned to the woman and her needs, along with a concern about the safety of those who might be offering her assistance. The following comment gives us some initial insight into this issue from the point of view of churchwomen themselves.

We need to make our people more educated within the church structure, within the, the body itself, where people can understand that it's safe to come to people within the church. Instead we hide because it's not, abuse is a nonaddressed issue. It's not something that's acceptable in Christians, so we hide. And we say, "Oh, I'm not a very good Christian if such and such has happened to me." So, so we hide and so nobody cares anything about those kinds of things. It's not a safe place to come because once you get there with those types of issues, nobody knows what to do with you.

(Woman #2, Focus Group #28)

Later on, this same woman said:

I hid from the church because I didn't feel safe, that wasn't a safe place for me to come and talk without feeling like I was being judged and condemned and put down. . . . I don't know if a lot of our pastors would even recognize abuse because they're not trained to. . . . They should be much, much, much more aware. . . . They've never lived or experienced it, so they don't know what to say.

(Woman #2, Focus Group #28)

Sometimes, women did in fact consider the church, pastor, and people to offer safety to a woman struggling to deal with her abusive partner and her own fear.

I guess I'd see the church perhaps as a, a safe haven. A place where if they're at the end of their rope and have nowhere to go I would hope that the church would be one place . . . where they could be given some love and immediate attention.

(Woman #2, Focus Group #17)

While women were sometimes divided among themselves as to *whether* the church was in fact a safe place, they were unanimous that it *ought* to be a place of safety and security, a safe haven offering refuge from the storms of life. As groups of women talked about responding to victims, they highlighted several features of the intricate balance between care and empowerment, vulnerability and strength, and the difficulty of predominantly male clerical leaders' responding to the needs of women who have been abused by men. Some women answered this dilemma by considering that a pastor can "create a safe place within himself, a place of confidence where someone feels freely able to share" (Woman #12, Focus Group #1); others felt that the pastor was not a likely choice: "I know I've had a pastor that I would have no more gone to with my troubles than I would have thought [of] going to the moon" (Woman #5, Focus Group #27). Still others were uncomfortable with a male pastor becoming a "female's confidante or pal" (Woman #8, Focus Group #4).

Most women, though, recognized that one pastor simply could not respond to the myriad individual needs presented within the congregation. And here was the point of entry for women ministering to the needs of other women. That brings us to the second theme to emerge out of the focus group discussions, the centrality of friendships.

The Friendship Model

. . . don't take advice from anyone, but you've always got a friend right here at my kitchen table.

(Woman #7, Focus Group #7)

Being a friend first to them. And sometimes, just by opening your door and asking them to come over for a coffee. . . . It doesn't matter what the home is like, you feel, there's usually something special in your home that makes it . . . special . . . the different things that are homemade. . . . When I go into a home, I look for what draws you, or attracts you. And oftentimes people will see that in your home, whether it's making it cozy or more loving or friendly or warm, or it's because you're doing a bit of baking, or whatever. And you trade recipes, you do things. And that's what makes a person maybe become a friend and warms you up and they have faith in your confidence or whatever, and you'll go from there . . . just a little bit of warmth and a little of love, just reaching out.

(Woman #10, Focus Group #1)

I think sometimes too if you know of a woman that's suffering from this that we need to show them a lot of love. Because I think a lot of times they're made to feel like, by the person that's abusing them, that they're worthless. And I think a lot of women that are abused are just, you know, they're told that they're no good for anything. And they're made to feel so low that they have to be shown love . . . and made to feel that they are worthwhile human beings and not just, you know, worthless.

(Woman #3, Focus Group #4)

I think there's a very definite role that we can play as women, yet not, not only in the listening. . . . There are women in the church [abused women] can come to without being ashamed, because I think shame is, is a big part of [it] . . . but we can also [help] in very practical and tangible ways. . . . We can become involved in, in their backup support, and with that, help with the care of children and all the practical food and shelter needs; I think that women have a very large role to play.

(Woman #10, Focus Group #5)

To which another person responded:

I think listen, let them vent, not pass an opinion, encourage them to seek help, and if they have an immediate physical need, try to meet that, if it includes shelter maybe for that night or something, if there's anything you can do about that, be a helpful person to guide them to the people that can counsel and can provide for them the support that [they need].

(Woman #2, Focus Group #5)

The friendship model translates compassion into concrete help for women in crisis. It transcends boundaries created by religious commitment, economic or social class differences, or language barriers created by educational or career differentials. According to the women who participated in our focus group research, friendship becomes the litmus test of the Christian as they attempt to translate the love of Christ into acts of kindness and emotional support and empowerment for other women.

Spiritual Support

You can spend time praying with that person when there aren't any answers and you've talked it all out and there doesn't seem to be a way. . . . You could spend time praying . . . bringing that person to the Lord.

(Woman #5, Focus Group #6)

I think that the only thing that you can do is to be a friend and to stay, stay very close and pray. . . . [Says another woman in the group,] Not to be abandoned, let them know they will not be abandoned.

(Woman #3, Focus Group #3)

I think the role of the church would be in a preventive sense to teach from the Bible the guidelines for husbands, wives, and children. (Woman #7, Focus Group #4)
And put [those guidelines] into practice as it's been taught.

(Woman #8, Focus Group #4)

To raise awareness more within the confines of the church. We tend in the church to feel we're a little bit sheltered from those sorts of things. . . . Even from the pulpit talking about it. So if there are people that are in the congregation that are actually . . . even suffering from, from different forms of abuse, they'll feel more comfortable to discuss it with someone.

(Woman #2, Focus Group #4)

Some of our earlier research, which probed the stresses women of faith faced in their daily lives (which was conducted among a sample of 287 conservative church women) had revealed that there was a pressing need for churches and their leaders to simply recognize that violence against women and children is a problem. In that project, some women charged that local churches and the denominations they represent support denial of past pain, and as a result individual men and women of faith need to identify their vulnerability, then seek help and begin the long and arduous healing journey. Moreover, they felt that as a "caring community" the church had some rather unique opportunities through which to offer victims of violence safety and to promote violence-free family living, both from the pulpit and within the regular routine of church life. Through a recognition of the shared boundaries between the secular and the sacred, these churchwomen felt that churches and government-funded agencies could work together in the fight to end violence against women and support victims in their search for healing and wholeness.

Guided by this earlier research, which touched only marginally on issues of abuse, the focus groups offered an opportunity for churchwomen to reflect more fully on the many ways that churches, and their leaders and the laypeople who attend them, respond to family violence. Not surprisingly, spiritual support emerged as one of the themes in the discussion. As the comments from individual women presented above reveal, spiritual support to a woman victim involves first and foremost prayer, and then the broader role of the church includes raising awareness of the problem of abuse as well as teaching appropriate family living.

As we noted earlier, churchwomen see their primary support to abused women accomplished through a model of friendship whereby they offer a *listening ear* to hear about the pain, and uphold the woman victim as she embarks on the path of recovery. By their own accounts, women offer very little direct advice to the women they support; rather, they attempt to help identify a woman's options for securing safety and security both at times of immediate crisis and for the future. And they are not reluctant to provide practical support that would *ensure* that safety. Particularly noteworthy are the number of churchwomen who have offered temporary refuge to a woman and her children fleeing a violent husband. Whether it was a couch for the night, a room for the weekend, or extended care for the children, significant numbers of churchwomen gave support, even as they prayed that it would be forthcoming.

In their book aptly subtitled *When Praying Isn't Enough,* Anne Horton and Judith Williamson argue that spiritual guidance alone is inadequate as the response of churches and the clerical elite to the contemporary problem of family violence. Our research offers tangible evidence that churchwomen help to enable their petitions to God on a victim's behalf, even as their prayers are being offered. We have no data that would support the contention that churchwomen are guilty of dismissing the problem of violence in the family context, or that they offer victims "pat answers" or advice that would further risk abused women's physical or emotional health. To be sure, there were wide differences between both individual women and the groups with which we had contact. Nevertheless, both rural and urban women, some attending churches tucked away in the suburbs and others located in coastal communities, discussed the issues we were raising with amazing candor and empathy. As researchers, we were convinced of the women's honesty and integrity as they offered us stories of personal pain and their outreach to others.

For most women, the role of the local church was straightforward: to recognize that violence in the family exists; to teach that it should not exist; and to offer victims of that violence safety and support. While the over two hundred women participating in our focus groups were almost unanimous that the "call for help" rested firmly and squarely on the shoulders of churchwomen like themselves, they acknowledged an important role for their clerical leaders. But here too they recognized the difficulties involved in a predominantly male religious elite's offering support to a predominantly female group of victims. The following comments illustrate the complexities involved.

Have more female pastors (Woman #1, Focus Group #26).

[Another woman chimes in,] I find they come because there is a woman [pastor] here, to talk and then go back to their own church. So I think the maleness of most pastors probably puts up one of the barriers (Woman #6, Focus Group #26).

Or the pastor's wife ends up doing a lot of counseling (Woman #7, Focus Group # 26).

To which another woman responded:

I agree with you entirely that women would probably find it easier to talk to women. But there must be some men that are easier to talk to than others, as well, so it's the way that the pastor, presents himself.

(Woman #10, Focus Group #26)

As we discussed in chapter 5, most clergy have some pastoral contact with abused women, and a minority of ministers have rather substantial contact with violent families, victims as well as perpetrators. While the number of female pastors in the region is minuscule, and certainly precludes any analysis of clerical response by gender, women ministers in other denominations in the region have told me privately that they are frequently called on by congregants from other churches to respond to abused women and their children. Sometimes the call comes directly from the woman victim; often, the crisis is brought to the woman minister's attention by a churchwoman or a male member of the clergy. As an antidote, I was having dinner one evening with a woman minister who pastors in a small town, and she was telling me that so many referrals (for counseling abused women) were coming her way from other clergy that she had to set up both a policy concerning her own time allocation for counseling and a long waiting list. In her own experience, the need for women clergy to minister to women victims was a pressing pastoral issue.

Stemming the Tide: Individual Examples of Support

Throughout our focus group interviews, we have collected literally scores of stories of how women of faith have attempted to meet the needs of abused women in their midst or in their local communities. Churchwomen themselves would be the first to claim that their support is "only a drop in the bucket," that the need far exceeds their individual or collective capacity to help. In fact, in one focus group, a woman exclaimed with exasperation, "If 99 percent of the people are violent and 1 percent isn't, there's just not enough to stop it all." While other women would be unwilling to accept either her statistical analyses of violence or her pessimism, there was definitely a feeling among churchwomen that while they were attempting individually to respond to the needs presented to them, their collective efforts and especially the response of the church was far from adequate or acceptable.

With that important caveat in mind, it is important to consider some of the myriad ways that women have ministered to other women at their point of need. As we traveled from focus group to focus group, we found churchwomen asking for ideas that other groups of women had put into practice. Part of my purpose in exploring some of these stories here is to encourage a process of cross-fertilization. As one woman from focus group 29 put it, "I would say that [we] can only do as much as [we] are informed about."

Listed below are ten examples drawn from women's personal accounts of their support for women who have been victimized by abuse in the family context.

I have been called in the early hours of the morning to help a friend of mine who was battered and my husband was out of town. And I arranged for her and the children, she had three children at the time, to take a cab to my home and we were making arrangements for her to go in to Hestia House. And you've got to be aware though that the other person . . . things got a little out of hand when [he] was banging on my door and knowing that his children were inside and his wife. And I mean the kids were crying. . . . You got to be prepared for what happens the minute you allow [an abused] family inside that door.

(Woman #6, Focus Group #6)

A woman was calling out of desperation because she'd been hit over the head with a frying pan by a husband who was drunk and lost control. And so my husband and I both went to the home and talked with the couple. I happen to have a little nursing background, so I helped her with her injury, which did leave a gash in her head and got that straightened out cleaned up and all. . . . My husband had talked to him and quieted him down.

(Woman #4, Focus Group #6)

Look after children, treating her to lunch or coffee, or giving her something clothingwise she might not have, or . . . buy her something. And encourage her.

(Woman #17, Focus Group #2)

I guess I can think of another situation where a husband was threatening an assault on his wife and she spent the night in our home. And I guess we helped separate them maybe.

(Woman #10, Focus Group #1)

Listen, love, pray, and support. . . . I had times of reaffirmation, times when they could call night and day. I had times when they came to my home and stayed to remove themselves from their situation. I developed a place of safety and support for them . . . I encouraged them to go for education on the type(s) of abuse . . . even caused them to be aware of the[ir] feelings that caused them to [be] powerless. I encouraged them to go to a Christian psychologist and to the pastor.

(Woman #12, Focus Group #1)

I was involved once with the police and the courts because a woman who was beaten came to me. And I took her to the police and so I was subpoenaed to be in court. . . . I think if somebody comes to you and they're beaten that, that you should go to the police with them.

(Woman #5, Focus Group #2)

We have moved women, we have gone and rescued women out of their home, we had the truck and gone, got somebody, got them out, got them to Chrysalis House.

(Woman #6, Focus Group #26)

Well, it was a neighbor. . . . I've taken the children out of the home when I knew things were really bad, I've laid beside her in bed and held her in my arms many times while she's cried, but not admitted what's actually gone on. . . . A couple of times, I sort of acted like I was really, really stupid, when I knew it was going on, and just walked in the house and pretended that I was so dumb, I didn't know what was going on, like you know what I'm saying, so that he couldn't do it, at least while I was there.

(Woman #1, Focus Group #20)

We put a woman up in our home one night when we lived in the parsonage, who was on the run. She had two small children with her, she was traveling under an assumed name, and she was on the run from, from her husband. She had crossed the border and, you know, she was traveling.

(Woman #4, Focus Group #7)

We helped her get her car fixed when it was broken.

(Woman #2, Focus Group #11)

The most unequivocal evidence for church support to battered women involved the assistance offered from one woman to another under the umbrella of Christian love and service. Perhaps more than other groups, churchwomen understand first-hand the limitations of clergy-only counsel, yet subscribe to a worldview where the spiritual journey permeates every facet of contemporary life. While their responses to women victims clearly involved empowerment for battered wives, the Christian worldview offered the framework through which these actions were mediated. In a sense, churchwomen appropriated feminist calls for social action even as they prayed that victims would have God's strength to leave the men who were abusing them. Nevertheless, given their focus on intact families, and their celebration of marital harmony, churchwomen felt equally comfortable praying that abusive men would stop their violence and that conflict would no longer characterize the home. Reconciliation, then, was always a goal of Christian intervention, but it was not *the only* goal. Ensuring a woman's safety and mental health took precedence over keeping families intact. For these women, spiritual support was an important part of the healing journey, but *praying was never enough*. Tied to their prayer life was a strong sense of individual and collective responsibility to ease the suffering of another woman.

Churchwomen and Support
for Transition Houses

Not only did women have individual stories to tell, there were numerous accounts of working together to support abused women or the local transition house. Since many of the women's groups were involved in the same forms of support, I have included a smaller number of collective accounts below, five in all.

Every year [we] had our little Christmas party and exchanged five-dollar gifts and all that stuff; we decided we didn't really need each other's candy or mug anymore. . . . Transition houses [were] just getting started . . . and we decided that we would . . . instead of giving each other five-dollar gifts, that we would give a . . . shower for the transition house, so, some glasses and cups, towels . . . and baking things like that, we just followed that up with regular visits to the transition house.

(Woman #5, Focus Group #14)

We painted, decorated and furnished a room at the [local transition] House.

(Focus Group #9)

[Women named Hestia House, where they take health care products for the women and other things for the children. They bring them on an individual basis to the women's group and then they send it as a group.] Support what facilities are already there.

(Woman #5, Focus Group #2)

We have a . . . Woman's Center, and we can support it. . . . We take flowers to the shelter on Mother's Day, and toys for the children.

(Focus Group #25)

And we take in movies for the kids to watch and videos. . . . A week ago I took in sixteen women's comfort kits and eight children's comfort kits and we still have supplies for two or three more. And these were drawstring bags, Nancy, that they could keep and they were made out [of] a nice material.

(Woman #1, Focus Group #2)

Are churchwomen and transition house workers partners or antagonists? At first glance, conservative churchwomen eager to uphold the virtues of happy family living[19] and transition house workers eager to ensure that women have complete control over their lives and destinies[20] seem to be on an ideological collision course. Yet, they agree on the primacy of safety, the need for practical support, and the importance of a healing journey if a woman victim of abuse is to become a survivor. Where they part paths is on the role of forgiveness, the possibility of reform and renewal in an abusive man's life, and the desirability of "till death us do part." It is incorrect, however, to postulate that churchwomen encourage other women to return to abusive environments where their safety and self-esteem cannot be assured. Moreover, while churchwomen are reluctant to see any marriage end, our data reveal that as a group they are supportive of women who leave abusive husbands, even while they recognize how difficult and emotionally painful that process can be for an abused wife.

This dilemma between the rhetoric of happy family living and the reality of abused women's lives is captured succinctly in the following comment:

> I think this is quite foreign territory in a way, that we're stepping in here. You know, the little bit I hear about men who abuse their wives, usually they say if a man beats you, he's not going to stop. And, as a church, we try to hold the family unit together, to really, really work hard and to try to work things out. So it puts us in a very precarious situation. . . . It's something I guess that as churchwomen we probably haven't given it as much thought as we should have. And even with the pastor, I mean, one of his roles is to . . . try to keep the family unit, it's the basis of our society, the family unit. And here's an area where probably [the family staying together] isn't what would be the best advice.
>
> (Woman #2, Focus Group #4)

For the most part, women in our focus group discussions talked about the complexities of the choices surrounding an individual abused woman (to stay or to leave) and how abused women themselves need to be supported in the choice only they can make.

> Personally I sit down and cry with her first. . . . They realize that you genuinely care and . . . you're trying to be . . . a listening ear (Woman #2). But too, I think that you have to say, "Well, you've got to get out of that situation" (Woman #5). But not everyone who comes for help is looking to get out of the situation (Woman #3). That's only one part of it.
>
> (Woman #4, Focus Group #17)

> I don't think I should tell anybody else what to do. But I should provide them with the information that they need in order to make an informed choice and support them no matter what the choice is that they make, whether I agree with their choice or not. That choice may be staying where they are, but [I'll] still be their support.
>
> (Woman #14, Focus Group #28)

In-depth interviews with a sample of these women confirmed the finding that churchwomen attempt to support abused women in their choice to stay or to leave, even as they strive to ensure her physical safety and mental health.[21] Particularly useful in conceptualizing the empowerment churchwomen offer abused women is Martha Mahoney's term *agency*.[22] While feminists have often thought of agency only in terms of the choice to leave an abusive husband, Mahoney argues that women can also exercise agency in the choice to stay and transform an abusive relationship. As a result, much of the support work that religious women perform can be understood within the feminist model of empowerment, rather than classifying it incorrectly as simply encouraging a woman's false consciousness—though no doubt that sometimes is the case. As we discussed in chapter 3, sometimes the choice to stay with a partner who has been abusive and work toward transformation can be an example of a woman's exercising agency in her own life. Seen in this perspective, staying may be not merely accepting what is, but enacting a process of reform. However optimistic churchwomen might be at an ideological level about renewal, though, their ongoing support of—and contact with—abused wives offers a reality check and tempers their optimism.

While the friendship model was the most explicit expression of their support for abused women, it had some costs associated with it. First and foremost was the risk of getting in over your own head.

And then when it gets to the point or she opens up to you and you know you can't take it any further, well then it's time for you to suggest that she, maybe she needs help and maybe she should speak to the pastor or speak to someone else, or whatever, and pass it on. But I think this is where we have to discern and know too how far we can go with that and know when we have to drop it and say, "I can't take it any further, I don't know what to do." And admit to it, and then pass it on.

(Woman #4, Focus Group #1)

My friend used to call me on a regular basis when her boyfriend would be beating her up. And she'd come down and stay for a day or two or whatever. And you'd be giving her all kinds of advice and of course she'd always go back. And I'd be thinking, "Well, I give her all kinds of advice and she chooses not to take it." And it was like constant, you know, it was all the time, all the time calling you. And it got so draining on me personally, mentally, physically . . . I had to point her somewheres else. Like I was depressed, and you know, like I was going through, through it with her. So I had to . . . [get] counseling [myself].

(Woman #17 Focus Group # 28)

In an attempt to address this concern, churchwomen talked about their desire not to feel overwhelmed by the myriad needs presented to them. Their solution to this potential problem area is captured in the phrase "sharing the load": women working together to carry the burden of other women's problems.

If you say . . . call me, you better mean it (Woman #17) You may need a support group yourself (Woman #15). You can't do it alone (Woman #2, Focus Group #28).

A ladies' morning out . . . [big burst of laughter from the other women in the group]. Well, it gives her a form to have that support and that feeling of, of sisterhood. I think women, because they are nurturing by nature, can have a special role to a woman, only to women, it's special. . . . She needs to know that there are choices. . . . Also for the children's sake, if the woman's being abused and she has no outlet for support, she might take it out on her kids 'cause she feels . . . trapped.

(Four women talking at once; Focus Group #16)

While churchwomen never named their collective efforts on behalf of abused women as *social action*, they were acutely aware of the cost of individual friendship. For them, the answer to feeling overwhelmed by the practical and emotional needs of particular victims of abuse was to think about how they as a group of churchwomen could share the responsibility of friendship, which they almost always referred to as a *ministry*. Within this framework, ministry meant ministering to women in need of ongoing support of both a practical and a spiritual nature: it sometimes included lodging, food, child care, emotional support, prayer, and spiritual counsel, and less frequently referral to a secular service provider (such as a social worker or lawyer), but it almost always included offering a safe environment where an abused woman could tell her story and share her pain.

In part a reflection of their experience in offering support to abused women and their children, many churchwomen were acutely aware of how very difficult it was to break the cycle of abuse and assist a woman to leave an abusive environment. Reflecting on her personal background as a child growing up in an abusive environment, one woman offered the following comments:

I mean, I was brought up in a home [where] my father abused my mother. And, she'd leave him maybe for two days and then she'd go back to him and go right back into it. And maybe a month later she'd pack up and take us all out again. So I mean there's no way anyone could convince her. Her family couldn't convince her, her children couldn't convince her, nobody could convince her."

(Woman #5, Focus Group #1)

As churchwomen talked about their individual and collective response to abused wives, it was clear that their support was contextualized within a fairly accurate understanding of the nature and frequency of violence in the lives of women. Their experience led them to view the journey from victim to survivor as a long and arduous one, but given their worldview evangelical women were quite optimistic that, with God's help, it was possible. Although some women who were victims of abuse—and beneficiaries of help from other churchwomen—talked about how important that support had been in their own lives, evangelical women themselves were rather critical of their own *inattentiveness* to the needs of those around them. As a group, they were not at all willing to see their individual or collective efforts as laudable, or even satisfactory. Because the *need* of abused women for support outmatched churchwomen's ability to *supply* that need, women in our focus group study were not very satisfied with their ministry performance in this area.

Themes in Assessment of Response

I mean they were really supportive. I mean they just, the women, just started to go down and pray for me right there. And I guess I was afraid they would [be] judging of what was going on because I was leaving him. And I knew he [the pastor] was really good to talk to and he just sat there—leave, but it [was] my choice.

(Woman #2, Focus Group #1)

I think we need to be, well, someone mentioned being [less] self-centered. We kind of look after our own little families, instead of being just that way we need to be on the outlook for others. Usually body language tells you if somebody is hurting or if they're not feeling good or if they've had a terrible day . . . so I have to shake myself once in a while and say, "Go and speak to that person," or "Do something for them." And it's a little extra work, but it's usually worth it in the long run.

(Focus Group #14)[23]

If the Lord gives us the opportunity to build those bridges, then we should act upon it. And if we sit on our blessed assurance and become full in our little nest and do nothing about it then we're defeating the purpose of sharing the gospel and sharing Christ and his love too.

(Woman #17, Focus Group #2)

Research on women in general,[24] and evangelical women in particular[25] suggests that responsibility for ensuring family unity and managing family tension is securely posited as being part of "women's role." In her study of three generations of women in a single-industry town in northern Canada, Meg Luxton argues that women are "tension managers," whereby they act as a giant sponge soaking up the cares, disappointments, and anger of other family members and thereby ensuring greater peace and tranquillity in the home environment. Some of the women in her study who had been victimized by their husbands felt responsible for the violence, believing that they had failed in their role as tension managers.[26] Other research suggests that women generalize their nurturance and care from the family environment to the broader social community.[27] Women within explicitly Christian churches are encouraged in their efforts to help others; in fact, some would argue that service to others is the hallmark of a woman's devotion to her God. It should not be surprising, then, that many women were unhappy with their level of support to abused women and their children. In an environment where family life is enshrined with sacred significance while families in crises are to be found everywhere, religious women feel that their service is no match for the need.

Teaming Up with Secular Care Providers

Recognizing the shared boundaries between religious and community responses to violence against women, churchwomen were anxious to collaborate where possible with resources in their local area, yet acutely aware of some of the tension possibilities inherent in such cooperation. For these religious women, cooperation meant working together, utilizing the resources each had to offer and making referrals when appropriate.

I mean churches weren't meant to keep themselves separated from the community. That's a part of what we're supposed to be, is to reach out into the community.

(Woman #1, Focus Group #27)

As long as we don't feel that we're just passing the buck to the secular community. . . . I think that we need stay involved as a church . . . our church family. . . . I don't think that one excludes the other, and we can work together.

(Woman #10, Focus Group #5)

I think that we could work together just so far. . . . Secular organizations will tie the hands of the church . . . ridicule them . . . probably we can go so far together and then they have to separate.

(Woman #6, Focus Group #8)

Yet, as the following example illustrates, one of the primary tension spots between churches and secular organizations concerning the family relates to the issue of divorce. Chapter 5 raised this issue from the perspective of the pastoral counselor, and chapter 7 will be devoted entirely to collaboration between churches and secular organizations—the possibilities and the problems. It is important to acknowledge at this point, however, that churchwomen themselves are aware of the opportunities that cooperation offers both victims of violence and the churches that are called on to meet these needs. As voluntary organizations, with a mission to preach the gospel and serve the world, establishing links or relationships with the community cannot be overlooked as a potential area for ministry opportunities. Churchwomen see themselves as part of that link.

When you go to somebody, a Christian counselor or a non-Christian counselor, sometimes I think we try to look toward just what our church is offering instead of, when there are things out there available in the secular world that can [be] beneficial too.

(Woman #10, Focus Group #1)

Later on this woman commented:

I would think that a counselor that's compassionate would be better than no counselor at all. . . . I think we as Christians, we encourage the husband and wife, if they can solve their problems to do so and to make a happy home instead of an unhappy one. And yet I think we live in a day and age that some of the non-Christians, the first answer is, separate. But maybe it's through that separation that the healing will happen. Maybe that's the only way the healing can happen.

(Woman #10, Focus Group #1)

However much churchwomen desire to see the establishment and maintenance of links with the secular community, there is no doubt that the relationship is at times difficult. At the heart of the matter is the question of spirituality, and the desirability or importance given to a person's spiritual journey. As the following comments illustrate, women who participated in our focus group research felt that many community agencies simply did not, or would not, acknowledge that there is a spiritual component to the process of healing.

> But there's a spiritual component as well, and I think that that sometimes is missed. When we think that . . . it is such an overwhelming problem . . . so we send them off to the experts, and I'm wondering if the spiritual component is left missing for a lot of women.
>
> (Woman #1, Focus Group #26)

> Just saying, like the spiritual side of things is overlooked in the secular, which is a need that some people might need to get complete healing, the whole process. [Other women add:] The power of prayer, A spirit of reconciliation, And forgiveness. [One woman goes on to explain:] And forgiveness in that situation so that she can carry on and not have that load, with or without the man.
>
> (Four women; Focus Group #16)

These difficulties notwithstanding, several women who were employed in the caring professions offered illustrations of both their occupational commitment to women's safety and health and their compassion as Christian women.

> As a nurse, I work night shifts alone in the emergency department and I've had an abused woman come in, where she's black-and-blue and bruised and she'll just say, "Oh just protect me from my husband." And I put her in a bed over in the corner and pulled the curtain and said, "Just have a good night's sleep here tonight and we'll deal with it in the morning," and she had a good night's sleep.
>
> (Woman #2, Focus Group #26)

> Now I've worked as an RN with the single-parent health center . . . You were forbidden to touch on the spiritual realm. . . . It's difficult being in [that] situation, without having conflict of ideology.
>
> (Woman #2, Focus Group #5)

Here we observe the tension that many churchwomen feel between their allegiance to their faith and their performance of occupational or professional roles that demand religious neutrality. Through their acts of care, churchwomen perceive they are engaged in *ministry* irrespective of what the secular world—or their profession—labels such service. But these women are aware, as well, that there is a delicate balance between overt Christian activities or religiously motivated service to others and tasks performed in accord with their occupational roles. As a result, they are careful to separate one from the other. Yet, as the following quote demonstrates, there are times when such lines of demarcation are broken through, and the secular world actually applauds the work of the sacred. One woman offered the following example of cooperation between her neighborhood church and the child welfare department in her local jurisdiction.

This family was in the church that was ministered to, social services was also involved and had been long before the church really got into the scene. And social services, after learning how the church handled things, actually came to the church and thanked them for their involvement. . . . But social services had an appreciation for the way the church handled the given situation. . . . They were literally at a standstill . . . they tried all of their resources. . . . This is where the church family came in, on a daily basis . . . some opened homes and others, you know, taking people out for coffee in the family and talking . . . ministering to this family, and it was neat.

(Woman #4, Focus Group #6)

This chapter has sought to tell the story of what happens when women look out for each other and respond to each other's needs under the umbrella of Christianity, or the ministry of the local Christian church. It seemed fitting to close the chapter with two case illustrations of groups of women who have sought to push their faith in God and in themselves to the limit, and in so doing to combine their personal and spiritual resources to reach out to others more needy than themselves.

Local Church Initiatives: Two Case Illustrations

The Young Moms Support Group of Riverside Baptist Church

The story of the Young Moms Support Group of Riverside Baptist Church all began when three middle-class, middle-aged Baptist women had a ministry idea that put their faith to the test.

They were members of a rather large evangelical church located in a downtown urban area, a church that was mission-minded and interested in outreach. But there was a problem: the upper-middle-class congregation had little contact with the needs of the downtown area where it was located. The physicians, nurses, university professors, students, and civil servants who sat in the pew had little in common with the men, women and children who lived in the local neighborhood.

Three housewives, motivated by a desire to share their faith and their time, decided that they wanted to make a difference in the lives of young mothers whom they considered to be "at risk." Their vision was to provide both material and emotional support for young women and their children whose existence was marked by poverty, violence, and despair.

"I want to be remembered as somebody who cared about people and somebody who tried to do what Jesus would do," said Jean, one of the originators of the program. The motivating factor for them was "love for the community" and "sacrificial care for their needs." The enthusiasm with which the women recounted their five-year history told the story from the heart: their compassion for women so unlike themselves transformed their personal existence as much as it did the women they had targeted for help.

At the very initial stage, the three women took their ideas to the board of deacons, an all-male group of elders responsible for church leadership. Here they received the formal approval necessary to launch a new ministry. "That's how it all began," said a bubbly middle-aged woman, who was as keen to tell the story of their group as I was to hear it. "We started with four young moms, and now we have thirty-four."

Five years later, placements in the program are filled by word-of-mouth alone, donations of food and clothing come regularly from church people, and the list of volunteers numbers in the dozens. Secular professionals not normally sympathetic to the mission of the church offer to donate an hour to talk to the young women about restraining orders, or writing a letter of application for their first job, or lodging a complaint against a landlord. But the ministry ideas are basically unchanged: to bring the love of Christ and the practical support of Christian women to young women in need.

The program operates on a nine-month basis, one morning a week. In its early days the program was run twice a week, with a short summer holiday, but the churchwomen feared burnout within themselves and tailored it accordingly. By their own words, the program involves "food and fellowship," but in actual fact it is a merger of spiritual support, child care, food donations, coffee time, Bible study, clothing gifts, craft activities, peer mentoring, and life skills training.

Each Thursday, events begin at 9 A.M., after volunteer drivers have brought the participating women and their children to the church's auxiliary building. Coffee, muffins, and fruit await the women, and a complete program of age-appropriate activities are available for the children. What began as "nursery" facilities for child care has expanded to include an internship program for a couple of education students at the local university. At 9:30, there is a guest speaker—a lawyer, a social worker, a teacher, a job consultant, or a nutritionist—and at 10:30, the women go "shopping for free" through the racks of clothing that have been provided by church people. At 11:00 both craft activities and a Bible study are organized, and women choose to participate in either of these or just "sit and chat" with one of the volunteers. At 11:30, the young women prepare to go home, and they are each offered a bag of groceries as they depart. Women volunteer drivers escort them home, or to a doctor's appointment, or to the social assistance office, as the case may be.

In all of my fieldwork experience over the last fifteen years, I have never met such an enthusiastic group of women as the volunteers at Riverside Young Moms Group. In fact, the experience alone had a profound effect on me and other members of our Research Team. It was the simplicity of the vision and its implementation that was so noteworthy. But it was far from a simple program. It included a strong social justice flavor, it was educational, it kept the spiritual journey alive, it was nonpretentious, it was cooperative, it was empowering for participants, it involved fairly extensive commitment from volunteers, and it was very, very practical. In a sense, it offered a bridge between the church and the community. The Young Moms Program at Riverside Baptist Church is an example of what a small group of women, motivated by a vision, can accomplish.

To be sure, there are challenges involved. Drawing boundaries is a case in point. To ensure the longevity of the program and an ample supply of volunteers, the organizers decided after the first year to restrict the program to one morning per week, and to stop the program early in the month of June for a summer recess. Moreover, they began to refer young women requiring "in-depth" counseling to either the senior pastor or a professional counselor paid by church funds, rather than assume too much emotional weight from the women they wanted to help. While women volunteers make themselves available to talk to women participants whenever their help is required, they do not encourage the young women to visit them at home, or to rely on them for transportation except to the program.

There is virtually no expectation that the young women will attend any other function at the church, though the organizers of the program are keen to encourage such involvement when it occurs. Some acknowledge that talk about God as a loving father is both painful and rare for young women who have been physically or sexually abused by their own father or other men in their adult life. Thus, the women-mentoring-women approach is both intentional and therapeutic. Several of the churchwomen who volunteer in the program shared in the focus group how much they had personally grown as a result of contact with young women at risk. In essence, getting to know several young women who were victims of childhood abuse, and who lived alone with their preschoolers in cramped apartments, caused these fairly affluent housewives to challenge their notions about happy family living. One woman volunteer mentioned how the strength of the women at Young Moms (both volunteers and participants) helped her through a personal crisis with her son and his eventual drug rehabilitation regime.

The seriousness of problems faced by many of the women who participate in the program means that the healing journey is slow and arduous. As a result, success is hard to measure. When women leave the program for a job, they rarely have contact with the volunteers again. Many times women who flee abusive relationships to begin a new life free from their abuser return to him at some point, and the volunteers fear that the independence they have nurtured has been all but lost. Yet, some women "graduates" of the program volunteer to come back and help years later. Some of the children get connected with the church Sunday school program, and others show improvement in their school performance. Many, many young women bring their friends along and come faithfully week after week. And for most of the volunteers that is evidence enough that the program is meeting a need or building a bridge between the church and the community.

Coastal Community Church Support Group

Coastal Community Church was a small fellowship of believers whose livelihood was derived from the sea. As fishing families they faced the vulnerability of depleting cod stocks, competition from the large trawlers called "seiners" that sucked fish off the ocean floor, aquaculture that bred fish but often pushed the "schools" to deeper waters, and the slow demise of community life as their children left the fish behind in search of a more prosperous living in the inland towns and cities.

But Coastal Community Church had a very important resource for women who suffered from present or past abuse: a support group of women victims and survivors who met together regularly for support and encouragement. The group's beginning was humble enough. "Six or seven women approached me after I had given an afternoon workshop at the church," said the organizer, a university-educated woman in her late thirties. "They were all victims of abusive homes, and they wished there was a Christian support group to help them in their efforts to deal with the past."

While she admitted to being overwhelmed by victims' requests to begin a support group on their behalf, Marianne, the organizer, was firm in her conviction of the need and her responsibility to do something about it. Several months later, having recruited two other women (a pastor's wife and a nurse) to help her facilitate the support group, the first meeting of Coastal Community Support Group was launched, with three facilitators and six women survivors. The ages and the backgrounds of the group members varied, as did their ways of coping with the abuse and its long-term implications on their lives. All the women were active in their churches and saw their faith as an important part of their own healing.

The initial commitment of group members and facilitators was for a twelve-week period, meeting weekly for an hour and a half. "As we shared some of the pain, shame, guilt, and anguish, an incredible bond began to form," reflected Marianne. "The bond that has developed . . . is literally unlike any other relationship I have ever experienced; it is precious and priceless." Central to the group's success was the assurance of absolute confidentiality and unconditional love and acceptance. "We have laughed, cried, prayed, confronted, teased, complained, rejoiced—most of all, we have been learning to love and to trust," she said confidently.

To be sure, the journey toward healing and recovery is very long and fraught with obstacles. Dealing with so much pain pushes both victims and facilitators to the boundaries of their emotional and spiritual resources. It blurs the roles of facilitator and group member. Many times the level of emotional suffering increases for victims as they start to share their pain. All group members begin to feel both a sense of personal vulnerability and the weight of another sister's anguish and abuse.

Compassion and care is not for the fainthearted. Yet, the story of Coastal Community Support Group reveals that where women listen to the needs of other women in their midst, great things can be accomplished. It is a story in which victims have the courage to give voice to their needs and where other Christian women respond out of love, giving of their time and emotional strength to bear another's burdens.

7

From the Steeple
to the Shelter

Challenges to Sacred and Secular Cooperation

The Path out of
Gethsemane's Garden

It seemed fitting to begin a book on violence and Christianity by reflecting on the pain and hope offered by the familiar story of Jesus in the Garden of Gethsemane. As I argued in the Preface, scenes from the Garden of Gethsemane—Jesus' anguish, the fervent prayer, disciples who were fast asleep, the kiss of death, the arrest—offer a moving portrayal of the partnership between God and human suffering. The story reminds believers, but especially women and children, of human vulnerability and the pain of betrayal and abandonment. But Gethsemane also represents hope, renewal, and strength to face the challenges that lie ahead and to draw on our spiritual and personal reservoirs in times of crisis.

To respond pastorally to a victim of violence is to support that individual in her quest to find strength to leave the garden and begin the journey toward human wholeness. The Gethsemane experience offers hope while never diminishing the reality of the suffering. These very motifs of pain and hope—core constructs within the Christian message—are the essential foundation on which faith communities can build their credibility to respond to the suffering created by violence. The story of the Garden of Gethsemane reminds us that there are resources both within and beyond the human person that can transform vulnerability to strength, fear to calm, victim to survivor.

The path out of Gethsemane's Garden involves a myriad of relationships as suffering is transformed into human agency and empowerment. For members of faith communities, that personal struggle has both temporal and spiritual overtones. As a result, cooperation and collaboration between the secular and the sacred in responding to the needs presented by victims is of utmost importance. Ultimately, the fight to reduce and indeed eradicate violence in human relationships necessitates a coordinated effort between all the major institutions within contemporary society. At present, not all secular and sacred caregivers feel it is possible to work together toward empowering victims and eliminating violence.

Throughout this chapter we will explore that reluctance in some detail. But our primary task will be to consider the potential of partnerships and the collaborative challenge to achieve them. Discovering common elements in the response of churches and secular agencies to victims of abuse is an important first step. Coordinated efforts, though, are built on an understanding of the unique contributions of different service providers. Ultimately, trust and respect are the piers on which bridges are built between the secular and the sacred.

The Importance of Partnerships

Despite increasing secularization in modern society, there are several compelling reasons why secular agencies ought to include faith communities in the fight to end violence against women and other forms of family violence. The first factor relates to the level of identification with a faith tradition. The majority of North Americans still identify with a faith tradition, even though they may have long since stopped attending church or synagogue. The 1991 Statistics Canada census data revealed that only 12% of Canadians report "none" when asked about their religious group identification. In his 1987 book, aptly titled *Fragmented Gods,* Reginald Bibby concludes that while commitment to specific faith traditions has changed, most Canadians—young and old alike—are continuing to claim allegiance to the religion of their parents. Similarly, Wade Clark Roof in *A Generation of Seekers*[1] argues that while American baby boomers do not share the commitment to organized religion that their parents did, their spiritual quest remains important to them.[2] Thus, ties of allegiance remain even as participation rates have dropped. At times of birth, marriage, and death, as well as other periods of life crises, large numbers of Canadians and Americans seek help and solace from their religious community, however nominally they participate within it.

While it is important to recognize that participation in specific religious traditions has undergone a tremendous change within the last fifty years, nonetheless, one in every five Canadians and one in every three Americans reported in 1993 that they attended their church or synagogue the previous week.[3] Moreover, the number jumps dramatically when one considers sporadic attendance or participation in specific celebrations like Christmas, Easter, or other festivals. With all the attention given to the secularization of modern society, it is easy to overlook the fact that religious institutions still serve a large percentage of the population and do so on a continuing, regular basis. Furthermore, those groups that tend to value separateness from the secular world are the same faith traditions for which attendance is most consistent among members. In Canada, almost one in two members from conservative Protestant churches attends church on a weekly basis.[4] And in the United States, we find the same pattern between church attendance and Christian fundamentalism.[5]

A second factor relates to the importance of the family within faith traditions. Believers feel a sense of belonging to their religious community. In part, it connects them to a tradition and a shared story through which they interpret the social and material world as well as their own daily reality. Tied closely to one's cultural or physical "roots" is the concept of family, those individuals who shape and nurture the sense of self and the context through which one experiences life. Most faith traditions depend on adults to pass on religious instruction and devotion to their children and thus keep the faith perspective alive. Therefore, it is not surprising that many spiritual communities are organized around the family life cycle: birth, "coming of age," marriage, death, and so on. While men typically perform the public functions, it is the lives of faithful women that ensure that the tradition lives on in the minds and hearts of their children.[6]

A third reason why secular agencies for women who have been battered ought to be concerned about establishing links with churches relates to the vulnerability of abused women in faith communities. Past research has shown that religion and religious participation are linked to specific attitudes about women,[7] gender roles,[8] and family life.[9] Women espousing a conservative religious tradition may be especially vulnerable when they have been abused.[10] While there is a growing body of religious literature condemning power abuse in a familial context,[11] there are two particular tenets within some faith traditions that may contribute to women's remaining in abusive situations: (1) the importance and desirability of remaining separate from the world; and (2) the doctrine of submission and attendant beliefs about appropriate gender roles.[12]

Studies have shown that abused women often feel isolated and alone.[13] The tendency of many conservative churches to endorse separation from the world means that these churchwomen may be even more liable to feelings of isolation and loneliness.[14] Moreover, their knowledge about the availability of secular resources such as the police, transition houses, and social workers may be very limited. Therefore, many churchwomen who are abused by their husbands will turn to church resources to deal with that abuse.[15]

Finally, partnership with churches involves tapping into the potential resources of these faith communities. Churches have four major strengths useful to secular agencies in attempting to stop violence in the family context: physical space; community-based mission; infrastructural support; and volunteers. Not only do many churches have a sanctuary that will seat hundreds of people, they have classrooms, multipurpose rooms, kitchen facilities, nurseries, gymnasiums, and so on. And in most faith communities, their physical space is not utilized to its maximum potential, except perhaps on their day of worship, Saturday or Sunday. On the other hand, many agencies that work with and for battered women struggle with inadequate space. Although many churches would not be in a position to provide temporary or permanent accommodation to abused women, they may be able to offer meeting rooms, venues for community workshops, and day-care facilities. Central to the gospel message are the notions of mission and evangelism, however those concepts are defined. Thus, a community-based mission is a second reason why secular agencies might look to religious organizations for help. For those churches directly espousing a philosophy of service to their local communities, responding to the needs of abused women and their children allows them an opportunity to implement such service goals.

A third advantage churches may provide to secular agencies revolves around the rather vast infrastructural support many churches have at their disposal. In a vein similar to educational institutions, churches provide regular opportunities for religious instruction to both children and adults. Moreover, religious professionals—like educators—also have clearly defined avenues for information gathering and dissemination that can be used as vehicles for in-service training. The power and potential of the Sunday sermon should not be underestimated. Moreover, many churches have developed home fellowship or cell ministries, whereby small groups of people assemble for study, fellowship, and support.[16]

Finally, churches have an army of volunteers, committed lay people who assemble regularly and are desirous of impacting their social world. With a generalized culture of volunteerism inherent in most religious traditions, cooperation can be sought and obtained in a rather straightforward manner. A recent study in Atlantic Canada found that the average evangelical woman held four volunteers jobs in her church.[17]

Reflecting on the religious call to service and the simultaneous call to piety, Richard Clark Kroeger and Catherine Clark Kroeger argue that Christian women have been commanded to pour out God's love to others and thereby respond to their spiritual, emotional, physical, and social needs.[18] The relationship between Christian mission and the culture of volunteerism is thus mutually reinforcing.[19]

With service as a hallmark of the churches' commitment to God, the secular world needs to rethink the potential of partnerships between churches and community agencies. Moreover, fiscal restraint and government downsizing make cooperation appear even more desirable. From the point of view of churches, the contemporary public obsession with reducing the deficit and government financial accountability may open doors for collaborative efforts that have been closed in the past.

The Road to Partnership

As the remainder of this chapter will examine, there are both signs of church sensitivity to the suffering of abuse victims and specific obstacles to be overcome if sacred and secular caregivers are to work together. Motifs of pain and hope characterize the analysis of how contemporary Christianity is responding to abuse within its own boundaries and within the larger society. While the potential for partnership is immense, the road to achieving it will be long and arduous. Building bridges between the sacred and the secular world must involve a clear recognition of the unique contribution, skills, and understanding that people from various professional and faith traditions bring to the problem of abuse. Bridge building does not necessarily involve accepting wholeheartedly, or endorsing, a particular perspective, but it does depend on recognizing its value and contribution under certain conditions or within specific contexts. Ultimately, it is based on trust and respect.

Signs of Church Sensitivity to the Suffering of Abuse Victims

Throughout the last three chapters we have been exploring how churches and their leaders respond to the needs of abused women, abusive men, and couples in conflict. We have considered in some detail the level and nature of the experience of clergy in counseling both victims and perpetrators of abuse. In chapter 6, we focused on women's ministries within the local church setting and examined the response of these organizations to the suffering of other women. Based on the data we have discussed more fully in earlier chapters, I would suggest that there are five major areas that reveal sensitivity within faith communities toward issues of violence against women and other forms of family violence.

"Women-Helping-Women": The Informal Support Network

The most dramatic demonstration of the sensitivity of faith communities to the needs of battered women and their children lies within the confines of a woman-only network of informal social support. Through our focus group research, we have learned that two in every three evangelical women report that they have sought the advice of another woman in their own church for a family-related problem, and likewise two in three women claimed to have sought the assistance of a Christian woman in a church other than the one they now attend. Clearly religious women seek out other women of faith when they have family-related problems and need help or advice.[20] These data reveal that evangelical women consider each other a source of social support and have experience receiving help "one from another" under the umbrella of their faith perspective.[21]

Women from conservative faith traditions appear uncomfortable seeking out secular service providers for help or advice.[22] However, disclosing personal traumas and family crises with other women who share your particular worldview empowers both "caregiver" and the "care receiver."[23] Ultimately, this reinforces the prevalent model of women only ministries operating in many conservative church settings. In part, it is the persistence of the single-sex ministry model that has created both the rationale and the "space" for women to offer support to one another at their point of need.[24] Empowerment between religious women of like faith, then, responds to individual women's needs even while it reinforces the religious ideology of the faith community. While conservative churchwomen may not be more vulnerable to abuse than other women,[25] their options appear more restricted once they have experienced their husband's battery.[26] The support they find within the faith community of women becomes an important ingredient in helping them to explore options and alternative courses of action as they work through their personal pain in their journey to human wholeness.

In this context, then, empowerment for churchwomen involves both religious and gender overtones. Sharing a specific outlook on the world enables religious women to disclose spiritual as well as emotional and physical pain and despair. It enables a level of personal intimacy not possible outside the faith perspective. Moreover, it makes possible the opportunity to question even the spiritual journey itself, something that may be perceived as inappropriate, or at least inadvisable, with a secular woman. While religious women do consult their pastors on family-related matters, the assistance they receive from one another occurs with greater frequency and intensity, enabling a longer-term impact.

Given their level of personal experience in *receiving* help from one another, it is not surprising that the majority of evangelical women report offering support to another woman at her point of need. What may be surprising, though, is the number who have assisted an abused woman. Fully 58 percent of the almost 250 women who participated in our focus group research claimed to have offered support to a woman who was abused by her husband. As we discussed in chapter 6, while most women referred to their role as *a listening ear,* many had provided overnight accommodations, looked after children, given financial help, provided transportation, or accompanied the woman to particularly difficult places, like a court appearance. Contrary to popular notions denigrating or denying the help religious women can and do offer one another, our data reveal that evangelical women practice a kind of support that does not demand that a victimized woman cut all ties with her abusive partner for the remainder of her life, nor does it insist that she remain indefinitely in a home that threatens her safety and mental health.[27] Through in-depth interviews with a selection of ninety-four women who participated in our focus group research, it was revealed that religious women who themselves are abused exercise a level of personal agency as they assess alternative courses of action for responding to their own victimization.[28]

Some of our earlier research on evangelical women in Atlantic Canada revealed that both evangelical and Roman Catholic women had grown impatient with their churches and ordained leaders on the issue of addressing the severity of violence in the family context.[29] For the most part, religious women—especially those from the more conservative faith traditions—used their personal life and day-by-day experiences to filter and interpret the religious teaching on the family they heard from clergy.[30] And amid the religious discourse, they were clearly appropriating selected feminist principles, at least in their understanding of the causes and consequences of wife abuse.[31] While religious women who suffer abuse stay married longer and go to greater lengths to save their marital relationship,[32] support from women of like faith is an integral resource when the battered churchwoman comes to a decision to leave her abusive marriage, temporarily or forever.

Churchwomen's Response to the Transition House Movement

One of the initial indicators of the link between churchwomen's groups and transition houses was raised during our telephone interviews with transition house workers. Somewhat to our surprise, we heard them tell us stories about how churchwomen's groups in local communities would raise funds for the transition house or offer to the women residents donated goods or services. The diversity of their provisions was in some ways as noteworthy as the consistency of the support. Sometimes a churchwomen's group would host a "shower" and donate the gifts to the transition house; sometimes churchwomen would recruit others within the church to help them decorate and furnish a room at the transition house; other women's groups would prepare "comfort kits" for women residents, composed of a variety of toiletry items; others hosted special fund-raisers (such as an Easter pancake breakfast) and donated the proceeds to the local transition house. While their monetary donations were always rather small in relation to the budget of the transition house, most women's groups in churches collect very little money over the course of a year, and what I think is noteworthy is that from the meager amounts they raise, the transition house was a regular benefactor.[33] Interestingly, but not particularly surprising, clergy we interviewed appeared totally unaware of the contact between churchwomen's groups (even where they pastored) and the transition house movement. For whatever reason—and on that it is tempting to speculate—churchwomen's groups and the women who led them were never very vocal with their ordained male leaders about the contact with and support for transition houses. It may be partly the understated way that women *do* ministry—these acts of kindness are simply the way women live their Christian lives. Nevertheless, some women leaders would have perceived a lack of support from clergy for their contact with transition houses and the secular workers there. While churchwomen's groups are fairly autonomous in terms of both programming and finances in the local church setting, through their annual reports or informal meetings with the clergy one might have expected that their support of the community transition house would have been mentioned. Apparently that was not the case.

In their relationships with the transition house movement, churchwomen as a group put aside some of their ideological reservations about feminist activism,[34] creating more flexible boundaries for cooperation and the provision of material and ideological support. As a group, churchwomen are extremely supportive of the work of transition houses, preferring to call it a "ministry."[35] Within their religious framework, helping another woman in need can be understood much more clearly as Christian service than as feminist action. Perhaps more fully than other church organizations, women-only groups know firsthand the limitations of clergy-only counsel and therefore are eager to supplement sacred support for women suffering as battered wives. As women, they understand the fear and vulnerability women so often feel at the hands of unrestrained male aggression. And no doubt they interpret the transition house movement and the feminists who lobby on its behalf as responsible for naming that fear and placing it in the public realm. Yet as members of a conservative faith community, they uphold the sanctity of the family unit, the undesirability of divorce, and a belief in God-ordained gender roles within the family constellation.[36] As such, they appropriate both secular and sacred wisdom into their understanding of abuse against women.

In many ways, churchwomen interpret the Christian call to compassion as their signal to support one another.[37] While the relationship between faith and social action is not new for women motivated by religious zeal,[38] it has been reshaped by certain contemporary cultural forces. As cultural sociologist Ann Swidler has argued, periods of social transformation are the breeding ground for culture's influence on social action.[39] In essence, political (e.g., feminist) and religious ideologies sometimes interface in a way that results in strategies for social action. I would argue that churchwomen's support for the transition house movement is one such example.

While the clearest sign of church sensitivity to the suffering of abuse victims is the large proportion of women who have offered personal support to an abused woman and her children, the ongoing contact between transition houses and churchwomen's groups offers evidence of collective action and an enormous potential for growth and development.

Clerical Experience in Counseling Victims of Abuse

Our research data collected from over three hundred clergy reveals that the majority of ministers report limited, but ongoing, pastoral experience in counseling abused women, abusive men, and couples in conflict. A minority of pastors—around one in every ten—have substantial experience responding to the many needs introduced by parishioners' experience of family violence. As we noted in chapter 4, the four situations ministers are most frequently faced with include: (1) a woman with an abusive husband or partner; (2) a woman who was abused in childhood by a parent; (3) a man who is abusive toward his wife or partner; and (4) a couple for whom violence is common in their relationship. While pastoral counseling experiences are highly clustered, almost all ordained clergy are called on to respond to the needs of women with abusive partners, with a majority doing so with some regularity (at least twice a year).

Throughout chapter 5, we examined what happens when an abused woman seeks pastoral counsel. Contrary to what some sources have suggested,[40] but for which there was little empirical data,[41] clergy do not tell battered women simply to return home to an unchanged abusive environment, or to suffer in silence. Rather, clergy cling to excessive optimism that (1) abusive men want to stop their violence; (2) abusive men can stop their violence with help; and (3) violent relationships can be transformed into healthy family living.[42] Yet, the fact that clergy report ongoing pastoral experience responding to the needs of abusers is noteworthy, for the reason that services for violent men are relatively rare and poorly funded.[43] As a result, clergy may be one of the very few community-based services for men who batter.[44]

While clergy are reluctant to see even a violent marriage terminated permanently and divorce proceedings begun, they are not unwilling to support—and many even encourage—an abused woman's temporary separation from her husband and the abusive man's seeking counsel. In the eventuality that the abuser is unwilling to get help, or his abusive behavior has not changed as a result of therapy, clergy advise permanent separation or divorce. In essence, it appears to be the deliberateness with which this course of action is advised that most differentiates clerical advice from secular counsel.[45]

Recognition of Training Needs

Only 26 out of 332 (8%) pastors in our survey study reported that they feel *well equipped* to respond to situations involving family violence, while 124 (37%) claimed that they are poorly equipped, with others falling between these two extremes.[46] Moreover, an overwhelming theme in both the clergy survey project and our interview study with ministers was the desire on the part of most pastors to receive further training in the area of counseling, and specifically in responding to victims of abuse. As we saw in chapter 5, while clergy themselves are cognizant of their own limitations in responding pastorally to victims of violence, they also are subjected to the growing demands for counseling services within their pastoral charge. The result is that the average ordained minister is called on regularly to provide counseling for which he or she is ill equipped in terms of both prior preparation and knowledge of other community resources.

The response by denominational executives to the training needs of clergy in the area of counseling abuse victims has been slow to emerge. Yet, recent years have witnessed the development of several in-service training programs,[47] clergy workbooks and manuals,[48] and denomination-specific pastoral training handbooks.[49] Some denominations have passed resolutions condemning violence between husbands and wives, while others have attempted to think creatively about resolving both the level and persistence of violence in households of faith. Although efforts such as these are important first steps, they clearly are inadequate *if* they represent the only response of a denomination to the suffering created by violence in the family context. But they send an important signal to clergy and lay people alike, and for that reason alone I believe they are extremely important and to be encouraged.

At the same time, the information clergy most desperately need is the knowledge of what resources are available in their local region,[50] an understanding of the mandatory reporting laws as they relate to child physical and sexual abuse,[51] and an appreciation of the depth of pain and despair that victims face.[52] Also, clergy need to appreciate the lay ministry of women in responding to the needs of other women in the church family. Moreover, they need help to identify what it is specifically that the *pastoral counselor* has to offer abuse victims.[53] And once these areas have been identified, the challenge is to network with other community agencies and professionals to provide a coordinated team approach.[54] But in order for a team approach to be effective, the different agencies and professionals working together must establish a level of trust and respect, an appreciation for the contribution each brings, and a willingness to relinquish control. Needless to say, team building is a complicated, time-consuming process. But, the experience of those who have worked together in the interests of children report that, in the final analysis, the coordinated approach saves time and money (through less duplication of services) and enhances the therapeutic process for the victim.[55]

Signs of Sensitivity: A Summary

Several signs of church sensitivity to the suffering of abuse victims have been identified. One of the most positive and progressive examples of support grows out of the unique experiences of women-only ministries within local churches, where women support each other out of a shared vision of "need" and "responsibility."[56] Having been the recipients of another woman's *listening ear,* many women of faith believe they have a mandate to help and care for one another. In fact, service to others is one of the hallmarks of a woman's faith journey. The strong link between women's informal networks of support and the single-sex ministries of local parishes in large measure circumvents the mainly patriarchal structure of modern churches. It provides "space" and "mission" for women to do what they claim they are most comfortable doing: providing nurturance and care for one another, much as mothers do for their children.[57]

As Winter, Lummis, and Stokes argue, many religious women are simply "defecting in place," connected to their faith community through their relationships with other women.[58] While these women understand their growing feminist consciousness to be in tension with the patriarchal structure of their faith tradition, they opt to either work for reform from within or to continue to celebrate their uniqueness as women of spirit under the umbrella of a local church or synagogue setting.[59]

Even amid the dominant discourse on gender and conservative Christianity there has been a small but growing literature that seeks to reconcile the ideological tenets of Christianity and secular feminism.[60] Known as Christian feminism, those writing within this paradigm merge the ideological presuppositions of feminism with mainstream Christian teaching. The organization Christians for Biblical Equality, begun by evangelical feminists, promotes in its mission statement the equality of men and women in church, home, and society. Yet, as sociologist James Davidson Hunter has cautioned, we should not overestimate the impact of Christian feminism on evangelical thought about gender.[61] These cautions notwithstanding, in small measure groups like Christians for Biblical Equality temper the teaching of the Christian family literature for those women and men who wish to ensure that their allegiance to evangelicalism remains strong, even while they cope with changing personal life circumstances and social realities.[62]

To be sure, there are other signs of sensitivity, not least of which involves the ordained clergy. Here, we find that a sizable minority of clergy are engaged in regular and ongoing support to abused women and couples in crisis. But the level of abuse prevalent in North America—and in our churches—far exceeds clerical response to it. Ill-equipped for the task, and overburdened by other demands, many clergy are simply unable to respond to all the requests that come their way; some are never asked; and, sadly, some cannot *hear* the cries for help.

The Collaborative Challenge

However encouraging these signs of sensitivity within faith communities to the suffering of victims may be, there are some real challenges to be faced on the road to partnership between the sacred and the secular in the fight to end violence against women in the family setting. Based on the series of studies reported in the preceding chapters, I would like to highlight five major obstacles that currently reduce or mitigate against the possibility of collaborative ventures between clergy and other workers in responding to the needs of abused women and their children.

Naming the Violence

First, and in many ways foremost, is the problem of finding the right words to name the problem of abuse.[63] Supporters of the transition house movement identify cases of husbands' and boyfriends' inflicting harm on their partners as wife abuse, and in so doing they *name* the problem as male violence against women. Transition house workers and the feminists who lobby on their behalf do not consider the abuse of wives to be a family issue.[64] Rather, they conceptualize women's victimization by the men who purport to love them as an example of unrestrained male aggression, a specific illustration of the pervasive power imbalance between men and women within a patriarchal culture.[65] According to this paradigm, violent men need to be restrained and women and child victims need support and safety. Action-oriented and woman-centered, transition houses seek to transpose women's fear into strategies for social change.[66] Central to this mandate is the need to ensure that violence perpetrated within the *personal,* domestic sphere, is redefined into the *public* domain as unrestrained male power. As support for the transition house movement has gained strength at the community level, there are fears that its political message has been in some ways sacrificed.[67] The transition house movement seeks to provide more than simply a Band-Aid approach to the pain and fear of individual women. At the theoretical level, at least, it offers a critique of contemporary society and the relationships of men and women within it.[68] Needless to say, it is here that churches and transition houses experience their most severe conflict.[69]

While the feminist movement sees wife abuse as a vivid demonstration of the power inequities between men and women within contemporary society, conservative Protestant ideology regards violence in marriage as a function of misconceptions about God's design for marital harmony. Consistent with this approach, then, clergy *name the problem* as family violence. As a result, the aggression and the issue are firmly placed within the family unit, to be resolved at that level.[70] Upholding the sanctity of the family unit and the sacredness of the marital vows, clergy are reluctant to lay responsibility for abuse solely with the abusive man, preferring, especially in cases involving less physical forms of aggression, to see both partners as contributing to marital disharmony. Since the problem is named in a way that eludes, or at least minimizes, blame, the solution clearly rests inside the family unit, within the husband-wife dyad. When clergy, then, talk about situations involving abusive men and abused women they call it *family violence.*

Clearly and unequivocally, there is a translation problem here. Transition house workers, or other secular professionals, and clergy do not have a common language with which they can talk about violent behavior in the family context. Not surprisingly, there is a fair degree of emotion associated with the words one uses to describe these aggressive acts. On the one hand, feminists are very sensitive to any reconceptualization of wife abuse that ignores or obscures the identity of the male perpetrator.[71] Within this framework, abuse is not a private matter between one man and one woman, it is a public display of gender inequity. On the other hand, conservative faith traditions, and the clergy who are ordained within them, are uncomfortable with any notion that would downplay the centrality of the family unit. While religious feminists have challenged many aspects of contemporary Christianity,[72] they have tended to leave the notion of family intact (though they have broadened its definition). Consistently throughout our fieldwork, clergy *reframed* questions about wife abuse into responses that considered the issue to be family violence.[73]

Naming the problem of violence between men and women within the family context has clear implications for how it is solved and the potential steps toward its resolution. It is no wonder that the words and the labels strike such an emotional chord.

The Role of Reconciliation

A second major obstacle to partnership between the secular and the sacred in responding to wife abuse concerns the role of reconciliation, or more specifically, whether reconciliation should be a main goal of intervention.[74] As we have noted in chapters 4 and 5, the majority of clergy in our research see reconciliation as both desirable and attainable. This is not to suggest that they ignore or downplay the fear or reality of violence when it has been directly presented to them. They simply believe that change can occur, and given their theological worldview this should not be surprising. Reconciliation is at the heart of the gospel message; the notion of personal salvation is the believer's response to the message, and transformation the work of grace. It would be surprising indeed if theologically conservative clergy were less than fully optimistic about the possibility of conversion in the life of an abusive man. As we saw in chapter 4, the response of conservative Protestant clergy to wife abuse is steeped in notions about the relationship between God and the individual. The abuser's behavior is conceptualized as sin, while guilt and fear are believed to impact on the victim's spiritual journey. Since the nuclear family is idolized in traditional religious communities, abuse is interpreted as spiritual confusion over God's plan for family life. Chapter 2 has highlighted the role and impact of the multimillion-dollar Christian family industry, including the selling of books, tapes, and videos for both adults and children.

When the abusive husband claims to have previously experienced spiritual renewal through personal salvation, clergy appear to be faced with three options: (1) they disbelieve his conversion claim; (2) they opt for the view that Christianity does not erase all traces of humanness; or (3) they become pessimistic that change is possible. Since clergy report far more experience dealing with cases where the woman is connected to the faith community and the husband is either nominally attached or hostile to her faith, pastors have much more limited experience in responding to extreme violence where *both* partners are actively involved in the church.[75]

Despite evidence in their pastoral practice to the contrary, clergy appear to endorse reconciliation as one of the main goals of intervention in the life of an abusive man and an abused woman. For counselors who work at a transition house, there is great reluctance to believe that abusive men desire to change their behavior, or could change it even if they so desired. The reality of revictimized women returning to the transition house in search of safety tempers any optimism with regard to reforming relationships that are abusive. Transition house workers have experienced too many examples of women who return home only to find an unchanged partner and an environment that continues to be violent.

Still, clergy are called on to minister to the needs of both men and women, aggressor and victimized. As a result, abusive men cannot and should not be ignored by clergy: their stories and history of victimization are relevant too. One of the unique opportunities available to spiritual counselors is to bring the message of God's love and forgiveness to an abusive man who wants to turn from his violent ways.

Low Rate of Referrals

In part a reflection of their predisposition to spiritualize wife abuse in cases involving church or Christian families, the data we have presented in chapters 4 and 5 lead us to conclude that many evangelical ministers are reluctant to refer victims of abuse to secular professionals or the agencies that employ them. Their reluctance stems from a rather deep-seated fear that counselors who do not share their theological worldview will be quick to suggest that an abused woman leave her husband and her faith community forever and begin a new life free from both of these restraining forces. Through our interviews with transition house workers we have learned that many secular counselors fear that an abused woman who turns to her church for help will both receive regressive advice and remain indefinitely in a marital union where her physical and mental health cannot be assured. In a sense, then, the reason for the low rate of referrals is bidirectional: while clergy want assurance that secular counselors will not automatically suggest that a woman of faith abandon her religious community in her search for healing, transition house counselors and other professionals want to be assured that religious caregivers do not neglect a woman's physical and emotional safety as they minister to her spiritual needs.[76] As we shall argue at a later point in this chapter, if clergy had a stronger sense of both their unique role as *pastoral* counselors and the presenting needs of abuse victims and perpetrators, such an impasse would be much less likely to occur. Moreover, if secular counselors were more knowledgeable about the services the church and clergy provide in response to the suffering of abuse, they would be far less likely to see incompatibility between the secular and the sacred. At that point, secular and sacred care could be regarded as supplementing each other rather than competing with each other. And should that occur, workers from each perspective could begin to collaborate and cooperate.

To be fair, professional workers who assist battered women may not appreciate how central a woman's beliefs and religious practices may be in the healing process.[77] Furthermore, they may not realize the support a faith community could offer an abused woman and her children.[78] Ultimately, they probably lack the knowledge and skills that would enable them to appropriate a woman's specific faith perspective to condemn the violence she has suffered.[79]

At one level, a low rate of referrals between the secular and sacred caregiving worlds can simply be understood as guarding one's own professional turf.[80] And this is understandable. Clergy find themselves operating in an institution that is losing members, money, and influence.[81] It is only natural that they would want to *protect* the boundaries separating the religious and the secular worlds.[82] Religious boundaries, however, are vanishing and the lines of separation are far less clear than they once were.[83] From the clerical perspective, I would argue that a low rate of referrals has far more to do with an emotional reaction to the integrity, motives, and advice of secular caregivers than guarding their professional jurisdiction. Clergy fear that women victims will be told to leave their faith behind as they embark on the journey to healing and wholeness. By their own accounts, ministers are overburdened and overwhelmed by the emotional and time demands of pastoral counseling. Lacking in counseling training, coupled with their relative unawareness of community resources, many clergy do not see the *need* to refer, and when they do, they lack a referral network. There is little evidence from our data— either from clergy accounts or from women's experience of receiving clerical help—that in the present context there is a desire to see abused women suffer in silence or perfect their salvation through personal pain. While that may have characterized the past,[84] what is more likely now is that clergy do not understand the depth of a woman's despair or simply cannot hear her cries for help. For many women, disclosing the abuse they have suffered is a painful and shameful process. Consequently, when they seek professional help, the abuse is masked by some other initial presenting problem. Thus it takes a skilled counselor to both recognize the signs of abuse and help a woman to disclose the violence she has endured.

Clerical fear of secular counselors centers around several issues believed to be at the heart of the secular response to abused women: a reluctance to believe that an abusive relationship can be transformed into a nonabusive relationship; an unwillingness to include the abusive man in the therapeutic process; the denial of spiritual healing and forgiveness; the transience of marital relationships; and the place of divorce in responding to marital conflict.[85]

Secular counselors, like the transition house workers in our research, tend to believe that clergy offer exclusively spiritual counsel to abuse victims, including the admonition to "pray" about the abuse and to return to their unchanged home with a mandate to "become a better wife and mother." They criticize clergy for the speed with which they offer forgiveness to the abuser and encourage the victim to do likewise. Moreover, there is a belief among transition house workers that clergy have an absolute standard against divorce. Other researchers have argued that secular counselors are more skeptical about the therapeutic role of forgiveness and display little adverse reaction to marital breakup and divorce.[86] In a sense, both secular and sacred caregivers are guilty of overdramatizing their differences and minimizing their areas of overlap.[87]

Despite what might appear to be rather irreconcilable differences, there is evidence that some clergy do refer victims and perpetrators of abuse to secular counselors for help. Chapter 4 revealed that clergy who reported more referral experience also reported greater counseling experience with victims, a working relationship with secular service providers (including a visit to the local transition house), larger church attendance figures, and enhanced formal training in pastoral counseling. Pastors with more experience counseling abused women and abusive men are those who are actively seeking out referral sources, visiting transition houses, talking with secular professionals, and reporting suspected cases of child abuse according to mandatory reporting laws. Where referrals are perhaps needed most—among those clergy with very limited counseling experience—they are least likely to occur. And, as we saw in chapter 5, there are a minority of ministers who have a rather fully developed referral network. In those cases, there was little evidence to suggest that the impetus for networking came from the secular world: rather, it was the more experienced pastor counselors who took it on themselves to initiate contact with community agencies and professionals and to begin making referrals and following them up.

Reluctance to Condemn Violence from the Pulpit

While 31 percent of clergy claim to have preached specific messages on wife abuse and/or child abuse and 40 percent indicate that they have discussed the problem of family violence in all of their premarital counseling, very few women parishioners seem able to recall any such sermons.[88] One of the consistent themes running through our focus group interviews with almost 250 churchwomen was the call for faith communities simply to recognize and denounce violence against women in the family setting, and then to begin to take practical steps toward responding to the victims. As a group, churchwomen are impatient with the silence of their clerical leaders on this important issue.

From the perspective of the preacher, the reluctance to condemn violence should not surprise us. Pastors find themselves preaching to dwindling numbers of men,[89] and there is strong pressure from international religious leaders not to scare the men away.[90] In fact, the Promise Keepers Movement was begun in 1991 with exactly that purpose in mind: to reach men with the evangelical gospel message and to bring these men into greater commitment ties to their local church, its (male) pastor, other men of like faith, and their families.[91] It may be possible that within such a movement, which focuses heavily on peer mentoring, men will challenge each other to live abuse-free lives. On the other hand, given their equally dominant sports motif, it is also possible that men's aggression will simply be ignored or valorized. Sociologists of religion have recognized for a long time the delicate balance between comfort and challenge in the admonitions given to religious followers.[92]

However silent Sunday sermons may appear to be on abuse in the family context, some clergy perceive that they are preaching against violence when their sermon is on the stoning of Stephen or Jesus' condemnation of the Pharisees when the adulterous woman was brought to him.[93] Despite this, the failure of clerical leaders to be direct in their condemnation of violence against women has been understood by some as support for it.[94]

It is also important to recognize that ministers sometimes find themselves in the uncomfortable situation of pastoring both "victim" and "perpetrator."[95] Whether it is possible or therapeutic for one counselor to provide independent support for both the abused woman and the abusive man is a contentious issue and one that we cannot resolve here.[96] Suffice it to note, however, that many experienced pastoral counselors opt to refer one of the parties to another service provider out of a desire to enhance the possibility of healing and restoration. Nevertheless, when it comes to the Sunday sermon, many clergy wish to avoid controversy. If pastors understood how important their condemnation of wife abuse from the pulpit could be in the healing process of a battered woman, or in the decision of a victim to disclose abuse, or for a perpetrator to seek help, they might be led to reconsider their silence.

Clergy Understanding of Abuse
in Christian Families

Without exception, evangelical clergy understand abuse within families of faith to be a spiritual issue and the abusive behavior on the part of the man a sign of spiritual immaturity and struggle with sin.[97] As we saw in chapter 4, some pastors claimed that an abusive Christian man was an oxymoron—either he was not really abusive or he was not really Christian. This tautological position is understandable: the Christian faith purports to offer believers a renewed heart and a changed life. Abuse within the Christian family context provides a disquieting reality check on the rhetoric of "happy family living."

As we discussed in chapter 4, the overwhelming majority of pastors in our studies believe that violence in families of faith stems from unresolved spiritual issues. As a group, clergy are reluctant to point to non-spiritual factors to account for why some men of faith batter their wives. Nevertheless, these same ministers are willing to employ social scientific explanations to account for abuse within families outside of their faith perspective. In essence, their vision is bifurcated: social science data can be appropriated to explain violent acts in families living in the neighborhood surrounding the church, but among families of faith aggressive acts are rooted in a spiritual warfare between the forces of good and evil.

This bifurcated vision easily leads to the conclusion that since the origin of violence derives from the spiritual realm, so too must its cure. As a result, their interpretation of violence in Christian families reinforces pastors' reluctance to refer parishioners to secular agencies for help. Moreover, in chapter 6, we saw that churchwomen too interpret the nature, causes, and level of violence in families of faith as differing from couples outside the community of believers. Though the pattern was not as marked for churchwomen as it was for clergy, there were, nevertheless, strong traces of it. As a result, women themselves are drawn to seek out help from their faith community when crises enters their lives. They too are reluctant to step outside their church network or religious worldview. Given the compounded effect of clergy and lay preference for counsel within the parameters of the faith perspective, it is no small feat to witness even modest patterns of referral from the sacred to the secular.

Discovering Common Ground

It would be presumptuous of me, to say the least, to suggest any one model or method for establishing partnership between the sacred and the secular in the fight to end violence against women and other forms of family violence. To be sure, not all secular service providers are willing to entertain the involvement of religious leaders; and not all clergy want such involvement. And where there is grave reluctance to cooperate or collaborate, the experience is almost doomed to failure from the beginning. Yet, despite that caveat, our data reveal that there is both a willingness and an openness on the part of many workers involved with abused women to work in a multidisciplinary fashion. The struggle to respond to the immense needs presented by abused women and their children—not to mention perpetrators' needs as well—has necessitated some laying aside of ideological and professional loyalties. Most services for abused women operate on "soft money," grants that are allocated on a year-by-year basis, subject to budgetary approval and political will. Fiscal restraints and the persistence of funding cuts to the delivery of social services has meant that even their relatively meager government funding cannot be assured. As a result, many services for battered women are more dependent than ever on voluntary contributions and fund-raising activities. While cooperation between the voluntary sector and various agencies (including the government's) has its ideological challenges, it is perceived by many as a fiscal necessity in the current economic climate. Translated, this means that churches and other community organizations must be able to build bridges toward each other in new and renewed ways.

There are several principles on which such cooperation might be built.

Ensuring the Physical Safety
of the Abused Woman and Her Children

The number-one priority in any response to violence against women must be to ensure the physical and emotional safety of the victimized family members. This is the core premise on which the transition house movement has been built. Women victims (and their dependent children) need a place of refuge where they can flee when the circumstances in their home jeopardize their mental or physical health. Clergy and lay religious alike need to be aware of the danger a violent home presents to a woman victim, and they must strive to provide her with options that would ensure her safety.

The Condemnation of Abusive Acts
on the Part of the Perpetrator

Central to the healing journey for both religious victims[98] and perpetrators[99] is the clear message that within their faith community—and to their ordained leaders—violence is unacceptable as a way to resolve conflict between family members. This same message of no tolerance for violence needs to be offered by secular caregivers as well. But it is important to point out that for religious victims, condemnation of the violence they have endured in *religious* language and within the confines of their faith perspective is a central part of the journey toward healing and wholeness.[100] Thus, it is not enough for a religious woman to hear her social worker condemn the violent acts; the pastor must condemn them too. To be sure, some victims will want little or no contact with their religious community or its leaders in some (or all) of the stages of their own road from victim to survivor; yet, for countless others, spiritual healing is a vital and necessary component of the overall journey, and should be an option for those victims and perpetrators who identify their faith as important.

The Centrality of Healing for the Victim

The impact of violence on an abused woman's life is profound, and the road toward wholeness is long and frought with complications. As a result, the support she will most likely need will include physical, emotional, financial, and spiritual components. Probably it will involve both professional counsel and the friendship and support of others. It will be painful for the woman victim, and at times it will be difficult for those offering her assistance as well. Sometimes a woman victim will exercise agency, tapping inner and external resources, thus leading to greater personal control over her own life and circumstances. Sometimes it will seem that the independence that was nurtured in an abused woman has been all but lost. In essence, the journey is long and painful: it is not a linear progression toward total recovery.

Empowering the Victim
by Offering Alternatives

Not all women victims want to leave their abusive husbands forever, and not all victims want to reconcile with abusive partners, but the desire of every abused wife is to live without the reality or fear of further abuse. Because we cannot (and should not) consider all victims of wife abuse as identical, it is imperative to suggest options and choices that will lead the particular victim to greater control over her life and ensure her safety and self-esteem. As we saw in chapter 3, abused Christian women take different paths toward wholeness: some leave a violent husband temporarily and return to him at a later point, and others leave their violent husband permanently because their abuser will neither seek help nor change his hurtful behavior. And there are many women, too, who remain victims most of their lives, suffering either in silence or without adequate support structures.

Understanding that Many Perpetrators
Are also Victims

While support to perpetrators must never undermine or dislocate the services available to victims, it is important to recognize that many abusive men are living the cycle of violence they experienced as children, and in so doing are teaching the next generation to continue the abuse. Thus, there are several compassionate and compelling reasons why abusers need counseling and ongoing support. For men connected to faith communities, either by their own allegiance or through the involvement of other family members, churches are uniquely positioned to offer some of that help. Moreover, the Promise Keepers Movement has the potential to offer clerical and lay assistance to men struggling to overcome their abusive past and/or abusive present.

Exploring the Common Ground

While the principles just cited are far from exhaustive, they do offer a beginning point for sacred and secular caregivers, and the organizations they represent, to think about cooperation and collaboration. But acknowledging principles without strategies to enact them is shortsighted. Are there some mechanisms or methods that differing agencies can employ to chart their shared focus? How can clergy and other professionals explore their common ground?

Allowing Opportunity for Informal Interaction
Between Sacred and Secular Caregivers

Groups of professional workers who have little contact with each other tend to define the others' role in stereotypical ways, like "All police officers are trigger-happy," "Social workers wear their hearts on their sleeves," and "Professors are dull, impractical, and absentminded." Some clergy are prone to believe that transition house workers are "man-hating women," while some transition house workers contend that clergy are "dangerous buffoons." Informal interactions in a neutral, nonthreatening environment can begin to "thaw the ice," break down the stereotypes, and thereby open the door for cooperation. That's why international leaders whose countries are at war begin their negotiations in another region of the world. Meeting in the same room is considered one of the first steps toward resolving a long-standing dispute.

Focusing on Areas of Overlap or Shared Vision

Consensus building, of course, takes more than just physically being in the same room with a group of people. Team building requires at least some form of shared vision. The importance of shared goals and objectives is well known, whether one is referring to an athletic team or making hamburgers. Thus, for sacred and secular cooperation to occur, the individuals involved need to see that they have some common ground on which to build. We have already considered what some features of that consensus building might be. But it is important to note that the focus needs to be on areas of overlap, rather than on points of departure.

Identifying the Unique Contributions
Different Perspectives Bring

While the focus needs to be on shared goals, it is important not to minimize or cloud the differences that might exist between sacred and secular caregivers. But *how* this is done is extremely important. Rather than interpreting differences in a negative light ("We disagree on so much"), professional diversity can be viewed as enriching the help available to victims of violence and their families. What becomes critical at this point is a recognition that violence against women has not been solved by one perspective or one profession. It is a problem of enormous magnitude, and therefore requires those working from within varying occupational spheres to share their knowledge. Only with this cumulative wisdom will ultimate solutions be found. As we observed in chapter 5, those clergy who are clear about their unique contribution to abuse victims (and perpetrators) appear to have little difficulty working within a team perspective. Obviously, not all clergy will be in a position to work in this way, and many may prefer not to. But if connections to the community are a priority for an individual minister, one way to augment this process is to be clear as to the efficacy and the limitations of his or her training and perspective.

Offering Flexibility for
Region-Specific Needs and Challenges

Part of the frustration some clergy report in their daily work is linked to their perception that denominational headquarters do not always fully recognize the fact that what works in one place doesn't always work in another location or region of the country. Just as there are rural/urban differences and variations based on either cultural or socioeconomic factors, the resources available for collaboration in one place may be absent in another. This is especially true of services for victims of abuse. Although some rural areas have a transition house in close proximity, others do not. While some parts of the country are well served by mental health facilities, others have long waiting lists. In some rural jurisdictions, the church is the main support service and the ordained clergy the persons from whom help is sought for a variety of spiritual and temporal problems. Any coordinated response between churches and the community will need to take into full account the resources and limitations available in the local region.

The task to reduce violence in our society is an enormous undertaking. When we think about the millions of women in North America alone who live in constant fear of their partner's rage, how can we be lulled into complacency? What can one woman, one pastor, or one church do, anyway? The stories of suffering shared on the pages of earlier chapters, and the responses to that suffering by pastors and laypeople alike, suggest that indeed one person can make a marked difference in the life of an abused woman and her children.

For women of faith who are abused by their partners, their despair impacts their spiritual journey as well. They have unique struggles to overcome in the healing process. We have met many survivors of abuse who credit others in their faith community for supporting them in their recovery. Whether it is offering a listening ear, overnight lodging, child care, or financial assistance, women of faith have an important role to play in helping one another overcome life's obstacles. Through pastoral visitation and counseling, clergy too augment the healing process. Sadly, though, many religious victims do not feel that it is safe to disclose their personal suffering to either others of like faith or their clerical leaders. They suffer without the support of the community of believers. Ensuring that abuse victims have the opportunity to disclose their suffering within the confines of their faith tradition is something that each of us—clergy and lay alike—can do. And likewise, many of us can play some role, even if it is limited, in the journey toward healing and human wholeness.

Building Bridges: A Collaborative Experiment

Bridge building is based on the premise that two rather discrete bodies of land should be joined together. In Eastern Canada, where our coastline extends for thousands of miles, there is a fairly well-developed ferry system. Both people and their vehicles are transported from the mainland to an island, or a peninsula, on a boat large enough to carry several cars and trucks. The ferry system is quaint, and people are often emotionally attached to it. For vacationers, it is definitely the preferred method of travel. Bridges, on the other hand, are far more convenient, accessible, and reliable and less influenced by the wind, the waves, and the whims of individual choice. Bridges offer a degree of permanence and connectedness that ferries do not. If the mission is urgent, one would always choose a bridge.

When it comes to responding to the needs of abused women and their children, the mission is indeed urgent and time is of the essence. That is why building bridges between sacred and secular caregivers has so much potential. Convinced of the efficacy of this approach, the Religion and Violence Research Team at the Muriel McQueen Fergusson Centre for Family Violence Research at the University of New Brunswick organized a day workshop to bring together a small group of clergy, churchwomen, and transition house workers from five communities around the Province of New Brunswick. Funded by the Women's Program of the Secretary of State Canada, this conference sought to explore ways in which churches and transition houses might work together collaboratively to better meet the needs of abused women.

The purpose of the workshop was to begin a process of developing region-specific community plans that would set out specific goals for building bridges between churches and transition houses. The day conference enabled workers from different perspectives to meet one another in an informal setting, to respond to our research findings, and to think creatively about how bridges might be built, reinforced, or repaired in their own local community.

The response of those who were invited to participate was overwhelming. We had organized the workshop, held on June 20, 1996, with some trepidation but much enthusiasm, and it exceeded even our highest expectations. Through small-group sessions, each community identified the major challenges ahead and brainstormed about how they might face those challenges. As this book goes to press, members of the Religion and Violence Research Team will be making site visits to follow up the success of implementing the various community plans and to assist those working groups who wish to put funding proposals forward that would enable their vision to expand beyond the volunteer realm. Three of the five invited communities have already hosted one collaborative event, such as an "information exchange," with other cooperative ventures now in the planning stages. While it is far too early to comment on the success of this approach, it is offered as one idea of putting into practice some of the principles we identified earlier.

It is just one experiment. But I am expecting to see some bridges across the community landscape as a result, bridges that extend from the steeple to the shelter.

NOTES

Notes for Introduction

1. The following are the members of the Religion and Violence Research Team: Dr. Nancy Nason-Clark, Department of Sociology, University of New Brunswick (coordinator); Dr. Lois Mitchell, chair of the Family Violence Committee of the United Baptist Convention of the Atlantic Provinces; Lori Beaman, LL.B., representative of the New Brunswick Coalition of Transition Houses; Sheila McCrea, M.Ed., Director of Women's Ministries, Atlantic District of the Wesleyan Church; and the Rev. Terry Atkinson, Baptist pastor and former chair of the Social Action Commission of the United Baptist Convention of the Atlantic Provinces. Three graduate students have been involved with the Team on a regular, ongoing basis: Amanda Henry, Christy Terris, and Lisa Hanson. Four other graduate students have worked on an ad hoc basis for Dr. Nason-Clark or the Team as research assistants: Danielle Irving, Dawne Clarke van Every, Diana Gentile, and Michelle Spencer. The Team has a wide variety of community partners from various denominations who are involved with individual projects.
2. This study has been undertaken by Lori Beaman as part of a Ph.D. degree in sociology at the University of New Brunswick. The research was supervised by Dr. Nason-Clark.
3. Study 5 was conducted as two distinct projects , one conducted by Amanda Henry in partial completion of her honor's degree in psychology and the other by Christy Terris in partial completion of her M.A. degree in sociology, both at the University of New Brunswick.
4. This study is still in progress; when completed it will encompass the experiences of approximately 1,000 church members and attendees.

Notes for Chapter 1

1. M. Straus, R. J. Gelles, and S. K. Steinmetz, *Behind Closed Doors: Violence in the American Family* (Garden City, N.Y.: Doubleday, Anchor, 1980); M. A. Straus, "Injury and Frequency of Assault and the 'Representative Sample Fallacy' in Measuring Wife Beating and Child Abuse," in *Physical Violence in American Families: Risk Factors and Adaptations to Violence in 8,145 Families,* ed. M. A. Straus and R. J. Gelles (New Brunswick, N.J.: Transaction, 1990), 75–91; Statistics Canada, "The Violence against Women Survey," *The Daily,* Nov. 18, 1993.
2. S. L. Feld and M. A. Straus, "Escalation and Desistance of Wife Assault in Marriage," *Criminology* 27 (1989): 141–61; M. A. Straus and R. J. Gelles, "Societal Change and Change in Family Violence from 1975 to 1985 as Revealed by Two National Surveys," *Journal of Marriage and the Family* 48 (1986): 465–79.
3. D. C. Bross et al., *The New Child Protection Team Handbook* (New York: Garland, 1988).
4. N. Nason-Clark, "Conservative Protestants and Violence against Women: Exploring

the Rhetoric and the Response," *Sex, Lies and Sanctity: Religion and Deviance in Modern America,* ed. M. J. Neitz and M. Goldman (Greenwich, Conn.: Jai, 1995): 109–30.

5. L. Timmins, ed., *Listening to the Thunder: Advocates Talk about the Battered Women's Movement* (Vancouver, B.C.: Women's Research Centre, 1995).
6. M. French, *The War against Women* (New York: Ballantine, 1992).
7. This is not to suggest that all personnel in the helping professions are attuned to issues of violence or helpful in their response to it.
8. W. Stacey, L. Hazlewood, and A. Shupe, *The Violent Couple* (New York: Praeger, 1994).
9. L. Freedman, "Wife Assault," in *No Safe Place: Violence against Women and Children,* ed. C. Guberman and M. Wolfe (Toronto: Women's Press, 1985): 41–60.
10. R. P. Dobash and R. E. Dobash, *Violence against Wives: A Case against the Patriarchy* (New York: Free Press, 1979).
11. M. Daly, *Beyond God the Father: Toward a Philosophy of Women's Liberation* (Boston: Beacon, 1973); R. Radford Ruether, ed., *Religion and Sexism: Images of Woman in the Jewish and Christian Traditions* (New York: Simon & Schuster, 1974); E. Schüssler Fiorenza and M. Shawn Copeland, *Violence against Women* (London: SCM Press, 1994); L. Gehr Livezey, "Sexual and Family Violence: A Growing Issue for the Churches," *Christian Century* (Oct. 28, 1987): 938–42; J. Brown and C. Bohn eds., *Christianity, Patriarchy and Abuse: A Feminist Critique* (New York: Pilgrim, 1989).
12. E. Hilberman, "Overview: The 'Wife-Beater's Wife' Reconsidered," *American Journal of Psychiatry* 137 (1980): 1336–47.
13. R. J. Gelles, "Family Violence," *Annual Review of Sociology* 11 (1985): 347–67; R. J. Gelles and M. A. Straus, "Violence in the American Family," *Journal of Social Issues* 35 (1979): 15–39.
14. One of the first studies in Canada to focus on battered women's experiences was published by the Women's Research Centre, Vancouver, B.C., titled "Battered and Blamed: A Report on Wife Assault from the Perspective of Battered Women"; see also D. Martin, *Battered Wives* (San Francisco: New Glide, 1981); A. Quinby, "Taking Back the Movement: Resisting Professionalization and Listening to Women," in Timmins, *Listening to the Thunder,* 263–80.
15. Nova Scotia Family Violence Prevention Initiative, Newsletters 1–5, 1994.
16. Gelles and Straus, "Violence in the American Family."
17. G. A. Walker, *Family Violence and the Women's Movement: The Conceptual Politics of Struggle* (Toronto: University of Toronto, 1990).
18. M. A. Straus, "Sociological Research and Social Policy: The Case of Family Violence," *Sociological Forum* 7 (1992): 211–37.
19. M. A. Straus, "Conceptualization and Measurement of Battering: Implications for Public Policy," in *Woman Battering: Public Responses,* ed. M. Steinman (Cincinnati, Ohio: Anderson, 1991), 19–47.
20. D. Prieur, "Patriarchy—Now You See It: Why We Need to Take Another Look at Women's Oppression in the Family," in Timmins, *Listening to the Thunder,* 247–62.
21. M. McCrea, "Safe on the Farm? Outreach to Women in Rural Southern Saskatchewan," in Timmins, *Listening to the Thunder,* 131–46; B. H. Morrow, "A Grass-Roots Feminist Response to Intimate Violence in the Caribbean," *Women's Studies International Forum* 17 (1994): 579–92; R. Thorne-Finch, *Ending the Silence: The Origins and Treatment of Male Violence against Women* (Toronto: University of Toronto, 1992); and L. Untinen, "Safety for My Sisters: A History of the Shelter Movement in Northwestern Ontario," in Timmins, *Listening to the Thunder,* 173–86.
22. There are over 2,000 domestic violence programs (primarily shelters) in the United States, and most are full to capacity with waiting lists; see C. M. Sullivan and M. H. Rumptz, "Adjustment and Needs of African-American Women Who Utilized a Domestic Violence Shelter," *Violence and Victims* 9 (1994): 275–86.

23. Dobash and Dobash, *Violence against Wives;* Timmins, *Listening to the Thunder.*
24. J. Barnsley, "Co-operation or Co-optation? The Partnership Trend of the Nineties," in Timmins, *Listening to the Thunder,* 187–214; D. R. Loseke, *The Battered Woman and Shelters: The Social Construction of Wife Abuse* (New York: State University of New York, 1992); Untinen, "Safety for My Sisters"; and Walker, *Family Violence and the Women's Movement.*
25. Timmins, *Listening to the Thunder.*
26. Prieur, "Patriarchy – Now You See It."
27. J. Stern and D. Leppard, "Breaking In: Ex-Residents Organizing in Nova Scotia," in Timmins, *Listening to the Thunder,* 147–72.
28. Ibid.; Straus et al., *Behind Closed Doors.*
29. *Fire in the Rose Project* (Ottawa: The Canadian Council on Justice and Corrections, 1994); D. Harrison and L. Laliberté, *No Life like It: Military Wives in Canada* (Toronto: James Lorimer, 1994).
30. K. Yllo and D. LeClerc, "Marital Rape," in *Abuse and Religion: When Praying Isn't Enough,* ed. A. Horton and J. Williamson (Lexington, Mass.: Heath, 1988), 49–58; Timmins, *Listening to the Thunder.*
31. *Fire in the Rose Project: What Is Abuse?;* quote on p.32.
32. *Fire in the Rose Project: Education and Action;* quote on p. 3.
33. Timmins, *Listening to the Thunder.*
34. M. Merritt-Gray and J. Wuest, "Counteracting Abuse and Breaking Free: The Process of Leaving Revealed through Women's Voices," *Health Care for Women International* 16 (1995): 399–412; C. Tan, J. Basta, C. Sullivan, and W.S. Davidson II, "The Role of Social Support in the Lives of Women Exiting Domestic Violence Shelters," *Journal of Interpersonal Violence* 10 (1995): 437–51.
35. Dobash and Dobash, *Violence against Wives.*
36. Ibid.; quote on pp. 33–34.
37. J. Bussert, *Battered Women: From a Theology of Suffering to an Ethic of Empowerment* (New York: Lutheran Church of America, 1986).
38. R. Clarke, *Pastoral Care of Battered Women* (Philadelphia: Westminster, 1986).
39. M. D. Pagelow and P. Johnson, "Abuse in the American Family: The Role of Religion," in Horton and Williamson, *Abuse and Religion,* 1–12; Schüssler Fiorenza and Copeland, *Violence against Women.*
40. Livezey, "Sexual and Family Violence."
41. E. Schüssler Fiorenza, *In Memory of Her: A Feminist Theological Reconstruction of Christian Origins* (New York: Crossroad, 1983); L. Scanzoni and N. Hardesty, *All We're Meant to Be: A Biblical Approach to Women's Liberation* (Waco, Tex.: Word, 1974).
42. Horton and Williamson, *Abuse and Religion.*
43. E. Pence, "Legal Remedies and the Role of Law Enforcement Concerning Spouse Abuse," in Horton and Williamson, *Abuse and Religion,* 69–78; Harrison and Laliberté, *No Life like It.*
44. Schüssler Fiorenza and Copeland, *Violence against Women.*
45. Amrit, "White Racism: Power + Prejudice = Racism," in Timmins, *Listening to the Thunder,* 77–82; C. Townsend Gilkes, "'Together and in Harness': Women's Traditions in the Sanctified Church," *Signs: Journal of Women in Culture and Society* 10 (1985): 678–99.
46. M. M. Gutierrez-Diez, "Reinventing the Experiment," in Timmins, *Listening to the Thunder,* 51–70; U. Narayan, " 'Male-Order' Brides: Immigrant Women, Domestic Violence and Immigration Law," *Hypatia* 10 (1995): 104–19.
47. J. Freeman, "From Pillar to Post: One Woman's Experience of Battering and the Systems That 'Help,' " in Timmins, *Listening to the Thunder,* 23–42.
48. Timmins, *Listening to the Thunder.*
49. K. Fischer and M. Rose, "When 'Enough Is Enough': Battered Women's Decision

Making around Court Orders of Protection," *Crime and Deliquency* 41 (1995): 414–29; Tan et al., "The Role of Social Support."
50. M. S. Copeland, "Reflections," in Schüssler Fiorenza and Copeland, *Violence against Women,* 119–22.
51. Statistics Canada, "The Violence against Women Survey."
52. L. McLeod, *Wife Battering in Canada: The Vicious Circle* (Ottawa: Canadian Advisory Council on the Status of Women, 1980).
53. Freedman, "Wife Assault."
54. M. Baker, *Families in Canada* (Toronto: Butterworths, 1984).
55. Straus, "Conceptualization and Measurement of Battering."
56. Dobash and Dobash, *Violence against Wives.*
57. Straus, "The Conflict Tactics Scale and Its Critics: An Evaluation and New Data on Validity and Reliability," in Straus and Gelles, *Physical Violence in American Families,* 49–73.
58. Straus and Gelles, "Societal Change and Change in Family Violence from 1975 to 1985"; Straus, "Injury and Frequency of Assault and the 'Representative Sample Fallacy.' "
59. Straus et al., *Behind Closed Doors.*
60. Straus and Gelles, "Societal Change and Change in Family Violence from 1975 to 1985."
61. C.A. Hornung, B.C. McCullough, and T. Sugimoto, "Status Relationships in Marriage: Risk Factors in Spouse Abuse," *Journal of Marriage and the Family* 43 (1981): 675–92; Martin, *Battered Wives;* L. Walker, *The Battered Woman Syndrome* (New York: Springer, 1984).
62. Gutierrez-Diez, "Reinventing the Experiment"; N. Kherbouche, "Uprooted and Abused: Muslim Women in Transition," in Timmins, *Listening to the Thunder,* 43–50.
63. D. Russell, *Rape in Marriage* (New York: Macmillan, 1982).
64. D. Finkelhor and K. Yllo, *License to Rape: Sexual Abuse and Wives* (New York: Holt, Rinehart & Winston, 1985).
65. K. Yllo and D. LeClerc, "Marital Rape," in Horton and Williamson, *Abuse and Religion,* 49–58; quote on p. 51.
66. Ibid.; quote on p. 53.
67. M. Fortune, *Sexual Violence: The Unmentionable Sin* (New York: Pilgrim, 1983).
68. Yllo and LeClerc, "Marital Rape"; Kherbouche, "Uprooted and Abused," discusses the case of Muslim women.
69. L. Walker, "Spouse Abuse: A Basic Profile," in Horton and Williamson, *Abuse and Religion ,* 13–20; Walker, *The Battered Woman Syndrome.*
70. M. Luxton, *More than a Labour of Love: Three Generations of Women's Work in the Home* (Toronto: Women's Press, 1980).
71. Walker, *The Battered Woman Syndrome.*
72. Walker, "Spouse Abuse."
73. J. Goodwin, "Family Violence: Principles of Intervention and Precention," *Hospital and Community Psychiatry* 36 (1985): 1074–79; K.D. O'Leary and A.D. Curley, "Assertion and Family Violence: Correlates of Spouse Abuse," *Journal of Marital and Family Therapy* 12 (1986): 281–89.
74. Straus et al., *Behind Closed Doors;* P. Jaffe et al., "Similarities in Behavioural and Social Maladjustment among Child Victims and Witnesses to Family Violence," *American Journal of Orthopsychiatry* 56 (1986):142–46.
75. Goodwin, "Family Violence: Principles of Intervention and Precention."
76. Straus et al., *Behind Closed Doors;* Jaffe et al., "Similarities in Behavioural and Social Maladjustment."
77. Jaffe et al., "Similarities in Behavioural and Social Maladjustment."
78. A. Rosenbaum and K.D. O'Leary, "Marital Violence: Characteristics of Abusive

Couples," *Journal of Consulting and Clinical Psychology* 49 (1981): 63–71; K. D. O'Leary and A. D. Curley, "Assertion and Family Violence."
79. Statistics Canada, "The Violence against Women Survey."
80. Kalmuss and Seltzer, "Continuity of Marital Behavior in Remarriage: The Case of Spouse Abuse," *Journal of Marriage and the Family* 48 (1986): 142–46.
81. J. Barling and A. Rosenbaum, "Work Stressors and Wife Abuse," *Journal of Applied Psychology* 71 (1986): 346–48.
82. D. Goldstein and A. Rosenbaum, "An Evaluation of the Self-Esteem of Maritally Violent Men," *Family Relations* 34 (1985): 425–28.
83. Ibid.
84. O'Leary and Curley, "Assertion and Family Violence."
85. J. Ptacek, "How Men Who Batter Rationalize Their Behaviour," in Horton and Williamson, *Abuse and Religion,* 247–58; quote on pp. 249–50.
86. Ibid.; quote on pp. 249–50.
87. Ibid.; quote on pp. 252–53.
88. Ibid.; see also R. J. Gelles, "Family Violence," *Annual Review of Sociology* 11 (1985): 347–67; Dobash and Dobash, *Violence against Wives.*
89. Walker, "Spouse Abuse"; Schüssler Fiorenza and Copeland, *Violence against Women;* M. Furlong, *Dangerous Delight: Women and Power in the Church* (London: SPCK, 1991).
90. M. Fortune, *Violence in the Family: A Workshop Curriculum for Clergy and Other Helpers* (Cleveland: Pilgrim, 1991); *Fire in the Rose Project;* J. Alsdurf and P. Alsdurf, "Wife Abuse and Scripture," in Horton and Williamson, *Abuse and Religion,* 221–28; K. Marshall Strom, *In the Name of Submission* (Portland, Ore.: Multnomah, 1986); S.R. McDill and L. McDill, *Shattered and Broken: Wife Abuse in the Christian Community; Guidelines for Hope and Healing* (Old Tappan, N.J.: Revell, 1991); S. Dowell and L. Hurcombe, *Dispossessed Daughters of Eve: Faith and Feminism* (London: SCM Press, 1981); P. Gundry, *Heirs Together* (Grand Rapids: Zondervan, 1980).
91. Walker, "Spouse Abuse"; Prieur, "Patriarchy—Now You See It"; Quinby, "Taking Back the Movement."
92. Ptacek, "How Men Who Batter Rationalize Their Behaviour"; quote on pp. 255–56.
93. Harrison and Laliberté, *No Life like It;* Timmins, *Listening to the Thunder.*
94. Prieur, "Patriarchy—Now You See It."
95. Stacey et al., *The Violent Couple.*
96. Walker, "Spouse Abuse."
97. O'Leary and Curley, "Assertion and Family Violence."
98. L.W. Bennett, "Substance Abuse and the Domestic Assault of Women," *Social Work* 40 (1995): 760–71; quote on p. 760.
99. Ptacek, "How Men Who Batter Rationalize Their Behaviour."
100. Gelles, "Family Violence"; Gelles and Straus, "Violence in the American Family."
101. Rosenbaum and O'Leary, "Marital Violence"; Statistics Canada, "The Violence against Women Survey."
102. Gelles, "Family Violence"; Gelles and Straus, "Violence in the American Family."
103. Martin, *Battered Wives;* Gelles, "Family Violence."
104. Bennett, "Substance Abuse and the Domestic Assault of Women."
105. McCrea, "Safe on the Farm?"; M. Casardi et al., "Characteristics of Women Physically Abused by Their Spouses and Who Seek Treatment Regarding Marital Conflict," *Journal of Consulting and Clinical Psychology* 63 (1995): 616–23.
106. Martin, *Battered Wives.*
107. Ibid.
108. Prieur, "Patriarchy—Now You See It"; Sullivan and Rumptz, "Adjustment and Needs of African-American Women."
109. Quinby, "Taking Back the Movement."

110. Fischer and Rose, "When 'Enough Is Enough.' "
111. Stern and Leppard, "Breaking In"; Freeman, "From Pillar to Post."
112. Untinen, "Safety for My Sisters"; Gutierrez-Diez, "Reinventing the Experiment."
113. E. Greenglass, *A World of Difference: Gender Roles in Perspective* (Toronto: Wiley, 1982).
114. Luxton, *More than a Labour of Love.*
115. Gelles, "Family Violence."
116. Sullivan and Rumptz, "Adjustment and Needs of African-American Women."
117. Quinby, "Taking Back the Movement."
118. Martin, *Battered Wives.*
119. Timmins, *Listening to the Thunder.*
120. Merritt-Gray and Wuest, "Conteracting Abuse and Breaking Free."
121. M. Marden and M. Rice, "The Use of Hope as a Coping Mechanism in Abused Women," *Journal of Holistic Nursing* 13 (1995): 70–82.
122. D. Hooker, "Some Contributions of Christianity to Psychotherapy," *Journal of Religion and Health* 18 (1979): 178–81.
123. A.Weaver, "Psychological Trauma: What Clergy Need to Know," *Pastoral Psychology* 41 (1993): 385–408.
124. Luxton, *More than a Labour of Love.*
125. Horton and Williamson, *Abuse and Religion.*
126. Martin, *Battered Wives.*
127. Prieur, "Patriarchy—Now You See It"; quote on p. 253.
128. Merritt-Gray and Wuest, "Counteracting Abuse and Breaking Free."
129. Fischer and Rose, "When 'Enough Is Enough.' "
130. M. McGuire, *Religion: The Social Context* (Belmont, Calif.: Wadsworth, 1992).
131. D. J. Rumberger and M. L. Rogers, "Pastoral Openness to Interaction with a Private Christian Counseling Service," *Journal of Psychology and Theology* 10 (1982): 337–45; R. A. Bell et al., "The Clergy as Mental Health Resource," *Journal of Pastoral Care* 30 (1976): 103–15; L. Bowker, "Battered Women and the Clergy: An Evaluation," *Journal of Pastoral Care* 36 (1982): 226–34; H. P. Chalfont et al., "The Clergy as a Resource for Those Encountering Psychological Distress," *Review of Religious Research* 31 (1990): 305–13; G. K. Lau and R. Steele, "An Empirical Study of the Pastoral Mental Health Involvement Model," *Journal of Psychology and Theology* 18 (1990): 261–69; F. Perlmutter, L. Yudin, and S. Heinemann, "Awareness of a Community Mental Health Center among Three 'Gatekeeper' Groups," *American Journal of Community Psychology* 2 (1975):23–33.
132. B. A. Hong and V. R. Wiehe, "Referral Patterns of Clergy," *Journal of Psychology and Theology* 2 (1974): 291–97; N. A. Clemens, R. B. Corradi, and M. Wasman, "The Parish Clergy as a Mental Health Resource," *Journal of Religion and Health* 17 (1978): 227–32; S. A. Clark and A. H. Thomas, "Counseling and the Clergy: Perceptions of Roles," *Journal of Psychology and Theology* 7 (1979): 48–56.
133. D. M. Moss III, "Priestcraft and Psychoanalytic Psychotherapy: Contradiction or Concordance?" *Journal of Religion and Health* 18 (1979): 181–88; P. Lyons and H. Zingle, "The Relationship between Religious Orientation and Empathy in Pastoral Counselors," *Journal of Psychology and Theology* 18 (1990): 375–80.
134. K. L. Sell and W. M. Goldsmith, "Concerns about Professional Counseling: An Exploration of Five Factors and the Role of Christian Orthodoxy," *Journal of Psychology and Christianity* 7 (1988): 5–21.
135. F. McBurney Martin, *Call Me Blessed: The Emerging Christian Woman* (Grand Rapids: Eerdmans, 1988); R. Morris, *Ending Violence against Families: A Training Program for Pastoral Care Workers* (Toronto: United Church of Canada, 1988); C. L. Scott, *Breaking the Cycle of Abuse: A Biblical Approach to Recognizing and Responding to Domestic Violence* (Weston, Ontario, Canada: David C. Cook, 1988); A. B. Spencer, *Beyond the Curse: Women Called to Ministry* (Nashville: Thomas Nelson, 1985).

136. Fortune, *Violence in the Family; Fire in the Rose Project;* Gethsemane's Comfort Workshops; Church Council on Justice and Corrections, *Family Violence in a Patriarchal Culture: A Challenge to Our Way of Living* (available from the Women's Inter-Church Council of Canada, Toronto, Canada).

137. Weaver, "Psychological Trauma"; quote on p. 402.

138. Brown and Bohn, *Christianity, Patriarchy and Abuse;* Livezey, "Sexual and Family Violence."

139. J. P. Bartkowski and K. L. Anderson, "Are There Religious Variations in Spousal Violence?" (paper presented at the annual meetings of the Association for the Sociology of Religion, New York City, Aug. 16–18, 1996).

140. M. Brinkerhoff, E. Grandin, and E. Lupri, "Religious Involvement and Spousal Violence: The Canadian Case," *Journal for the Scientific Study of Religion* 31 (1992): 12–31.

141. Nason-Clark, "Conservative Protestants and Violence against Women"; L. Beaman, "Feminist Practice, Evangelical Worldview: The Response of Conservative Christian Women to Wife Abuse" (Ph.D. diss., University of New Brunswick, Fredericton, N.B., Canada, 1996).

142. Pagelow and Johnson, "Abuse in the American Family."

143. Horton and Williamson, *Abuse and Religion.*

144. Chalfont et al., "The Clergy as a Resource."

145. A. Wood and M. McHugh, "Woman Battering: The Response of the Clergy," *Pastoral Psychology* 42 (1994): 185–96; Horton and Williamson, *Abuse and Religion;* Clarke, *Pastoral Care of Battered Women.*

146. *Fire in the Rose Project.*

147. V. Whipple, "Counselling Battered Women from Fundamentalist Churches," *Journal for Marital and Family Therapy* 13 (1987): 251–58.

148. *Fire in the Rose Project.*

149. Horton and Williamson, *Abuse and Religion.*

150. Whipple, "Counselling Battered Women from Fundamentalist Churches"; J. Sacks, "Religious Issues in Psychotherapy," *Journal of Religion and Health* 24 (1985): 26–30.

151. M. J. Meadow, "Dealing with Religious Issues in Counseling and Psychotherapy: A Symposium," *Journal of Religion and Health* 18 (1979): 176–78; O. Strunk Jr., "The World View Factor in Psychotherapy," *Journal of Religion and Health* 18 (1979): 192–97; W. Schofield, "Discussion: Psychology, Inspiration and Faith," *Journal of Religion and Health* 18 (1979): 197–202.

152. Sell and Goldsmith, "Concerns about Professional Counseling."

153. N.T. Ammerman, *Bible Believers: Fundamentalist in the Modern World* (New Brunswick, N.J.: Rutgers Univ. Press, 1987).

154. Wood and McHugh, "Woman Battering" ; C. L. Scott, *Breaking the Cycle of Abuse;* Nason-Clark, "Conservative Protestants and Violence Against Women."

155. Horton and Williamson, *Abuse and Religion.*

156. Fortune, *Violence in the Family;* J. Alsdurf and P. Alsdurf, "A Pastoral Response," in Horton and Williamson, *Abuse and Religion,* 165–72; Schüssler Fiorenza and Copeland, *Violence against Women;* K. Gerdes and M. Beck, "A Qualitative Study of Latter-Day Saints Women Who Were Sexually Abused as Children" (presented at the annual meetings of the Society for the Scientific Study of Religion, St. Louis, Mo., Oct. 27–29, 1995).

157. Livezey, "Sexual and Family Violence"; quote on p. 941.

158. Hornung et al., "Status Relationships in Marriage."

159. Bowker, "Battered Women and the Clergy."

160. Horton and Williamson, *Abuse and Religion.*

161. Pagelow and Johnson, "Abuse in the American Family," 1–12; quotes on p.5.

162. Bowker, "Religious Victims and Their Religious Leaders: Services Delivered to One

Thousand Battered Women by the Clergy," in Horton and Williamson, *Abuse and Religion,* 229–34.

163. Ibid.
164. A. Horton, M. Wilkins, and W. Wright, "Women Who Ended Abuse: What Religious Leaders and Religion Did for These Victims," in Horton and Williamson, *Abuse and Religion,* 235–46.
165. Ibid.
166. Ibid.; quote on p. 242.
167. Ibid.
168. Ibid. quote on p. 240.
169. M. Langston, G. Privette, and S. Vodanovich, "Mental Health Values of Clergy: Effects of Open-mindedness, Religious Affiliation, and Education in Counselling," *Psychological Reports* 75 (1994): 499–506; Weaver, "Psychological Trauma"; G. Domino, "Clergy's Knowledge of Psychopathology," *Journal of Psychology and Theology* 18 (1990): 32–39.
170. Martin, *Battered Wives.*
171. D. G. Jansen, G. P. Robb, and E. C. Bonk, "Clergymen as Counselor Trainees: Comparisons with Counselors Rated Most and Least Competent by Their Peers," *Journal of Clinical Psychology* 28 (1972): 601–3.
172. D. Hooker, "Some Contributions of Christianity to Psychotherapy," *Journal of Religion and Health* 18 (1979): 178–81.
173. N. Nason-Clark, "Are Clergywomen Changing the Face of Ministry: An Exploration of American and British Realities," *Review of Religious Research* 28 (1987): 330–40; M. Furlong, *Dangerous Delight: Women and Power in the Church* (London: SPCK, 1991).
174. K. Higgins, "Clergywomen in the United Church and Transition Houses" (unpublished paper, University of New Brunswick, Fredericton, Canada, 1994); S. E. Martin, "The Response of the Clergy to Spouse Abuse in a Suburban County: A Research Note," *Violence and Victims* 4 (1989): 217–25.
175. Pence, "Legal Remedies and the Role of Law Enforcement"; Bross et al., *The New Child Protection Team Handbook.*
176. Horton and Williamson, *Abuse and Religion.*
177. Whipple, "Counselling Battered Women"; R. Bullis and M. Harrigan, "Religious Denominational Policies on Sexuality," *Families in Society: The Journal of Contemporary Human Services* (1992): 304–12; Sell and Goldsmith, "Concerns about Professional Counseling."
178. J. Miner Holden, R.E. Watts, and W. Brookshire, "Beliefs of Professional Counselors and Clergy about Depressive Religious Ideation," *Counselling and Values* 35 (1991): 93–103.
179. Horton and Williamson, *Abuse and Religion.*
180. A. Horton, "Practical Guidelines for Professionals Working with Religious Spouse Abuse Victims," in Horton and Williamson, *Abuse and Religion,* 89–100.
181. Pagelow and Johnson, "Abuse in the American Family."
182. R. R. King, "Evangelical Christians and Professional Counseling: A Conflict of Values?" *Journal of Psychology and Theology* 6 (1978): 276–81.
183. *Fire in the Rose Project;* Fortune, *Violence in the Family.*
184. N. Nason-Clark, "Religion and Violence Against Women: Exploring the Rhetoric and the Response of Evangelical Churches in Canada," *Social Compass,* 46 (1996): 515–36; Pagelow and Johnson, "Abuse in the American Family."
185. M. Fortune, "Forgiveness the Last Step," in Horton and Williamson, *Abuse and Religion,* 215–20; Alsdurf and Alsdurf, "A Pastoral Response."
186. Horton, "Practical Guidelines for Professionals."
187. Bowker, "Battered Women and the Clergy"; Nason-Clark, "Religion and Violence Against Women."

188. Fischer and Rose, "When 'Enough Is Enough'"; D.W. Delaplane, "Stand by Me: The Role of the Clergy and Congregations in Assisting the Family Once It Is Involved in the Legal and Treatment Process," in Horton and Williamson, *Abuse and Religion,* 173–80; Fortune, *Violence in the Family;* M. Fortune, "Reporting Child Abuse: An Ethical Mandate for Ministry," in Horton and Williamson, *Abuse and Religion,* 189–98.

189. *Fire in the Rose Project;* J.A. Kowalski, "Developing a Religious and Secular Partnership," in Horton and Williamson, *Abuse and Religion,* 199–206.

190. M. N. Eilts, "Saving the Family: When Is the Covenant Broken?" in Horton and Williamson, *Abuse and Religion,* 207–14.

191. Fortune, "Reporting Child Abuse."

192. Alsdurf and Alsdurf, "Wife Abuse and Scripture."

193. Fortune, *Violence in the Family.*

194. Fortune, "Forgiveness the Last Step"; C. Doran, "A Model Treatment Program That Would Work toward Family Unity and Still Provide Safety," in Horton and Williamson, *Abuse and Religion,* 277–84.

195. Fortune, "Forgiveness the Last Step"; McDill and McDill, *Shattered and Broken;* Strom, *In the Name of Submission.*

196. Alsdurf and Alsdurf, "A Pastoral Response."

197. Ibid.

198. Martin, "The Response of the Clergy to Spouse Abuse in a Suburban County"; Wood and McHugh, "Woman Battering"; Weaver, "Psychological Trauma."

199. See Bowker, "Battered Women and the Clergy."

200. Martin, "The Response of the Clergy to Spouse Abuse in a Suburban County."

201. Wood and McHugh, "Woman Battering."

202. L. Beaman and N. Nason-Clark, "Partners or Protagonists? Exploring the Relationship Between the Transition House Movement and Conservative Churches," *Affilia,* vol 12, No. 2, Summer 1997: 176–196. Nason-Clark, "Religion and Violence Against Women"; T. Hulme, "Mental Health Consultation with Religious Leaders," *Journal of Religion and Health* 13 (1974): 114–27; Langston et al., "Mental Health Values of Clergy"; R.D. Gorsuch and W. D. Meylink, "Toward a Co-Professional Model of Clergy-Psychologist Referral," *Journal of Psychology and Christianity* 7 (1988): 22–31; Martin, "The Response of the Clergy to Spouse Abuse in a Suburban County"; Sacks, "Religious Issues in Psychotherapy"; Chalfont et al., "The Clergy as a Resource"; B. Beitman, "Pastoral Counselling Centers: A Challenge to Community Mental Health Centers," *Hospital and Community Psychiatry* 33 (1982): 486–87.

203. Horton et al., "Women Who Ended Abuse"; Whipple, "Counselling Battered Women from Fundamentalist Churches."

204. Kowalski, "Developing a Religious and Secular Partnership"; Horton and Williamson, *Abuse and Religion;* McDill and McDill, *Shattered and Broken;* Bullis and Harrigan, "Religious Denominational Policies on Sexuality."

Notes for Chapter 2

1. R. Balmer, "American Fundamentalism: The Ideal of Femininity," in *Fundamentalism and Gender,* ed. J. S. Hawley (New York: Oxford, 1994), 47–62.

2. K. McCarthy Brown, "Fundamentalism and the Control of Women," in Hawley, *Fundamentalism and Gender,* 175–202.

3. Nason-Clark, "Conservative Protestants and Violence Against Women."

4. To be sure, there is not complete agreement among writers in this area. Christian feminism is a case in point. Later in the book, we will explore the impact of evangelical feminists and the broader organization, Christians for Biblical Equality.

5. Ammerman, *Bible Believers;* M.J. Neitz, *Charisma and Community: A Study of Religious Commitment* (New Brunswick, N.J.: Transaction, 1987); T. Heaton and M.

Cornwall, "Religious Group Variation in the Socioeconomic Status of Family Behaviour of Women," *Journal for the Scientific Study of Religion,* 28 (1990): 283–99; N. Nason-Clark, "Gender Relations in Contemporary Christianity," *The Sociology of Religion: A Canadian Focus,* ed. W.E. Hewitt (Toronto: Butterworths, 1993): 215–34.

6. Ammerman, *Bible Believers.*
7. J. D. Hunter, *Evangelicalism: The Coming Generation* (Chicago: Univ. of Chicago Press, 1987); G. Rawlyk, *Is Jesus Your Personal Saviour? In Search of Canadian Evangelicalism in the 1990s* (Kingston, Ont.: McGill-Queen's Univ., 1996).
8. J. S. Hawley and W. Proudfoot, "Introduction," in Hawley, *Fundamentalism and Gender,* 3–46; quote on p.32.
9. R. Balmer, "American Fundamentalism"; quote on p. 55.
10. S. Gerami, *Women and Fundamentalism: Islam and Christianity* (New York: Garland, 1996).
11. D. Renee Kaufman, *Rachel's Daughters: Newly Orthodox Jewish Women* (New Brunswick, N.J.: Rutgers Univ. Press, 1992); L. Davidman, *Tradition in a Rootless World: Women Turn to Orthodox Judaism* (Berkeley: Univ. of California Press, 1991).
12. N. T. Ammerman and W.C. Roof, eds., *Work, Family, and Religion in Contemporary Society* (New York: Routledge, 1995).
13. P. Long Marler, "Lost in the Fifties: The Changing Family and the Nostalgic Church," in Ammerman and Roof, *Work, Family, and Religion in Contemporary Society,* 23–60.
14. W.C. Roof and L. Gesch, "Boomers and the Culture of Choice," in Ammerman and Roof, *Work, Family, and Religion in Contemporary Society,* 61–80.
15. B. Hertel, "Work, Family and Faith: Recent Trends," in Ammerman and Roof, *Work, Family, and Religion in Contemporary Society,* 81–122.
16. Ammerman and Roof, *Work, Family, and Religion;* J. Porter and A. Albert, "Subculture or Assimilation? A Cross-Cultural Analysis of Religion and Women's Role," *Journal for the Scientific Study of Religion* 16 (1977): 345–59; L. Molm, "Sex Role Attitudes and the Employment of Married Women: The Direction of Causality," *The Sociological Quarterly* 19 (1978): 522–33; M. McMurry, "Religion and Women's Sex Role Traditionalism," *Sociological Focus* 11 (1978): 81–95.
17. W. P. Blitchington, *Sex Roles and the Christian Family* (Wheaton, Ill.: Tyndale, 1980); quote on pp.13–14.
18. Nason-Clark, "Conservative Protestants and Violence Against Women."
19. N. Nason-Clark, "Clerical Attitudes Towards Appropriate Roles for Women in Church and Society" (Ph.D. diss., London School of Economics and Political Science, London, England, 1984); Ammerman, *Bible Believers;* Hunter, *Evangelicalism.*
20. J. Lipman-Blumen, *Gender Roles and Power* (Englewood Cliffs, N.J.: Prentice-Hall, 1984).
21. The back cover of their 1995 publication, *The Spirit-Filled Family,* says that Tim LaHaye's books alone have sold over 8 million copies. Beverly LaHaye is the founder and president of Concerned Women for America.
22. J. C. Dobson, *Love Must Be Tough: New Hope for Families in Crisis* (Dallas, Tex.: Word, 1996); J. C. Dobson, *Straight Talk: What Men Need to Know; What Women Should Understand* (Dallas, Tex.: Word, 1995).
23. T. LaHaye and B. LaHaye, *The Spirit-Filled Family* (Eugene, Ore.: Harvest House, 1995).
24. While the Christian family literature recognizes that divorce is permitted by scripture in cases involving adultery, authors are generally reluctant to advise it and do so only after other means of relationship repair have been exhausted.
25. LaHaye and LaHaye, *The Spirit-Filled Family*; quote on p. 103.

26. G. Smalley, *Making Love Last Forever* (Dallas, Tex.: Word, 1996); quote on p. 56.
27. Ibid.; quote on p. 48.
28. Blitchington, *Sex Roles and the Christian Family;* quote on p.50.
29. O. R. Johnston, *Who Needs the Family? A Survey and a Christian Assessment* (London: Hodder and Stoughton, 1979).
30. J. Walker, *Husbands Who Won't Lead and Wives Who Won't Follow* (Minneapolis, Minn.: Bethany House, 1989); quote on p. 138.
31. J. Hurley, *Man and Woman in Biblical Perspective: A Study in Role Relationships and Authority* (Leicester, England: InterVarsity, 1981).
32. J. C. Dobson, *Straight Talk;* quote on p. 184.
33. Smalley, *Making Love Last Forever.*
34. Nason-Clark, "Conservative Protestants and Violence Against Women."
35. W. H. Lockhart, "Redefining the New Christian Man: An Investigation into Books Related to the Promise Keepers Movement" (paper presented at the annual meetings of the Association for the Sociology of Religion, New York City, Aug. 16–18, 1996).
36. T. Elmore, *Soul Provider* (San Bernardino, Calif.: Here's Life, 1992).
37. Lockhart, "Redefining the New Christian Man."
38. G. Inrig, *Whole Marriages in a Broken World: God's Design for a Healthy Marriage* (Grand Rapids: Discovery House, 1996).
39. Smalley, *Making Love Last Forever*; quote on p. 14.
40. Smalley, *Love Is a Decision;* G. Smalley, *Hidden Keys of a Loving, Lasting Marriage* (Grand Rapids: Zondervan, 1988); videotapes released in 1991.
41. Smalley, *Making Love Last Forever*; quote on p. 202.
42. G. R. Collins, *Family Shock: Keeping Families Strong in the Midst of Earthshaking Change* (Wheaton, Ill.: Tyndale, 1995).
43. James Dobson, *Love Must Be Tough.*
44. Ibid.; quote on p. 231.
45. Ibid.; quote on p. 174.
46. T. LaHaye and B. LaHaye, *Spirit Controlled Family* (Eastbourne, England: Kingsway, 1978); T. LaHaye and B. LaHaye, *The Battle for the Family* (Old Tappan, N.J.: Fleming H. Revell, 1982); LaHaye and LaHaye, *The Spirit-Filled Family.*
47. Dobson, *Love Must Be Tough;* quote on p. 19.
48. Smalley, in *Hidden Keys of a Loving, Lasting Marriage* (pp. 229–30), tells the story of Gail and Mike, a couple who would have violent fights, with Gail coming out losing since she was shorter and weighed less than her husband. When Gail began applying Smalley's advice, what he calls the biblical principle of a quiet spirit, her inner beauty—and inner calmness—won out. In this example, the only one offered explicitly about abuse, she submitted herself to God, became anxious for nothing, and this peace guarded her heart. By focusing on Mike's needs, the newfound calmness crowded out her fear of Mike and the future.
49. Dobson, *Love Must Be Tough;* quote on p. 160.
50. Ibid.; quote on p. 164.
51. Ibid.; quote on p. 164.
52. Horton and Williamson, *Abuse and Religion.*
53. In his study of 1,044 senior pastors, George Barna in *Today's Pastors* (Ventura, Calif.: Regal, 1993) found that nearly one quarter of his sample were unable to identify their spiritual gifts.
54. Barna, *Today's Pastors.*

Notes for Chapter 3

1. There are four parts to this chapter: opening narratives; introduction; the experiences of abused women; and the healing process. The third section was written by Lori Beaman, one of the author's former Ph.D. students.

2. Dobash and Dobash, *Violence against Wives;* Walker, *Family Violence and the Women's Movement.*
3. Brown and Bohn, *Christianity, Patriarchy and Abuse;* Schüssler Fiorenza and Copeland, *Violence against Women;* Fortune, *Violence in the Family.*
4. R. Radford Ruether, *Women-Church: Theology and Practice* (San Francisco: Harper, 1985); Schüssler Fiorenza and Copeland, *Violence against Women.*
5. A tenth woman was included despite the fact that she did not characterize herself as an abused wife. The justification for including her is based on the description of the husband's behavior.
6. Horton et al., "Women Who Ended Abuse," also found that abused Christian women claim to gain strength from their faith.
7. M. R. Mahoney, "Victimization or Oppression? Women's Lives, Violence and Agency," *The Public Nature of Private Violence: The Discovery of Domestic Abuse,* ed. M. A. Fineman and R. Mykituk (New York: Routledge, 1994).
8. Alsdurf and Alsdurf, "A Pastoral Response"; Bussert, *Battered Women.*
9. Schüssler Fiorenza and Copeland, *Violence against Women;* Horton and Williamson, *Abuse and Religion.*
10. Beaman, "Feminist Practice, Evangelical Worldview."
11. Gundry, *Heirs Together;* M. Langley, *Equal Women: A Christian Feminist Perspective* (Hants, United Kingdom: Marshalls, 1983); Martin, *Call Me Blessed.*
12. Beaman, "Feminist Practice, Evangelical Worldview."
13. Brown and Bohn, *Christianity, Patriarchy and Abuse.*
14. R. H. Albers, *Shame: A Faith Perspective* (Binghamton, N.Y.: Haworth, 1995).
15. Ibid.; quote on p. 139.
16. McDill and McDill, *Shattered and Broken.*
17. Ibid.; quote on p. 149.
18. Fortune, "Forgiveness the Last Step."
19. Ibid.; quote on p. 216.
20. Ibid.; quote on p. 218.
21. Ibid.; quote on p. 220.
22. When Jesus was asked how many times a brother ought to forgive another brother, "seventy times seven" was the reply (Matt. 18:21–22).

Notes for Chapter 4

1. Ammerman, *Bible Believers;* S. Warner, *New Wine in Old Wineskins: Evangelicals and Liberals in a Small-Town Church* (Berkeley: Univ. of California, 1988).
2. Statistics Canada, "The Violence against Women Survey."
3. N. L. Eiesland, "A Strange Road Home: Adult Female Converts to Classical Pentecostalism," in *Mixed Blessing: Gender and Religious Fundamentalism Cross Culturally,* ed. J. Brink and J. Mencher (New York: Routledge, 1997), 91–115; Balmer, "American Fundamentalism."
4. Timmins, *Listening to the Thunder;* E. R. Hamlin and K. L. Pehrson, "Family Services: A Proposed Model for Coordinating Spouse Abuse Services," *Journal of Family Social Work* 1 (1996): 19–31.
5. I use the terms "Atlantic Canada" and "Eastern Canada" interchangeably to refer to New Brunswick, Nova Scotia, Prince Edward Island, and Newfoundland.
6. Schüssler Fiorenza and Copeland, *Violence against Women;* Horton and Williamson, *Abuse and Religion;* Brown and Bohn, *Christianity, Patriarchy and Abuse.*
7. Weaver, "Psychological Trauma"; Domino, "Clergy's Knowledge of Psychopathology."
8. Wood and McHugh, "Woman Battering"; Bowker, "Battered Women and the Clergy"; Martin, "The Response of the Clergy to Spouse Abuse in a Suburban County."

9. To date there are no direct studies that have been published of the rates of violence against women in conservative faith communities, though C. Ellison and his colleagues have presented conference papers on spouse and child abuse; Statistics Canada, "The Violence against Women Survey"; Brown and Bohn, *Christianity, Patriarchy and Abuse;* Fortune, "Forgiveness the Last Step"; L. McLeod, *Battered but Not Beaten . . . Preventing Wife Battering in Canada* (Ottawa: Canadian Advisory Council on the Status of Women, 1987); Horton and Williamson, *Abuse and Religion.*
10. In this region very few evangelical clergy would be uncomfortable with a complete prohibition of alcohol consumption.
11. K. Tingley, "Women in Transition: From Homemaker to Paid Employment" (M.A. thesis, University of New Brunswick, Fredericton, N.B., Canada, 1996).
12. S. Hale, *Controversies in Sociology: A Canadian Introduction,* 2d ed., (Toronto: Copp Clark, 1995); P. Phillips and E. Phillips, *Women and Work: Inequality in the Labour Market* (Toronto: James Lorimer, 1983); P. Armstrong and H. Armstrong, *The Double Ghetto: Canadian Women and Their Segregated Work,* rev. ed. (Toronto: McClelland & Stewart, 1984).
13. We received a total of 573 responses from pastors concerning how they account for violence in Christian families. Of these, 56.9% of the responses (n=326) offered an explanation that reflected largely spiritual factors, 13.6% (n=134) combined spiritual and secular factors, and 29.5% (n=169) listed nonspiritual factors.
14. Nason-Clark, "Conservative Protestants and Violence Against Women"; Nason-Clark, "Religion and Violence Against Women."
15. L. Beaman, "Making the Social Justice Priority List: Responses to Wife Abuse in an Evangelical Church" (presented at the annual meetings of the Society for the Scientific Study of Religion, Albuquerque, N.M., Nov. 4–6, 1994).
16. It is tempting to conclude that there is a "conspiracy of silence" on this issue; see Fortune, *Violence in the Family;* Gethsemane's Comfort Workshops; *Fire in the Rose Project.*
17. Of course, it is not enough for clergy to simply "ask" if abuse is present, they also need to recognize and respond to the "signs" or "signals" indicative of abuse.
18. L. Beaman, "Negotiating the Options: How a Program for Men Who Batter Negotiates Its Identity in a Network of Community Agencies" (M.A. thesis, University of New Brunswick, Fredericton, N.B., Canada, 1992).
19. Fortune, "Reporting Child Abuse"; Ptacek, "How Men Who Batter Rationalize Their Behaviour."
20. Nason-Clark, "Religion and Violence Against Women."
21. Horton and Williamson, *Abuse and Religion;* Morris, *Ending Violence against Families;* Whipple, "Counselling Battered Women"; Scott, *Breaking the Cycle of Abuse.*
22. Schüssler Fiorenza and Copeland, *Violence against Women;* Brown and Bohn, *Christianity, Patriarchy and Abuse;* Wood and McHugh, "Woman Battering."
23. Alsdurf and Alsdurf, "A Pastoral Response"; Bowker, "Religious Victims and Their Religious Leaders."
24. Wood and McHugh, "Woman Battering"; Schüssler Fiorenza and Copeland, *Violence against Women;* Brown and Bohn, *Christianity, Patriarchy and Abuse.*
25. Nason-Clark, "Religion and Violence against Women."
26. C. Terris, "Cares, Conflict and Counselling: A Study of Evangelical Youth and Their Youth Pastors" (M.A. thesis, University of New Brunswick, Fredericton, N.B., Canada, 1996).
27. Three ministers were unable to estimate the proportion of their time spent in counseling.
28. Religion and Violence Research Team, Muriel McQueen Fergusson Centre for Family Violence Research, University of New Brunswick, *Family Violence and the United Baptist and Wesleyan Churches of Atlantic Canada: First Phase Report,* 1994. Available from the author.

29. Sell and Goldsmith, "Concerns about Professional Counseling"; Hong and Wiehe, "Referral Patterns of Clergy."
30. Weaver, "Psychological Trauma"; King, "Evangelical Christians and Professional Counseling."
31. Martin, "The Response of the Clergy to Spouse Abuse in a Suburban County"; Bell et al., "The Clergy as Mental Health Resource"; Langston et al., "Mental Health Values of Clergy."
32. Gorsuch and Meylink, "Toward a Co-Professional Model of Clergy-Psychologist Referral"; Wood and McHugh, "Woman Battering."

Notes for Chapter 5

1. According to the 1991 Statistics Canada census, the population of Canada is 27.3 million, of which 13.8 million are female. Over 10% of Canadians attend a Christian service once a week, with more women participating than men (R. Bibby, *Fragmented Gods: The Poverty and Potential of Religion in Canada* [Toronto: Irwin, 1987]; R. Bibby, *Unknown Gods: The Ongoing Story of Religion in Canada* [Toronto: Irwin, 1993]). The population of the United States stands at over 250 million and church attendance patterns are higher than in Canada.
2. Statistics Canada, "The Violence against Women Survey"; Straus et al., *Behind Closed Doors.*
3. Schüssler Fiorenza and Copeland, *Violence against Women;* Horton and Williamson, *Abuse and Religion;* Beaman, "Feminist Practice, Evangelical Worldview."
4. Brown and Bohn, *Christianity, Patriarchy and Abuse.*
5. Some clergy gave percentages that did not total 100%.
6. Approximately 21% and 20% of pastoral respondents reported "high" risk for the wife and husband respectively.
7. A further four mentioned going to a physician, two suggested a lawyer, two another pastor, and one a friend.
8. With regard to perspective, 54% of clergy reported great difference, 27% moderate difference, and 19% little difference. Concerning process, 27% of clergy reported great difference, 42% moderate difference, and 30% little difference. Finally, related to outcome, 14% cited great difference, 18% moderate difference, and 67% little difference.
9. For partly the same reason, police agencies are reluctant to intervene in what they term "domestic disputes."
10. Concerning perspective, 52% of clergy reported great difference, 20% moderate difference, and 27% little difference. In terms of process, 26% reported great difference, 36% moderate difference, and 38% little difference. Finally, related to outcome, 10% reported great difference, 10% moderate difference, and 80% great difference.
11. While it is beyond the scope of this study, the issue of 24-hour clerical availability brings considerable stress to the clergy family, for often it is the minister's wife who receives and screens the calls and has to pick up the slack at home when her husband is responding to a crisis (see J. Finch, *Married to the Job: Wives' Incorporation in Men's Work* [London: George Allen & Unwin, 1983]).
12. While a couple of clergy alluded to personal fear during their interviews, other clergy in the region have approached me after a workshop to report cases where they were personally threatened by an abusive man or accused of marital infidelity with the abused wife. In one case, a pastor told about an abuser who came to the parsonage with a shotgun in hand.
13. Personal communication with two therapists involved in Context, a program for men who batter in Nova Scotia, Nov. 17, 1994.
14. Beaman, "Negotiating the Options."

Notes for Chapter 6

1. At the beginning of each focus group all women and all focus groups were given a number by the research assistant who was observing the focus group session. See opening of chapter 2.
2. Nason-Clark, "Are Clergymen Changing the Face of Ministry?"
3. Balmer, "American Fundamentalism."
4. Hawley, *Fundamentalism and Gender*.
5. Marler, "Lost in the Fifties"; Brown, "Fundamentalism and the Control of Women"; Nason-Clark, "Conservative Protestants and Violence Against Women."
6. Ammerman, *Bible Believers;* Neitz, *Charisma and Community;* Heaton and Cornwall, "Religious Group Variation"; D. Kraybill, *The Riddle of Amish Culture* (Baltimore: Johns Hopkins Univ. Press, 1988); Davidman, *Tradition in a Rootless World;* Kaufman, *Rachel's Daughters;* S. Palmer, *Moon Sisters, Krishna Mothers, Rajneesh Lovers: Women's Roles in New Religions* (Syracuse: Syracuse Univ. Press, 1995).
7. Ammerman and Roof, *Work, Family, and Religion in Contemporary Society*.
8. Balmer, "American Fundamentalism."
9. Martin, *Battered Wives.*
10. Horton and Williamson, *Abuse and Religion.*
11. Marler, "Lost in the Fifties."
12. Nason-Clark, "Conservative Protestants and Violence Against Women."
13. Beaman, "Feminist Practice, Evangelical Worldview."
14. D. Smith, *The Conceptual Practices of Power: A Feminist Sociology of Knowledge* (Toronto: Univ. of Toronto, 1990).
15. Straus et al., *Behind Closed Doors;* Fortune, *Violence in the Family; Fire in the Rose Project*.
16. Smalley, *Making Love Last Forever* and *Hidden Keys of a Loving, Lasting Marriage;* Dobson, *Love Must Be Tough* and *Straight Talk;* LaHaye and LaHaye, *The Spirit-Filled Family; The Battle for the Family,;* and *Spirit Controlled Family;* Collins, *Family Shock* and *Christian Counseling*.
17. Scott, *Breaking the Cycle of Abuse;* McDill and McDill, *Shattered and Broken;* Fortune, *Violence in the Family;* Horton and Williamson, *Abuse and Religion*.
18. The 314 examples do not refer to specific instances of support per se, but rather to the types of support they were offering, e.g., "Take abused woman to the emergency department of the hospital."
19. L. Beaman and N. Nason-Clark, "Partners or Protagonists?"; Ammerman and Roof, *Work, Family, and Religion in Contemporary Society;* Ammerman, *Bible Believers;* Neitz, *Charisma and Community;* S. Rose, "Women Warriors: The Negotiation of Gender in a Charismatic Community," *Sociological Analysis* 48 (1987): 245–58. Kaufman, *Rachel's Daughters,* and Davidman, *Tradition in a Rootless World,* discuss orthodox Jewish women, and Palmer, *Moon Sisters, Krishna Mothers, Rajneesh Lovers,* considers new religious movements.
20. McLeod, *Wife Battering in Canada;* Walker, *Family Violence and the Women's Movement*.
21. Beaman, "Feminist Practice, Evangelical Worldview."
22. Mahoney, "Victimization or Oppression?"
23. It was unclear from the tape (and hence the typed transcript) which woman was speaking at this point in focus group 14, for several women were speaking at once.
24. Luxton, *More than a Labour of Love*.
25. Ammerman and Roof, *Work, Family, and Religion in Contemporary Society;* Ammerman, *Bible Believers*.
26. Luxton, *More than a Labour of Love*.
27. R. Wuthnow, *Learning to Care: Elementary Kindness in an Age of Indifference* (New York: Oxford, 1995); Nason-Clark and Beaman, "Jugglers for Jesus."

Notes for Chapter 7

1. W. C. Roof, *A Generation of Seekers: The Spiritual Journeys of the Baby Boom Generation* (San Francisco: Harper, 1993).
2. R. Bellah et al., *Habits of the Heart: Individualism and Commitment in American Life* (Berkeley: University of California, 1996).
3. Bibby, *Unknown Gods*.
4. Ibid; Bibby, *Fragmented Gods*.
5. Ammerman, *Bible Believers;* McGuire, *Religion;* Hunter, *Evangelicalism*.
6. Nason-Clark, "Gender Relations in Contemporary Christianity"; Ammerman, *Bible Believers;* Davidman, *Tradition in a Rootless World;* Kraybill, *The Riddle of Amish Culture;* R.C. Kroeger and C.C. Kroeger, *I Suffer Not a Woman* (Grand Rapids: Baker, 1992).
7. McMurry, "Religion and Women's Sex Role Traditionalism"; Heaton and Cornwall, "Religious Group Variation in the Socioeconomic Status of Family Behaviour of Women."
8. Nason-Clark, "Are Clergywomen Changing the Face of Ministry"; Nason-Clark, "Gender Relations in Contemporary Christianity."
9. Ammerman, *Bible Believers;* Neitz, *Charisma and Community;* Ammerman and Roof, *Work, Family, and Religion in Contemporary Society*.
10. Whipple, "Counselling Battered Women"; Horton and Williamson, *Abuse and Religion*.
11. Gundry, *Heirs Together;* Martin, *Battered Wives;* McDill and McDill, *Shattered and Broken;* Scott, *Breaking the Cycle of Abuse;* Spencer, *Beyond the Curse*; Fortune, *Violence in the Family; Fire in the Rose Project*.
12. Nason-Clark, "Conservative Protestants and Violence Against Women"; Beaman, "Feminist Practice, Evangelical Worldview."
13. Martin, *Battered Wives;* Straus et al., *Behind Closed Doors*.
14. N. Nason-Clark and B. Bélanger, "Jugglers for Jesus: Identifying Career and Family Juggling Patterns amongst Conservative Religious Women" (presented at the annual meetings of the Society for the Scientific Study of Religion, Raleigh, N.C., Oct. 29–31, 1993).
15. McDill and McDill, *Shattered and Broken;* Scott, *Breaking the Cycle of Abuse;* Horton and Williamson, *Abuse and Religion*.
16. R.Wuthnow, *I Come Away Stronger: How Small Groups Are Shaping American Religion* (Grand Rapids: Eerdmans, 1994).
17. N. Nason-Clark, "Guarding the Turf: Exploring Clergy Reluctance to Refer Women Who Have Suffered Abuse to Secular Agencies" (presented at the Canadian Sociology and Anthropology Association, Calgary, June 4–7, 1994).
18. Kroeger and Kroeger, *I Suffer Not a Woman*.
19. R. Wuthnow, *Learning to Care*; R. Wuthnow, *Acts of Compassion: Caring for Others and Helping Ourselves* (Princeton, N.J.: Princeton Univ. Press, 1991).
20. Nason-Clark, "Religion and Violence Against Women."
21. Nason-Clark and Bélanger, "Jugglers for Jesus."
22. Whipple, "Counselling Battered Women"; Ammerman, *Bible Believers;* Kaufman, *Rachel's Daughters;* Davidman, *Tradition in a Rootless World;* Nason-Clark, "Conservative Protestants and Violence against Women."
23. Nason-Clark, "Religion and Violence Against Women."
24. Kaufman, *Rachel's Daughters*.
25. Brinkerhoff et al., "Religious Involvement and Spousal Violence."
26. Nason-Clark, "Conservative Protestants and Violence Against Women."
27. Ibid.
28. Beaman, "Feminist Practice, Evangelical Worldview."
29. E. A. Soucy, N. Nason-Clark, and L. Beaman, "Religion and Wife Abuse in Atlantic

Canada: The Response of Catholic and Evangelical Women" (presented at the annual meetings of the Atlantic Association of Sociologists and Anthropologists, Halifax, Nova Scotia, Oct. 13–6, 1994).
30. Nason-Clark, "Conservative Protestantism and Violence Against Women."
31. Nason-Clark, "Religion and Violence Against Women"; Beaman, "Feminist Practice, Evangelical Worldview."
32. Horton et al., "Women Who Ended Abuse."
33. One of my first professional experiences of churchwomen's donations to the Transition house movement occurred when the proceeds of a "love offering" at a churchwomen's convention (where I was the plenary speaker, but not on the subject of violence) were to be channeled to the local transition house.
34. Beaman, "Feminist Practice, Evangelical Worldview."
35. Beaman and Nason-Clark, "Partners or Protagonists?"
36. Nason-Clark, "Gender Relations in Contemporary Christianity."
37. Kroeger and Kroeger, *I Suffer Not a Woman;* Wuthnow, *Learning to Care;* Wuthnow, *Acts of Compassion;* N. Searle, "The Women's Bible Study: A Thriving Evangelical Support Group," in Wuthnow, *I Come Away Stronger,* 97–124.
38. B. DeBerg, *Ungodly Women: Gender and the First Wave of American Fundamentalism* (Minneapolis: Fortress, 1990); O. Banks, *Faces of Feminism* (Oxford: Blackwell, 1986).
39. Bellah et al., *Habits of the Heart.*
40. Schüssler Fiorenza and Copeland, *Violence against Women;* Brown and Bohn, *Christianity, Patriarchy and Abuse;* Wood and McHugh, "Woman Battering."
41. Alsdurf and Alsdurf, "A Pastoral Response"; Bowker, "Religious Victims and Their Religious Leaders"; Bowker, "Battered Women and the Clergy."
42. Nason-Clark, "Religion and Violence Against Women."
43. Beaman, "Negotiating the Options."
44. Fortune, "Forgiveness the Last Step"; Ptacek, "How Men Who Batter Rationalize their Behaviour."
45. Nason-Clark, "Religion and Violence Against Women."
46. Ibid.
47. E.g., *Fire in the Rose Project;* clergy workshops produced by Fortune and the Centre for the Prevention of Sexual and Domestic Violence; *Gethsemane's Comfort Workshops,* P. Halsey, *Abuse in the Family: Breaking the Church's Silence,* produced by the United Methodist Church, and materials produced for the Purple Packet.
48. Fortune, *Violence in the Family;* D. M. Whitman, *Challenging the Darkness: Child Sexual Abuse and the Church* (Bellingham, Wash.: Discovery Counseling Resources, 1991).
49. Morris, *Ending Violence Against Families;* M. Miller, *Family Violence: The Compassionate Church Responds* (Waterloo, Ontario: Herald, 1994).
50. Perlmutter et al., "Awareness of a Community Mental Health Center"; Weaver, "Psychological Trauma."
51. Fortune, "Reporting Child Abuse."
52. *Fire in the Rose Project.*
53. *Gethsemane's Comfort Workshops.*
54. One of the specific goals of the series of Gethsemane's Comfort Workshops in Nova Scotia was to help clergy to network more effectively with the justice system. The Building Bridges Workshop, which was developed by our Religion and Violence Research Team, sought to facilitate community-specific networking opportunities for transition house workers, church women, and clergy. The concept of a coordinated interagency team approach to cases of child abuse has been well documented, as have its merits; e.g., Bross et al., *The New Child Protection Team Handbook.*
55. Bross et al., *The New Child Protection Team Handbook.*
56. Nason-Clark, "Religion and Violence Against Women."
57. B. Miedema and N. Nason-Clark, "Mothering for the State: Three Stories of Working

Class Foster Parents," in *Success Stories in Feminising Canadian Institutions,* ed. K. Blackford and S. Kirby, forthcoming.

58. M. T. Winter, A. Lummis, and A. Stokes, *Defecting in Place: Women Claiming Responsibility for Their Own Spiritual Lives* (New York: Crossroad, 1994).

59. Kaufman, *Rachel's Daughters;* Furlong, *Dangerous Delight: Women and Power in the Church* ; Dowell and Hurcombe, *Dispossessed Daughters of Eve;* R. Wallace, *They Call Her Pastor: A New Role for Catholic Women* (Albany, N.Y.: State Univ. of New York, 1992).

60. Scanzoni and Hardesty, *All We're Meant to Be;* D. Pape, *God and Woman: A Fresh Look at What the New Testament Says about Women* (London: Mowbrays, 1976); Gundry, *Heirs Together;* Malcolm, *Women at the Crossroads;* Martin, *Call Me Blessed;* Spencer, *Beyond the Curse;* Kroeger and Kroeger, *I Suffer Not a Woman* ; Langley, *Equal Women.*

61. J. D. Hunter, *Culture Wars: The Struggle to Define America* (New York: Basic, 1994); Hunter, *Evangelicalism.*

62. Lockhart, "Redefining the New Christian Man."

63. Beaman and Nason-Clark, "Partners or Protagonists?"

64. Thorne-Finch, *Ending the Silence;* Loseke, *The Battered Woman and Shelters.*

65. J. Barnsley, *Feminist Action, Institutional Reaction: Responses to Wife Assault* (Vancouver, B.C.: Women's Research Centre, 1985); Martin, *Battered Wives;* Walker, *Family Violence and the Women's Movement.*

66. Ibid.; Timmins, *Listening to the Thunder*; Nason-Clark, "Religion and Violence Against Women."

67. Walker, *Family Violence and the Women's Movement;* Loseke, *The Battered Woman and Shelters;* Barnsley, *Feminist Action, Institutional Reaction;* Quinby, "Taking Back the Movement."

68. Prieur, "Patriarchy—Now You See It."

69. Kherbouche, "Uprooted and Abused."

70. Nason-Clark, "Religion and Violence Against Women."

71. Walker, *Family Violence and the Women's Movement;* Timmins, *Listening to the Thunder.*

72. Scanzoni and Hardesty, *All We're Meant to Be;* Pape, *God and Woman;* Gundry, *Heirs Together;* Malcolm, *Women at the Crossroads;* Martin, *Call Me Blessed;* Spencer, *Beyond the Curse;* Langley, *Equal Women.*

73. N. Nason-Clark and L. Beaman, "Religion and Wife Abuse: Examining the Relationship between Transition House Workers and Clergy" (presented at the annual meetings of the Society for the Scientific Study of Religion, Raleigh, N.C., Oct. 29–31, 1993).

74. Nason-Clark, "Religion and Violence Against Women"; Nason-Clark, "Conservative Protestants and Violence Against Women."

75. This is not to suggest that physical violence does not occur in families where both husband and wife report equal commitment to the faith tradition, or that pastors are not called on to see such families. It is simply that pastors have more experience dealing with women whose husbands do not share their level of faith or its practice.

76. N. Nason-Clark and L. Beaman, "Religion and Violence Against Women in Atlantic Canada: Looking at the Response of Evangelical Churches" (invited presentation, Canadian Psychological Association, Charlottetown, P.E.I., June 15–17, 1995).

77. Horton, "Practical Guidelines for Professionals"; Kherbouche, "Uprooted and Abused."

78. Soucy et al., "Religion and Violence Against Women in Atlantic Canada"; Beaman, "Feminist Practice, Evangelical Worldview."

79. Whipple, "Counselling Battered Women."

80. Nason-Clark, "Guarding the Turf."

81. Bibby, *Unknown Gods.*

82. Ammerman, *Bible Believers;* Kraybill, *The Riddle of Amish Culture.*
83. D. R. Hoge, B. Johnson, and D. A. Luidens, *Vanishing Boundaries: The Religion of Mainline Protestant Baby Boomers* (Louisville, Ky.: Westminster/John Knox, 1994).
84. Alsdurf and Alsdurf, "A Pastoral Response" ; Bowker, "Religious Victims and their Religious Leaders."
85. Nason-Clark, "Religion and Violence Against Women."
86. Fortune, "Forgiveness the Last Step"; Kowalski, "Developing a Religious and Secular Partnership."
87. Pence, "Legal Remedies and the Role of Law Enforcement"; Horton, "Practical Guidelines for Professionals."
88. In a smaller study of 94 evangelical women who had participated in our focus group research, only a couple of women recalled ever hearing a sermon where wife abuse was directly condemned; see Beaman "Feminist Practice, Evangelical Worldview."
89. Bibby, *Fragmented Gods*; and Bibby, *Unknown Gods.*
90. Elmore, *Soul Provider;* A. Janssen, ed., *Seven Promises of a Promise Keeper* (Colorado Springs, Col.: Focus on the Family, 1994).
91. Lockhart, "Redefining the New Christian Man"; D. Irving, "The Promise Keepers," unpublished manuscript, Sociology 3335, University of New Brunswick, Fredericton, N.B., Canada, 1996.
92. C. Glock, B. Ringer, and E. Babbie, *To Comfort and to Challenge: A Dilemma of the Contemporary Church* (Berkeley: Univ. of California Press, 1967); P. Berger, *A Rumor of Angels: Modern Society and the Rediscovery of the Supernatural.* (Garden City, N.Y.: Anchor, 1970).
93. I am grateful to a clergyman from Saint John, N. B., who made this point during a small-group discussion session at the Building Bridges Workshop, held in Fredericton, N.B., June 20, 1996.
94. Pagelow and Johnson, "Abuse in the American Family"; Brown and Bohn, *Christianity, Patriarchy and Abuse;* Schüssler Fiorenza and Copeland, *Violence against Women.*
95. Nason-Clark, "Religion and Violence Against Women"; Gethsemane's Comfort Workshops.
96. Horton and Williamson, *Abuse and Religion.*
97. Nason-Clark, "Religion and Violence Against Women."
98. Fortune, "Forgiveness the Last Step."
99. Ptacek, "How Men Who Batter Rationalize Their Behaviour."
100. Whipple, "Counselling Battered Women"; Kherbouche, "Uprooted and Abused."

SUBJECT INDEX

abuse,
  context of, 1, 4, 41–47
  definition, 3
  feminist analysis, 3, 4, 11, 111
  intergenerational transmission of, 9
  pastoral responses to, 16–18, 83–107
  prevalence of, 1, 5–7, 58–59, 62,
    111–12
  religion and, 13–19, 139–159
  religious service providers and, 14–16,
    139–59
  responding to, 16–18, 83–106, 109–37
  understanding, 47–50, 59–68, 111,
    114–16
  women living with, 8, 11–13, 41–47,
    59–68, 116–37, 142–44
abused Christian women, 16–18, 37–55,
    109–37
abusive cycle, xvi, 1, 8, 54
abusive men, 8, 10–11, 16, 17, 42–47,
    59–68, 70, 106–7, 114, 128, 146, 156
agency, exercise of, 45–50, 128–29, 156
Albers, Robert, 52
Albert, Alexa, 23 n.16
Alsdurf, James and Phyllis, 11 n.90, 15
    n.156, 17 n.185, n.192, 18, 48 n.8, 70
    n.23, 146 n.41, 152 n.84
Ammerman, Nancy Tatom, 14 n.153, 22
    n.5, n.6, 23, 24 n.19, 58 n.1, 109 n.6,
    n.7, 127 n.19, 131 n.25, 140 n.5, 141
    n.6, n.9, 143 n.22, 151 n.82
Amrit, 5 n.45
Anderson, Kristin, 14
Armstrong, Pat and Hugh, 63 n.12

Babbie, E., 153 n.92
Baker, M. 7 n.54
Balmer, Randall, 21, 22, 58 n.3, 109 n.3, n.8
Banks, Olive, 145 n.38
Barling, J., 10 n.81

Barna, George, 32, 33 n.54
Barnsley, Jan, 3 n.24, 149 n.65, n.67
Bartkowski, John, 14
Beaman, Lori, 14 n.141, 19 n.202, 37 n.1,
    40, 51 n.10, 52 n.12, 66 n.15, 70 n.18,
    83 n.3, 105 n.14, 111 n.13, 127 n.19,
    128 n.21, 131, n.27, 141 n.12, 144
    n.28, n.29, n.31, 145 n.34, n.35, 146
    n.43, 148 n.63, 150 n.73, 151 n.76,
    n.78, 153 n.88
Beck, Martha, 15 n.156
Beitman, Bernard, 19 n.202
Belanger, Brenda, 141 n.14, 143,
    n.21
Bell, Roger, 13 n.131, 81 n.31
Bellah, Robert, 140, n.2, 145 n.39
Bennett, Larry, 11
Berger, Peter, 153 n.92
betrayal, ix, x, 3, 139
Bibby, Reginald, 83, n.1, 140, 151 n.81,
    153 n.89
Blitchington, Peter, 23–5
Bohn, Carole, 2 n.11, 14 n.138, 43 n.3, 52
    n.13, 58 n.6, 59 n.9, 70 n.22, n.24, 83
    n.4, 146 n.40, 153 n.94
Bowker, Lee, 13 n.131, 15, 17 n.187, 18
    n.199, 58 n.8, 70 n.23, 146 n.41, 152
    n.84
bridge building, xix, 131, 135–36, 140,
    155, 159
Brinkerhoff, M., 14, 143 n.25
Brookshire, W., 16
Bross, Donald, 1 n.3, 16 n.175, 147 n.54,
    n.55
Brown, Joanne, 2 n.11, 14 n.138, 43 n.3,
    52 n.13, 58 n.6, 59 n.9, 70 n.22, n.24,
    83 n.4, 146 n.40, 153 n.94
Brown, Karen McCarthy, 22, 109 n.5
Bullis, Ronald, 16 n.177, 19 n.204
Bussert, Joy, 4 n.37, 48 n.8

Casardi, Michele, 11 n.105
Chalfant, H. Paul, 13 n.131, 14 n.144, 19 n.202
Christian family literature, 21–35
Christians for Biblical Equality, 22 n.4, 148
Church Council on Justice and Correc-
tions, 14 n.136
Clark, Stephen, 13 n.132
Clarke, Rita-Lou, 4 n.38, 14 n.145
Clemens, Norman, 13 n.132
clergy
counseling experience, 58, 70–79,
83–107, 146–47
referral patterns, 76–77, 79–81, 88–89,
95–96, 151–53
Collins, Gary, 26, 113, n.16
Copeland, Mary Shawn, 2 n.11, 4 n.39, 5
n.44, n.50, 11 n.89, 15 n.156, 43 n.3,
n.4, 45 n.4, 51 n.9, 58 n.6, 70 n.22,
n.24, 83 n.3, 146 n.40, 153 n.94
Cornwall, Marie, 22 n.5, 109 n.6, 141 n.7
counseling, 32–34, 58, 70–79, 83–107
Curley, A.D., 9, 10 n.84, 11 n.97

Daly, Mary, 2 n.11
Davidman, Lynn, 22, 109 n.6, 127 n.19,
141 n.6, 143 n.22
DeBerg, Betty, 145 n.38
Delaplane, D., 17 n.188
Dobash, R.P and R.E., 2 n.10, 3 n.23, 4
n.35, n.36, 7 n.56, 11 n.88, 43 n.2
Dobson, James, 20, 22, 24, 27–33, 40, 113
n.16
Domino, George, 16 n.169
Doran, Constance, 17 n.194
Dowell, Susan, 11 n.90, 148 n.59

Eiesland, Nancy, 58 n.3
Eilts, M., 17 n.190
Ellison, Christopher, 59 n.9
Elmore, Timothy, 25 n.36, 153 n.90

family
as sacred, 1, 109, 131
values, 21–23, 57, 64, 109, 113
patterns, 23–25
family violence, see abuse
Feld, S., 1 n.2
Finch, J., 101 n.11
Finkelhor, D., 8
Fiorenza, Elisabeth Schüssler, 2 n.11, 4
n.39, n.41, 5 n.44, 11 n.89, 15 n.156,
43 n.3, n.4, 45 n.4, 51 n.9, 58 n.6, 70
n.22, n.24, 83 n.3, 146 n.40, 153 n.94

Fire in the Rose Project, 4 n.29, n.31, n.32,
11 n.90, 14 n.136, n.146, n.148, 17
n.183, n.189, 67 n.16, 113 n.15, 141
n.11, 147 n.47, 147 n.52
Fischer, Karla, 5 n.49, 12 n.110, 15 n.129,
17 n.188
Focus on the Family, 27–32, 74
forgiveness, 17, 53–55, 127, 133, 151–52
Fortune, Marie, 8, 11 n.90, 14 n.136, 15
n.156, 17, 43 n.3, 54–5, 59 n.9, 67
n.16, 70 n.19, 113, n.15, n.17, 141
n.11, 146 n.44, 147 n.47, n.48, n.51,
152 n.86, 155 n.98
Freeman, Janet, 5 n.47, 12 n.111
Freedman, Lisa, 2 n.9, 7 n.53
French, Marilyn, 1 n.6
friendship, 75, 90, 97, 100, 106, 116, 119,
121–23, 139–30
Furlong, Monica, 11 n.89, 16 n.173, 148
n.59

Garden of Gethsemane, viii–x, 139
Gelles, Richard, 1 n.1, 2 n.13, 3 n.16, 7 n.58,
n.60, 10, 11 n.88, n.100, n.102, n.103,
12
gender inerrancy, 22
gender roles, 21–25, 28
Gerami, Shahin, 22 n.10
Gerdes, Karen, 15 n.156
Gesch, Lyn, 23
Gethsemane's Comfort Workshops, 14
n.136, 67 n.16, 147 n.47, n.53, 153
n.94
Gilkes, Cheryl Townsend, 5 n.45
Glock, Charles, 153 n.92
Goldsmith, W. 13 n.134, 14 n.152, 16
n.177, 81 n.29
Goldstein, D.,10 n.82, n.83
Goodwin, J., 9 n.73, n.75
Gorsuch, Richard, 19 n.202, 81 n.32
Grandin, Elaine, 14
Greenglass, Esther, 12 n.113
Gundry, Patricia, 11 n.90, 51 n.11, 141
n.11, 148 n.60, 149 n.72
Gutierrez-Diez, Marilyn Maiza, 5 n.46, 7
n.62, 12 n.112

Hale, Sylvia, 63 n.12
Halsey, Peggy, 147 n.47
Hamlin, E.R., 58 n.4
Hardesty, Nancy, 4. n.41, 148 n.60, 149
n.72
Harrigan, Marcia, 16 n.177, 19 n.204
Harrison, Deborah, 4 n.29, n.43, 11 n.93

Hawley, John Stratton, 22, 109 n.4
Hazlewood, Lonnie, 2 n.8, 11 n.95
healing journey, xvi, 50–53
Heaton, Tim, 22 n.5, 109 n.6, 141 n.7
Hertel, Bradley, 23
Hilberman, E., 2 n.12
Higgins, Kelly, 16 n.174
Hoge, Dean, 152 n.83
Holden, Janice Miner, 16
Hong, Barry, 13 n.132, 81 n.29
Hooker, Douglas, 13 n.122, 16 n.172
Hornung, C.A., 7 n.61, 15 n.158
Horton, Anne, 4 n.30, n.42, 13 n.125, 14,
    15, 16, 17 n.179, n.180, 19 n.203,
    n.204, 31 n.52, 47 n.6, 58 n.6, 59 n.9,
    70 n.21, 83 n.3, 110 n.10, 113 n.17,
    123, 141 n.10, n.15, 144 n.32, 151
    n.77, 152 n.87, 153 n.96
Hulme, Thomas, 19 n.202
Hunter, James Davidson, 22 n.7, 24 n.19,
    140, n.5, 148 n.61
Hurley, James, 31
Hurcombe, Linda, 11 n.90, 148 n.59

Inrig, Gary, 26
Irving, Danielle, 25, 153 n.91

Jaffe, Peter, 9
Janssen, A., 183 n.90
Jansen, David, 16 n.171
Johnson, Benton, 152 n.83
Johnson, O.R., 25 n.29
Johnson, P., 4 n.39, 14 n.142, 15 n.161, 17
    n.181, n.184, 153 n.94

Kalmuss, D., 9
Kaufman, Debra Renee, 22, 109 n.6, 127
    n.19, 143 n.22, n.24, 148 n.59
Kherbouche, Nacera, 149 n.69, 151 n.77
King, Robert, 17, 81 n.30
Kowalski, J.A., 17 n.189, 19 n.204, 152
    n.86
Kraybill, Donald, 109 n.6, 141 n.6, 151
    n.82
Kroeger, Richard Clark and Catherine
    Clark, 141 n.6, 142, 145 n.37, 148 n.60

LaHaye, Tim and Beverley, 24, 28 n.46,
    33, 113, n.16
Laliberte, Lucie, 4 n.29, n.43, 11 n.93
Langley, Myrtle, 148 n.60, 149 n.72
Langston, Michael, 16 n.169, 19 n.202, 81
    n.31
Lau, Godwin, 13 n.131

LeClerc, Donna, 4 n.30, 8
Leppard, Denise, 3 n.27, 4 n.28, 12 n.111
Lipman-Blumen, Jean, 24 n.20
Livezey, Lois Gehr, 4 n.40, 14 n.138, 15
Lockhart, William, 25, 26 n.37, 148 n.62,
    153 n.91
Loseke, Donileen, 3 n. 24, 149 n.64, n.67
Luidens, Donald, 152 n.83
Lummis, Adair, 148
Lupri, Eugen, 14
Luxton, Meg, 8, 12 n.114, 13 n.124, 131
Lyons, Peter, 13 n.133

Mahoney, Martha, 48, 128
Malcolm, Kari Torjesen, 148 n.60, 149
    n.72
Marden, Mary, 13
marital counseling, 32–34, 75–81, 83–107
marital rape, 8
marriages
    Christian model for, 21–25, 34–35
    in trouble, 26–27, 30–32, 37–40, 58,
        70–79, 83–107
Marler, Penny Long, 23, 109 n.5, 110, n.11
Martin, Del, 3 n.14, 7 n.61, 11 n.103, 12,
    13 n.126, 16 n.170, 109 n.9, 141 n.11,
    n.13, 149 n.65
Martin, Faith McBurney, 13 n.135, 51
    n.11, 148 n.60, 149 n.72
Martin, Susan, 14 n.174, 18, 19 n.202, 58
    n.8, 81 n.31
McCrea, Marilyn, 3 n.21, 12 n.105
McDill, S.R., and Linda, 11 n.90, 18
    n.195, 19 n.204, 53, 113, n.17, 141
    n.11, n.15
McGuire, Meredith, 13 n.130, 140, n.5
McHugh, Maureen, 14 n.145, n.154, 18,
    58 n.8, 70 n.22, n.24, 81 n.32, 146
    n.40
McLeod, Linda, 6 n.52, 59 n.9, 127 n.20
McMurry, M., 23 n.16, 141 n.7
Meadow, Mary Jo, 14 n.151
Merritt-Gray, Marilyn, 4 n.34, 13
Meylink, Willa, 19 n.202, 81 n.32
Miedema, Baukje, 148 n.57
Miller, Melissa, 147 n.49
Molm, Linda, 23 n.16
Morris, Roberta, 13 n.135, 70 n.21, 147
    n.49
Morrow, Beatty Hearn, 3 n.21
Moss, David, 13 n.133
motherhood, 21–25, 28
Muriel McQueen Fergusson Centre for
    Family Violence Research, xv, 159

mutual submission, 34–5, 45, 51

Narayan, Uma, 5 n.46
naming the violence, 3, 148–50
Nason-Clark, Nancy, 1 n.4, 14 n.141, n.154,
    16 n.173, 17 n.184, 19 n.202, 22 n.3,
    n.5, 24 n.18, n.19, 25 n.34, 66 n.14, 70
    n.20, n.25, 109 n.2, 109 n.5, 110, n.12,
    127 n.19, 131, n.27, 141 n.6, n.8, n.12,
    n.14, 142 n.17, 143 n.20, n.21, n.22,
    n.23, n.26, 144 n.27, n.29, n.30, n.31,
    145 n.36, 146 n.42, n.45, n.46, 147
    n.56, 148 n.57, n.63, 149 n.66, n.70,
    150 n.73, n.74, 151 n.76, n.80, 152
    n.85, 153 n.95, 154 n.97
Neitz, Mary Jo, 22 n.5, 109 n.5, 111, n.12,
    127 n.19, 141 n.9
Nova Scotia Family Violence Prevention
    Initiative, 3 n.15

O'Leary, K.D., 9, 10 n.84, 11 n.97, n.101

Pagelow, M.D., 4 n.39, 14 n.142, 15 n.161,
    17 n.181, n.184, 153 n.94
Palmer, Susan, 109 n.6, 127 n.19
Pape, Dorothy, 148 n.60, 149 n.72
Pehrson, K.I., 58 n.4
Pence, Ellen, 4 n.43, 16 n.175, 152 n.87
Perlmutter, Felice, 13 n.131, 147 n.50
Phillips, Paul and Erin, 63 n.12
Porter, Judith, 23 n.16
Prieur, Deborah, 3 n.20, n.26, 11 n.91,
    n.94, 12 n.108, 13, 149 n.68
promise keepers, 25–26, 153
Proudfoot, Wayne, 22
Ptacek, James, 10, 11, 70 n.19, 146 n.44,
    155 n.99
Purple Packet, 147 n.47

Quinby, Ajax, 3 n.14, 11 n.91, 12 n.109,
    n.117, 149 n.67

Rawlyk, George, 22 n.7
reconciliation, 126, 150–51
referrals, xvi, 76–77, 79–81, 88–91,
    96–97, 102, 130–31, 136, 151–54
Religion and Violence Research Team, vii,
    xv n.1, xvi, 79, n.28, 147 n.54, 159
research methods, xv–xviii, 58
Rice, M., 13
Ringer, B., 153 n.92
Rogers, Martha, 13 n.131
Roof, Wade Clark, 23, 109 n.7, 127 n.19,
    131, n.25, 140, 141, n.9

Rose, M. 5 n.49, 12 n.110, 13 n.129, 17
    n.188
Rose, Susan, 127 n.19
Rosenbaum, A., 9, 10 n.81, n.82, n.83, 11
    n.101
Ruether, Rosemary Radford, 45 n.4
Rumberger, Daniel, 13 n.131
Rumptz, Maureen, 3 n.22, 12
Russell, Diana, 8

Sacks, Joseph, 14 n.150, 19 n.202
sacred support services, xvi, 16–19, 40–41,
    78–79, 111, 116–27, 130–37, 139–
    59
Scanzoni, Letha, 4 n.41, 148 n.60, 149
    n.72
Schofield, William, 14 n.151
Scott, C.L., 13 n.135, 14 n.154, 70 n.21,
    113 n.17, 141 n.11, n.15
Searle, Natalie, 145 n.37
secular support services, xvi, 16–19,
    40–41, 76, 116, 127–30, 132–34,
    139–59
Sell, Kenneth, 13 n.134, 14 n.152, 16
    n.177, 81 n.29
Seltzer, J., 9
sexual violence, 8
shame, 52, 60, 108, 121, 137, 152
shelter, see transition house
Shupe, Anson, 2 n.8, 11 n.95
Smalley, Gary, 24–6, 28 n.48, 113 n.16
Smith, Dorothy, 112, n.14
Soucy, E.A., 143 n.29, 151 n.78
Spencer, A.B., 13 n.135, 141 n.11, 148
    n.60, 149 n.72
Stacey, William, 2 n.8, 11 n.95
Statistics Canada, 6 n.51, 9, 11 n.101, 58
    n.2, 59 n.9, 83, n.2
Steele, R., 13 n.131
Steinmetz, Susan, 9, 10
Stern, Jo, 3 n.27, 4 n.28, 12 n.111
Stokes, Allison, 148
Straus, Murray, 1 n.1, 3 n.16, n.18, n.19, 4
    n.28, 7 n.55, n.57, n.58, n.59, n.60, 9,
    10, 11 n.100, n.102, 83 n.2, 113 n.15,
    141 n.13
Strom, Kay Marshall, 11 n.90, 18 n.195
Stunk, Orlo Jr., 14 n.151
submission, 4, 17, 18, 24, 28, 34–5, 41,
    44–46, 51, 65, 141
suffering servant, 43–50, 52, 55, 83
Sullivan, Cris, 3 n.22, 12
survivor, x, 109–37, 155, 158
Swidler, Ann, 145

Tan, Cheribeth, 4 n.34, 5 n.49
Terris, Christy, 71 n.26
Thomas, A. 13 n.132
Thorne-Finch, Ron, 3 n.21, 149 n.64
Timmins, Leslie, 1 n.5, 3 n.23, 4 n.33, 5 n. 48, 11 n.93, 13 n.119, 58 n.4, 149 n.66, n.71
Tingley, Kate, 63 n.11
transition house, xvii, 3, 5, 12, 18, 46–47, 76, 79, 88, 93, 96, 104–5, 110, 116, 118, 125–30, 139–47, 149, 152, 157–59

Untinen, Leni, 3 n.21, n.24, 12 n.112

victim, x, 109, 130, 155
violence, *see* abuse
violent-free family living, xvi, xvii, 16, 122–23

Walker, Gillian, 3 n.17, n.24, 43 n.2, 149 n.65, n.67, n.71
Walker, James, 25
Walker, Lenore, 8, 11 n.89, n.91, n.96
Wallace, Ruth, 148
Warner, Stephen, 58 n.1

Watts, R., 16
Weaver, Andrew, 13 n.123, 14, 16 n.169, 18 n.198, 58 n.7, 81 n.30, 147 n.50
Whipple, Vicky, 14 n.147, n.150, 16 n.177, 19 n.203, 70 n.21, 141 n.10, 143 n.22, 151 n.79, 155 n.100
Whitman, D. Mitchell, 147 n.48
Wiehe, V., 13 n.132, 81 n.29
Wilkins, Meland, 15, 16
Williamson, Judith, 4 n.30, n.42, 13 n.125, 14, 15, 17 n.179, 19 n.204, 31 n.52, 58 n.6, 59 n.9, 70 n.21, 83, n.3, 110, n.10, 113 n.17, 123, 141 n.10, n.15, 153 n.96
Winter, Miriam Therese, 148
Wood, Alberta, 14 n.145, n.154, 18, 58 n.8, 70 n.22, n.24, 81 n.32, 146 n.40
Wright, Wendy, 15, 16
Wuest, Judith, 4 n.34, 13
Wuthnow, Robert, 131 n.27, 142 n.16, n.19, 145 n.37

Yllo, Kersti, 4 n.30, 8

Zingle, H. 13 n.133